ENCYCLOPEDIA
OF ACTIVITIES
FOR TEACHING
GRADES K-3

ENCYCLOPEDIA
OF ACTIVITIES
FOR TEACHING
GRADES K-3

Hal Malehorn

Parker Publishing Company, Inc.
West Nyack, New York

© 1975, *by*

PARKER PUBLISHING COMPANY, INC.

West Nyack, N.Y.

Library of Congress Cataloging in Publication Data

Malehorn, Hal,
   Encyclopedia of activities for teaching grades K-3.

   1. Creative activities and seat work--Handbooks,
manuals, etc. 2. Educational games--Handbooks, manuals,
etc. I. Title.
LB1537.M25 1975   372.1'3   74-32312
ISBN 0-13-274985-8

Printed in the United States of America

Using This Book
to Help You Teach

Encyclopedia of Activities for Teaching Grades K-3 is the most complete collection of early childhood instructional ideas ever assembled in a single volume. It includes nearly 2,000 individual suggestions listed in 700 citations. It contains appropriate learning experiences for all principal areas of the curriculum and for all types of young children.

The *Encyclopedia* is a *practical* book. It is filled with useful items that have been classroom-tested. Most of the activities listed require very little preparation time, and they are so simple that even the busiest teacher can use them effectively. Many of the suggestions describe how to use either free or inexpensive instructional materials. Scores of the teaching objects that are described can be made easily from discarded items or from other objects readily at hand.

The *Encyclopedia* is a *versatile* book. The scope and the variety are vast, and most of the activities can be adapted for all ages of children ranging from Kindergarten through Grade Three. The ideas are as useful for individual instruction as they are helpful for group settings. They fit as well into traditional classrooms as they do in "open" classrooms. Use this volume to develop a new basic instructional program or to add interest to an established one. Share these helpful techniques with colleagues; include them in curriculum guides and courses of study; or, simply select single learning experiences from time to time as you need them.

The *Encyclopedia* is a *handy* book. The table of contents identifies eight separate areas of the curriculum. Each of these main sections contains several related subtopics. Note at the top of every page of text the guide words directing attention to individual entries. Check the key words that label all these entries in alphabetical order. See how easy it is to find specific citations quickly. Notice that the explanations for each activity are written concisely and simply, yet they are complete and to-the-point.

The *Encyclopedia* is an *interesting* book. The author's belief is that learning should be fun. The suggestions in this work will motivate young children to learn—and to be happy about it. Here are a few sample activities that will inspire fresh enthusiasm and stimulate thinking:

1. Dry and wax flowers and leaves for colorful decorations.
   See: SCIENCE—*Plants* (Preservation)
2. Make an animal poster to remind children to brush their teeth.
   See: PHYSICAL EDUCATION—*Health* (Grooming)
3. Build a "Mess Monster" for eating trash pollution.
   See: SOCIAL STUDIES—*Environment* (Litter)
4. Use water pistols as a painting experience.
   See: ART—*Painting* (Squirting)
5. Draw silly pictures with elements of musical notation.
   See: MUSIC—*Notation* (Note Picture)
6. Construct a humorous inchworm to show linear distance.
   See: NUMBERS—*Measurement* (Measuring Tapes)
7. Play "Hopscotch" with a unique twist.
   See: READING—*Aids and Games* (Jumpscotch)
8. Invent a story about a comic strip character.
   See: LANGUAGE ARTS—*Composition* (Cartoons)

Finally, the *Encyclopedia* is an *"open"* book. With hundreds of applications for self-selected, self-paced, and self-evaluated learning, this book is ideally suited to either customary procedures or the newly-developing "open education" approach. In addition, it is a reference designed to open your own teaching style: it will encourage you to add your own original variations to insure a constantly growing collection of effective teaching methods. As you develop the rewarding habit of looking for better ways of teaching, the *Encyclopedia* will stimulate your imagination and strengthen your commitment to the education of young children.

Hal Malehorn

Contents

Simple DESIGN Experiences (16)

Blindfold Designs ● Carpenter's Chalk ● Chalkboard Designs ● Classified Advertisements ● Crayon Etchings ● Crayon Resists ● Dot Designs   Embossed Foil ● Geometric Designs ● Graph Paper ● Grated Crayons ● Junk Sculpture ● Line Designs ● Melted Crayons ● Mosaics ● Oversize Drawings ● Outline Designs ● Rubber Cement Drips ● Rubbings ● Sculpture Exploration ● Sketching People ● Squiggle Designs ● Stencils ● String Sculptures ● Tracings ● Wet Chalk ● Weaving

MOTIVATING Art Activities (23)

Art Day ● Clean-Up ● Coloring Books ● Competitions ● Demonstrations ● Discards ● Exchanges ● Folders ● Grading ● Masterpieces ᴄ Messiness ● Modeling ● Preparation ● Scheduling ● Scrapbook ● Variations

Involving Pupils in PAINTING (27)

Additives ● Blotting ● Blowing ● Brayer ● Brushes ● Dye ● Finger Painting ● Marbelizing ● Mixing ● Pooling ● Printing ● Smearing ● Soap Flake Painting ● Spatter ●

Squirting • Stippling • String Painting • Twirling • Watercolors • Water Painting

What to Make with PAPER (34)

Accordian Folds • Animals • Attachments • Box Sculpture • Braiding • Cages • Caterpillars • Cellophane Squares • Collages • Cones • Corrugations • Crumpling • Curling • Cylinders • Exploded Designs • Fades • Fringes • Impaled Designs • Incising • Mobiles • Papier Mache • Positives and Negatives • Punch • Sacks • Scoring • Shoeboxes • Strips • Stuffing • Tape • Tissue Paper • Torn Paper

part two

LANGUAGE ARTS: Promoting Expressive Abilities 43

COMPOSITION: Writing and Telling Stories (44)

Animals • Booklets • Cartoons • Corrections • Descriptions • Experience Charts • Favorites • Feelings • Fragments • Group Writing • Heroes • Imaginary Roles • Letters • Magic • Monsters • Newspapers • Pictures • Question Chart • Reminder Chart • Roller Strips • Sensory Situations • Sequels • Shape Books • Show and Tell • Space Stories • Story Balloons • Story Folders • Surprise Box • Tape Recorders • Telephone Stories • Television Stories • Whoppers

Hints to Help HANDWRITING (55)

Applications • Cleanliness • Demonstrations • Display • Evaluation • Hidden Letters • Historical Handwriting • Implements • Lefthandedness • Models • Motivation • Names • Papers • Pencil Positions • Progress • Relation • Riddles • Sequence • Signatures • Similarities • Spacing • Surfaces • Tracing • Visual Aids

Strategies for Good SPELLING (62)

Absurdities • Anagrams • Battleship Game • Bees • Body Spelling • Color Coding • Demons • Display • Game *part three*

MUSIC: Enjoying Songs and Dances 71

Creative MOVEMENT Opportunities (72)

Teaching Basic MUSICOLOGY (83)

Responding to RHYTHMS (87)

Simple SINGING Activities (93)

Incremental Songs • Legendary Songs • Listening • Musical Directions • Musical Recall • New Songs • Nursery Rhymes • Old Favorites • Original Tunes • Original Words • Personal Records • Programs • Rehearsals • Resource Helpers • Roll Call • Rounds • Serenading • Silent Singing • Solo Singing • Song Chart • Song Illustrations • Vocal Control • Vocal Diction • Vocal Literature • Vocal Range

part four

Devices for Teaching COMPUTATION (102)

Adding Board • Adding Graphs • Adding Hands • Adding Machines • Address Cards • Beanbag Toss • Bingo Cards • Bounce Box • Bowling Box • Combination Wheels • Cuisenaire Strips • Dice Tossing • Equivalence Beam • Fishing Game • Flap Cards • Flashcards • Jumbo Numerals • Ladders • Lift-Up Cards • Magic Squares • Matching Laces • Operator Game • Pathways Game • Pegboard Adder • Practice Grids • Programmed Cards • Puzzles • Yarn Cards

Interesting Ways with COUNTING (110)

Action Counting • Calendar Counting • Carton Counters • Counting Chains • Counting Fives's • Counting Frame • Counting Man • Counting Objects • Counting Pairs • Dot-to-Dot Cards • Finger Counters • Greater and Lesser • Hundred's Board • Incidental Counting • Large Numbers • Number Booklets • Number Cartons • Number Dials • Number Labels • Number Line • Number Poems • Number Tapping • Number Walk • Odd and Even • Page Numbers • Personal Numbers • Place Holders • Seriation Cards • Seriation Labels • Seriation Rods • Seriation Songs • Story Numbers

MEASURING Time, Money, Distance (121)

Actual Sales • Calendar Clocks • Calendar Matching • Clock Addition • Clock Games • Clock Manipulables • Clock Mix-Ups • Estimation • Fractions • Graph Games • Graphing • Linear Measurements • Measurement Devices •

Measuring Tapes ● Measurement Terms ● Measuring Things ● Mileage ● Money Counting ● Money Replicas ● Personal Measurements ● Prices ● Recipe Measurements ● Story Clocks ● Tally Marks ● Television Times ● Timing Practice ● Weighing

part five

PHYSICAL EDUCATION: Training Safe and Sound Bodies 131

FITNESS Equipment and Activities (132)

Animal Stunts ● Balance Beam ● Balance Bench ● Balance Square ● Balls ● Balloons ● Barrels ● Beanbags ● Bouncing Board ● Calisthenics ● Climbing Apparatus ● Hoops ● Jumping ● Ladders ● Mats ● Obstacle Course ● Parachutes ● Pre-Sports ● Relays ● Ropes ● Scooters ● Tires and Tubes ● Wands

HEALTH: How the Human Mechanism Works (147)

Balanced Diet ● Body Machines ● Body Parts ● Bones ● Circulation ● Clothing ● Dictionary ● Eyes ● Grooming ● Growth ● Hair ● Microorganism ● Nerves ● Posture ● Respiration ● Scents ● Senses ● Speech Mechanism ● Tasting ● Teeth ● Touching

Instructing Students in SAFETY (155)

Bicycles ● Buses ● Electrical Hazards ● Emergency Drills ● Fire Prevention ● First Aid ● Helpers ● Nursery Rhymes ● Pedestrian Safety ● Plants ● Playground ● Poisons ● Safety Alphabet ● Safety Belts ● Seasonal Hazards ● Signs and Signals ● Situations ● Snow Play ● Traffic

part six

READING: Introducing Children to Books 161

Fun with Reading GAMES and AIDS (162)

Accordion Folds ● Bingo ● Blocks ● Broadcaster ● Card Games ● Circle Games ● Concentration ● Dominoes ●

Fishing • Hopscotch • Interest Cards • Labels • Match
Race • Money • Musical Squares • Pass-Around •
Pathways • Pinned Tags • Postman • Programmer •
Puzzles • Scrapbooks • Shifty Cards • Signs • Snatch •
Target Toss • Toy Catalog • Trains • Treasure Box •
Treasure Hunt • Word Worms

MANAGEMENT: Organizing and Stimulating Reading (172)

Auctions • Author Talk • Bad Reading Habits • Book Care •
Book Clubs • Book Criteria • Book Day • Book Fairs •
Book Racks • Book Store • Competition • Difficult Books •
Exchange Readers • Field Trips • Flashcards • Grouping •
Home Help • Modeling • Oral Reading • Partner Reading •
Reading Circle • Reading Materials • Reluctant Readers •
Scheduling • Show Cards • Testing • Voting Favorites

Ideas for Developing Reading SKILLS (181)

Comprehension Activities • Phonics Aids • Phonics Games •
Sequence Activities • Sequence Aids • Word Study Activities

part seven

SCIENCE: Examining the Physical World 189

Wondering About AIR and WATER (190)

Aerodynamics • Air Absorption • Air Expansion • Air
Pressure • Air Space • Air Weight • Atomizers • Buoyancy
• Clouds • Condensation • Dissolved Minerals •
Evaporation • Precipitation • Suction • Surface Tension •
Water Pressure • Weather • Wind

What to Teach About ANIMALS (196)

Ages • Babies • Categories • Companions • Compassion
• Defenses • Diseases • Enemies • Entertainers •
Environments • Footprints • Handling • History •
Movement • Observations • Products • Sizes • Sounds •
Speeds • Transportation • Varieties • Workers

PHYSICS: Experiments with Forces (202)

Convection ● Electrical Circuits ● Electrical Speed ●
Electrical Storage ● Freezing ● Friction ● Gases ● Gears ●
Gravity ● Inclined Plane ● Insulation ● Levers ● Light
Absorption ● Light Composition ● Magnetism ●
Magnification ● Pulleys ● Reflection ● Refraction ● Screws
● Shadows ● Sound Amplification ● Sound Production ●
Sound Reception ● Sound Recording ● Sound Transmission ●
Spectrum ● Vibrations ● Wheels

Investigating PLANTS (210)

Ages ● Arbor Day ● Capillarity ● Crops ● Decorations ●
Directional Growth ● Distribution ● Dyes ● Edible Parts ●
Enemies ● Environments ● Expansion ● Fossils ●
Gardening ● Germination ● Identification ● Landscaping ●
Leaf Activities ● Moisture ● Overcrowding ● Parts ●
Preservation ● Roles ● Seasons ● Soil ● Trees ● Watering
● Window Boxes

part eight

SOCIAL STUDIES: Encouraging Awareness of Others 219

COMMUNITIES and the World of Work (220)

Advertisements ● Banking ● Budgeting ● Circus ● Clothing
Manufacture ● Community Changes ● Division of Labor ●
Economic Needs ● Elections ● Farms ● Food Processing ●
Interdependence ● Job Change ● Job Dignity ● Job Directory
● Job Hands ● Local Industry ● Purchasing ● Role Play ●
Sales ● Store Play ● Tools ● Traffic Play ● Traffic Survey
● Transportation Play ● Transportation Toys ● Uniforms ●
Work Conditions ● Worker Displays ● Work Hats

ENVIRONMENTS and Ecological Responsibility (229)

Beautification ● Compost ● Conservation ● Dust Pollution ●
Endangered Species ● Garbage ● Interdependence ● Litter ●
Natural Elements ● Noise Pollution ● Open Space ● Paper

part one

ART:
Exploring Media

Simple DESIGN Experiences

BLINDFOLD DESIGNS Have a fun activity in which children are asked to draw with chalk, crayon, or charcoal while they are blindfolded. Younger children can be asked to merely explore the medium, while the older primary children can be instructed to draw representational products. For the blindfold, have the child don a paper sack, or tell the child to put his hand and the paper inside a large box so he cannot see what he is doing.

CARPENTER'S CHALK To add variety to chalk experiences, let the children use the large cakes of carpenter's chalk which is commercially available in white, yellow, and blue. This chalk is sold in powdered form at hardware stores and lumberyards. Instruct the children to use paper that contrasts with the pastel colors. Show the children how to use the powdered chalk like Indian sandpainting techniques. If powdered chalk is not available, make your own by rubbing pastel chalks over a vegetable grater or other rough surfaces.

CHALKBOARD DESIGNS Use the chalkboards in the classroom for free design activities, especially when the children have extra time, or where paper may be in short supply. Be sure that the children use chalk that is intended for chalkboard use, since some types do not wipe or wash off the chalkboard without leaving lines. As a further application of this approach, provide for the children their own individual slates made of scraps of chalkboard material.

Or, adapt pressed fiberboard or cardboard to this same purpose, covering the surface with blackboard paint that is commercially available at hardware or paint stores.

CLASSIFIED ADVERTISEMENTS   Use the classified section of the local newspaper for design activities. One possibility is to convert the columns of the paper into vertical representations of the skyscrapers of a large city, using black paint to suggest their shapes. Use classified ads also as the background experience for making other designs with chalk, paint, crayon, or charcoal. Or, locate pictures in the newspaper pages, and paint over each picture with colors chosen by the students.

CRAYON ETCHINGS   Use different colors of crayons to thoroughly cover a surface on a paper, then crayon on top of this foundation with black crayon. Take a sharp object, such as the point of a pair of scissors, and then scratch a design. An interesting variation of this approach is to use colored holiday greeting cards as the background, and crayon over them with black crayon, scratching the design suggested with a sharp instrument.

CRAYON RESISTS   Make a design on a piece of paper with crayon, and then wash over the design with thinned tempera paint or watercolors. As an interesting version of this activity, have the children use a candle scrap or a piece of paraffin, or light-colored crayons to make an "invisible" design. When the design is finished, brush contrasting paint over it, and the invisible designs will suddenly appear.

DOT DESIGNS   Show the children how to hold the crayon, chalk, or paintbrush vertically, and rotate it to make a round spot on the paper. Combine these dots into a design. A comparable effect is made as the child holds the piece of crayon or chalk flat on the paper and twists it as he presses it against the surface. This will leave either a large circular spot, if the children twist the crayon or chalk all the way around, or it will leave a butterfly-like design 'f the crayon or chalk is twisted just a bit. As another dot design experience, let the children punch holes in scraps of construction paper with a commercial paper punch, and then use these small round pieces of paper as pasted items on paper.

EMBOSSED FOIL   Give each child a piece of aluminum foil and show the class how to use blunt instruments such as lollipop sticks to emboss a design on the surface of the foil. Place several paper towels under the foil to allow the indentations to be seen. Show the children how to press gently so as not to tear the foil. When the group has experimented with this process, reverse it by obtaining a variety of textured objects that the children can press the foil over to make another type of embossed image.

GEOMETRIC DESIGNS   Use a compass with a blunt point to make a variety of circles on a piece of paper. Have a collection of colored pencils for the children to use for this purpose. After the children have made an interesting overlapping design, suggest that they color in certain parts of it, if they care to. Another geometric activity is that which involves the child in tracing regular shapes, such as circles, squares, and triangles, to make overlapping designs to be colored or painted. Or, show the children how to make figures, such as people, houses, or vehicles, using only geometric shapes as the basic parts.

GRAPH PAPER   Use graph paper with ½-inch squares or larger. Let the children fill in these squares with crayons or colored pencils. Show them some Oriental and American Indian designs that use squares of this type. Use this same graph paper to outline interesting objects, such as, for example, a picture of a crooked house that has a serrated roofline, or a car with square wheels, or an angular sun.

GRATED CRAYONS   Use a food grater or a pencil sharpener to make bits of crayon that can be placed between sheets of waxed paper or plastic wrap. Add other flat items, such as leaves, colored tissue paper, colored cellophane, weeds, butterfly wings, feathers, or grasses. When the assemblage is ready, press the paper with a warm iron and hang the finished product in a window. As a variation of this approach, give the children oil pastel crayons and have them write and draw directly on the surface of the waxed paper before the iron is used.

JUNK SCULPTURE   Help the children to invent a model of an original invention or a machine. Give the class small pieces of wood, metal, or plastic to glue or nail to a board. Bottle caps and spools serve as gears and pulleys, washers can become wheels. As a variation, some children might want to make a robot or a monster. Another type of junk sculpture is that which involves children in impaling toothpicks into styrofoam balls, plastic meat trays, cardboard boxes, or other discarded materials. Similarly, crumple up balls of aluminum foil or window screening and have the children impale twigs, lollipop sticks, or other objects in an interesting arrangement.

LINE DESIGNS   Give the children paper and a variety of materials to create two-dimensional line designs. This could be yarn glued to the paper, or toothpicks, matchsticks, or cotton roving. String and rubber bands are other possibilities. To add interest to this approach, have the children glue the elements together on a piece of waxed paper. When the glue is dry, peel off the paper. This produces an item that can be suspended as part of a mobile, for example.

MELTED CRAYONS   Involve the children in an encaustic crayon activity without danger from the heat that is usually necessary. Find an old muffin tin that will fit over the flat side of a gallon can which has one side removed. Get a 100-watt bulb, place it inside the tin can, and place the muffin tin over the bulb. The heat will be just enough to melt scraps of crayons that are put into the compartments of the muffin tin. Give the children cotton swabs and let them paint pictures on paper. As the crayon cools it will make a bumpy surface very much like oil painting.

MOSAICS   Keep a box or drawer full of many different kinds of scraps that can be used for collages and mosaics. Multicolored paper squares are only one possibility. Suggest that the children glue these to the paper in overlapping designs to give the surface added texture. Seeds, leaves, grasses, and other natural items offer other possibilities. For these materials use the lids of shallow boxes as the space to be filled. Think also in terms of food items, such as dry cereal, macaroni, or beans. Still another idea is to use different sizes of nails and have the child make a three-dimensional mosaic of nail heads. Or, invert a large nail, and let the children hit it repeatedly on a piece of wood to make still another kind of pattern.

OVERSIZE DRAWINGS   Give the students large sections of newsprint or classified ads from the newspaper and encourage them to make large sweeping movements with their arms. This should encourage them to be more free with their drawing and painting.

Another possibility is to have them draw on the paper, using various art media, with the accompaniment of music with a definite rhythm. A different type of oversize drawing is one in which the children draw large versions of each other: have individual children lie down on the floor on large pieces of paper, then outline their bodies. Let the children fill in the details and add paints, if desired.

OUTLINE DESIGNS   Use dark paint to outline colorful paint blobs that are placed on paper. With black paint make a series of parallel outlines moving farther and farther out from the original spot of color on the surface, or ask the children to write or print their own names on the paper, and use the dark paint technique to outline these names to make an abstract design.

RUBBER CEMENT DRIPS   Using a plastic squeeze bottle filled with rubber cement, dribble a thin stream of cement onto a piece of paper. Instruct the children to color in the areas outlined by the random dribbles. When the children are done coloring in these areas, show them how to rub off the rubber cement, leaving a series of white lines all through the design. For a similar effect have the children dribble thinned white glue in the same way they dribbled the rubber cement; the difference, of course, is that the white glue cannot be peeled away.

RUBBINGS   Assemble a collection of commonplace objects that have interesting textural possibilities: keys, coins, screening, combs, wood grain, rough fabric, office supply items. Show the children how to hold their crayons, chalk, or charcoal flat-side-down, and rub over paper which has been placed over arrangements of these objects. Help the children to identify interesting textures out-of-doors as you take them outside to make rubbings of things they find there: traffic signs, tree bark, pebbles in the concrete, metal grates, bricks, etc.

SCULPTURE EXPLORATION   Give the children wide experience in manipulating objects in the third dimension. From time to time have them use items that are used over and over again, each time to produce a different design experience. The most obvious possibility is building blocks. The toys which children often have in school for playtime are other suggestions: Tinker Toys, Lego blocks, Lincoln logs, and other building materials are very useful here.

Or, use spring-type clothespins; connect these onto each other or place them along the edges of cartons and cans. Scraps of flannel-board material can also expose the young child to design possibilities with almost endless variations.

SKETCHING PEOPLE Young children are only beginning to express interest in drawing people, and they tend not to know how to do it well. One suggestion is that they use stick figures or ovals for the various body parts. Help them to observe some of the main details of the body, including where the arms and legs bend. Apply this knowledge of the body parts to making simple puppets that can be connected with brass fasteners. Another activity with drawing people is that in which each child is given a duplicated picture of a funny face or of a cartoon character. Ask each child to decorate his own picture however he wants to—by adding glasses, curly hair, whiskers, funny hats, bandages. Some of these additions can be items that are glued to the picture surface for a third dimension.

SQUIGGLE DESIGNS Stimulate the children's imagination as they are challenged to incorporate random lines and objects into a design. Give each child a piece of paper and an implement with which to draw. Place on each child's paper some random line or squiggle, and challenge him to make a design based on that one element. A similar approach is to give to each child a small geometric piece of colored paper, or a button, and ask him to do the same. Note the variety of ideas in response to the situation.

STENCILS Show the children how to cut out cardboard stencils and then trace around them, repeating the patterns in overlapping or adjacent designs. These stencils can be tracings around cookie cutters, geometric shapes, or random designs. Use different colors of crayon or chalk for each repeat of the design. Use these stencils as both positive and negative design experiences. In addition to tracing around them, use chalk or crayon to rub over them onto a paper surface; or place the paper over the stencil, and rub over it with the crayon or chalk held flat in the hand.

STRING SCULPTURES Notch a cardboard circle and give the children colored string or yarn to cover randomly the surface of this circle. Do the same with notched cardboard rectangles. Or, find twigs which lend themselves to the "eye of God" design activity. A similar idea is to use colored rubber bands of varying lengths and thicknesses and stretch them over sturdy cardboard shapes.

TRACINGS Young children enjoy tracing as an art activity. They like to trace around things, especially their body parts. Have them trace around their hands, for instance, and convert the tracings into tree branches, adding blots of paint, tissue scraps, or sponge paintings at the end of each finger. Or, change these tracings, with the addition of color, into turkeys or butterflies. Also trace around shoes and feet and incorporate these tracings into other designs. Common objects found in the home or in the school can also be traced: kitchen implements or office supply items can easily become part of larger designs.

WET CHALK Add variety and reduce dust by having the children use wet chalk in their design experiences. Or, wet the paper on which the drawing is being done. If it is quite wet, the colors will tend to bleed and blend. As another possibility, wet the paper with different substances: liquid starch brushed over the paper is one possibility. Buttermilk produces an effect somewhat like oil paints.

WEAVING Incorporate design into a variety of weaving activities: Let the children stitch with colored string, weaving in and out of the holes on hardware cloth or window screening. Or have them cut paper strips for weaving into mat-like designs. Strings wound around a cardboard box also serve as a handy loom for children's weaving activities.

MOTIVATING Art Activities

ART DAY   Arrange an occasional "Art Day" to direct special attention to materials and methods not only for your children, but also for the other children in the school. Exhibit the art work in the hallways, and on folding partitions made of sections of decorated refrigerator cartons. Put up posters advertising the event, and send invitations to parents. Place publicity with local news media. Explain some of the basic art processes and give each visitor a student-made souvenir.

CLEAN-UP   Assign regular responsibilities for the clean-up at the conclusion of art activities. Explain to the children that the experience is not done until the materials are put away. Have each child know what is expected of him individually. Prepare the materials so the clean-up is simple: for example, fingerpainting can be done on metal trays that have low edges, and when the children are done, the whole tray can be taken to the sink and rinsed off. Similarly, plastic baggies can be placed inside cans into which paint is poured, and when the paint is used up, the baggies can simply be discarded and new ones can be placed in the cans.

COLORING BOOKS   Art specialists generally suggest avoiding coloring books for young children, since the models of art experiences that are presented in the books tend to condition the children's notions about drawing. One alternative activity, in the event that the children need manipulative skill in handling their crayons, is to ask them to make their own random scribble designs and fill in the spaces between their loops. This should help minimize their dependency on the representational art work of others.

COMPETITIONS Contests in art are not particularly appropriate, partly because such competitions tend to be principally coloring contests, and secondly, children's art is difficult to evaluate. More important, a child's main competition should come from within himself as he strives to set his own standards and to improve upon them. Let each child choose *his* best for a display, and if prizes are awarded, *each* participant should receive one.

DEMONSTRATIONS Invite local resource persons to come to the classroom and demonstrate various processes. Contact local potters, weavers, seamstresses, or other artisans. Survey the parents of your children to find those with art as a hobby or as a profession. Get in touch with art teachers from junior high schools, high schools, and colleges. Where resource people cannot come to you, take the children on a trip to a local studio.

DISCARDS Teach children responsibility for conserving materials by utilizing all the scraps from art activities. Maintain a scrap box or a drawer in which there are bits of paper, cloth, junk, small boxes, felt, and other salvaged items. Give the children free access to this collection whenever they have free time for exploring art. Encourage them to bring discarded items to add to the assortment.

EXCHANGES Check the current professional magazines for names of teachers who seek to exchange art objects with other classes in distant cities. Set up a regular procedure for exchanging items with these persons. Or, on a smaller basis, make arrangements with other teachers in your school or in your community to swap art work of children of comparable ages.

FOLDERS Maintain a collection of representative work from each child in the class. Keep these items for display purposes and for sharing with parents at conference time. Help the children make folders for flat work from heavy paper, oilcloth, or vinyl. Lace these folders together with yarn or string. Add the child's name or initials with fabric tape. Where it is not feasible to have folders, store art work rolled up and placed inside tubes that have been salvaged from gift wrappings at holiday times.

GRADING   Since art is a very personal statement, it should not be graded with a letter. It should be sufficient to report, instead, the child's responses to different media, his interpretations, and comments. Noticeable skills should be recorded on a checklist, along with notations concerning his general work habits, attitudes, effort, and interest.

MASTERPIECES   Develop an appreciation for the traditionally great art products by maintaining a junior gallery of art masterpiece reproductions that are cut from magazines, glued to wood or cardboard, and then shellacked for permanence. Let the children arrange these items in a special corner, or check them out to take home. Contact a local library or art department for similar checkout privileges.

MESSINESS   Some young children are very reluctant to get themselves dirty, and they may need some encouragement to participate fully in pasting, painting, and clay activities. Reinforce the notion that it is permissible to get dirty in the process. Show the child that you expect some untidiness as a natural outcome, and accept occasional spills and other accidents as additional learning experiences. Let the uncertain child ease into messy experiences. For example, the first finger painting activity might well involve only the forefinger used as a paintbrush. Provide adequate protection for clothing in the form of aprons or smocks. Let the children begin by holding messy materials in clothespins—for instance, during sponge painting. Also, provide short brushes for spreading paste.

MODELING   Demonstrate a personal enthusiasm for art, and participate in different activities as a teacher-learner in order to help anticipate some of the problems the child may encounter. However, try to avoid providing finished products that might serve as the models for the child to imitate. Instead, try to show that you respect the subject and each individual process.

PREPARATION   Provide sufficient materials and adequate instruction in their use. Distribute the materials in the order in which they are to be used, and do so promptly after the explanation. Give only the most essential directions in order not to curtail initial interest in exploring the medium under discussion. Introduce the class to only one art medium at a time.

SCHEDULING   Try to plan classroom art activities at times when the children would logically next move into an individual experience, such as playtime, rest time, or snack time. This will avoid having all children finish at the same time, and yet will aid clean-up by having a high-interest activity immediately following art. Also plan your activities to avoid having a large group of children involved at the same time, if this is at all possible. It is better to explain the basic procedures to all, but stagger the participations so only a small group are working on the medium at one time, especially when the medium is very messy or when it requires much intensive supervision.

SCRAPBOOK   Maintain a classroom scrapbook of different types of art work contributed by children during the school year. Be sure that all children in the group are represented, and that a wide variety of experiences are included. Keep this collection as a permanent exhibit for visitors. Include examples of materials that have been displayed in the classroom for all the children to enjoy.

VARIATIONS   Encourage the children to think in terms of alternatives and variations in art activities. Help them to think beyond your literal instructions. Present them with different shapes of paper, for example, rather than asking them to work only with rectangular pieces. Suggest that they try to see in how many different ways they can produce an effect with the medium at hand. Let them have many different kinds of paint, many different kinds of paper, and the freedom to explore all possibilities.

Involving Pupils in PAINTING

ADDITIVES Vary the painting experiences by adding different ingredients. For example, if powdered tempera is mixed with buttermilk instead of with water, it produces a chalky effect. Canned
milk of the condensed variety produces a glossy effect when it is
mixed with tempera paint. Wallpaper paste added to powdered
paint makes a thicker medium that simulates oil paints.

BLOTTING An interesting experience with paint is to drop a blob of
paint on a piece of paper folded in half. Then fold over the other
half of the paper onto the blob, and rub it with the hands to spread
the blob of paint. Open up the paper to dry. A different version of
this activity is to fold the paper into quarters, and place two
different blobs of paint on two different sections of the paper. Then
fold the paper together and press down. Open up the paper and fold
it the other dimension, mixing the colors that have already been
mixed to get interesting variations in colors. Still another possibility is to use blotting paper to pick up random pools of watercolors.

BLOWING Place pools of dark paint on light paper, or vice versa,
and give each child a soda straw. Instruct him to blow his paint in
different directions to produce a branch-like effect. When this
paint is dry, let him take a paintbrush and add a pretty blob of color
at the end of each of the strands of paint on the original part. As
variations, add bits of fabric or powder puffs of cotton at the tips of

these branches. Let the older children try the blowing technique with ink instead of paint.

BRAYER   The brayer allows the child to roll out paints on a smooth surface and then transfer the paint to a paper. If the regular printing inks are not available, mix tempera paint into a thick consistency and roll the brayer over it. For variety, also roll the brayer over string which will adhere to the brayer and make an interesting repeat design as the brayer is then run over the paper. Another adaptation of the brayer idea is to make a design with the finger or with a stick or some other device, marking on the surface of the rolled-out paint. Then place a clean piece of paper over the design and lift a monoprint from it; newsprint is especially appropriate for monoprints.

BRUSHES   Give the children opportunities to explore paint as a medium with different kinds of brushes. One-inch enamel brushes from a hardware store come in handy for spreading large amounts of paint. Using the standard-sized art brushes for young children, show them how to use the brush to produce different effects: for example, the brush can be rolled along the paper as the child holds it between his fingers, or the brush can be pressed down and then lifted, to produce a brush-print. It can be twirled to make a round spot. It can be used almost dry for a feathery effect. It can drizzle and drip paint onto a surface.

DYE   Tie together, or fold, the corners of paper towels or discarded sheeting, and dip them into commercial dyes or thinned paints. Have several different primary colors, and experiment with dipping the material into two or more colors. Vary the dyeing process with older primary children by having cotton swabs dipped into commercial dye solutions. Using white fabrics or white construction paper, the children should be able to paint on the surface; there will be a darker shade everywhere the swab touches.

FINGER PAINTING   This activity is one of the staples of the preschool children, and there is no reason why primary children cannot enjoy it as well. There are many good suggestions for enhancing this type of art experience:

Body Parts: Because fingerpainting is so familiar to some students, it is appropriate to introduce different body parts that can become involved in the painting process. For example, let the children use just one finger just like a paint brush, dipping it into thick tempera or commercial finger paints and painting on paper with just the one finger. Or, have the child dip different fingers into different colors of paint and use the hand just like a palette, one color at a time. Let the child also explore the effects of using a fist, knuckles, a forearm, elbows, finger tips, thumbs, palms, or the heel of the hand. After the children have experimented with these body parts, let them transfer the paint onto paper, making prints of each of the body parts involved. If the weather is warm, ask them to take off their shoes and socks and use their toes and feet in a related activity.

Media: Help the children to consider finger painting with substances other than commercial finger paints. Use liquid starch as one possibility. Place a small pool of starch in the center of the finger painting surface and sprinkle dry tempera paint in the middle of the puddle, allowing the individual child to mix his own paint with his hands. Regular wheat paste can be mixed to the consistency of thick cream and tempera paints can be added for a good medium. Liquid detergent is also an acceptable substitute. Spray shaving cream foam onto a smooth surface for tactile exploration, adding food coloring for pastel paints. Mix media by wiping away wet color with a disposable tissue; this will leave a streak of white in the design on the paper. Or, add bits of colored tissue, sand, salt, or dry powdered paint to the wet surface to add texture. When individual children are reluctant to finger paint, introduce small amounts of different substances, such as catsup, jam, mustard, cold cream, mayonnaise, peanut butter, hand lotion, margarine, petroleum jelly, whipped soap flakes, or even pudding.

Prints: Let the child make a design in finger paints on a smooth surface. Then, using a large piece of newsprint, lay the paper on the design and smooth it with the hands. Lift it off as a monoprint. In this way the same painting surface can be used repeatedly, saving paint, and giving each child a copy of his own design. Another type of print is made by laying the newsprint very gently onto the design done in the finger paints. Then, using clean hands, make another design with just the index finger, drawing directly on the paper as it lies on top of the finger painted surface. Lifting off the print, you will find a combination of the original design and the new one as well.

Papers: Glazed shelf paper in rolls is less expensive than commercial finger painting paper, and may be easily cut to different sizes if it is stored in a box with a serrated cutting edge. Add texture to finger painting paper by crumpling it into a ball and then smoothing it out again before painting on it; the paint tends to seep into the cracks in the paper, making a crackled effect. Discover images in these random wrinkles and outline them with black paint when the finger painting is dry. Glossy magazine pages also serve well as finger painting papers. Choose colors of paper that contrast with the colors of the paints. Waxed paper may also be used as a finger painting surface, particularly when the painting is done with liquid starch or liquid detergent.

MARBELIZING   Make an interesting design on paper surfaces by floating enamel paints on an inch of water in an old roasting pan. Place a spoonful of enamel onto the surface of the water and swirl the water gently to mix the paint. Place the paper on the surface of the water, and lift it off quickly. The enamel should adhere in a swirled pattern. When the process has been tried successfully, mix two primary colors of enamel and try it again as a color mixing experience.

MIXING   Purchase paints in the three primary colors, plus black and white. Have the children experiment with color mixing to obtain the secondary and tertiary colors. Provide activities in which the children can produce tints of basic colors by adding white, and also make shades of colors by adding black. Let the more mature children make charts showing gradations of these colors.

POOLING   Give each child a large piece of paper and on it place a small pool of paint. Show him how to tilt the paper to puddle the paint as it runs back and forth on the paper. As an interesting version of this activity, wet the paper first, and let the paint make a fairyland of colors as two or more colors are used in the process. The approach is most successful when glazed paper is a part of the procedure.

PRINTING   Fold an absorbent paper towel and place it in the bottom of a shallow plastic container and saturate the towel with paint, turning it into a stamp pad. Encourage the children to find objects to make prints with, dipping the objects into the paint and then pressing them firmly on the paper. Let the children experiment to find the right amount of paint for each item. Show them how to make repeat patterns, or overlapping designs with different colors of paint. Some of the more commonplace things to print with might include:

VEGETABLES AND FRUITS

lemon half	potato slice	cabbage wedge
apple half	carrot slice	turnip half
grapefruit half	orange half	celery stalk
beet half	bell pepper half	ear of corn

NATURAL ITEMS

pine cone	smooth stone	cattail
moss	bark	leaf
shell	nut half	fern

OFFICE AND HOUSEHOLD OBJECTS

small box	styrofoam	cork
corrugated paper	cookie cutter	eraser
wadded foil	alphabet block	kitchen utensil
rubber scrap	dribbled glue	sponge
wood scrap	felt scrap	towel tube
wood knot	spice can	bottle
stopper	comb	fork

SMEARING   Place a blob of paint on a paper and give the child a comb or a notched piece of cardboard and show him how to drag it around through the paint to spread it in an interesting fashion. When the child has completed this exploration, introduce a second and a third color for further experimentation. Another type of smear painting is made by covering one sheet of paper with paint and then dragging another sheet of paper over the top of it, catching the paint in a random design. If the paint is rather thickly applied on the base sheet, it will peak and leave a more interesting design.

SOAP FLAKE PAINTING   Add paint to a mixture of soap flakes dissolved in warm water, thick enough to peak when beaten with a hand beater. Let the children put their hands in this mixture and spread the paint on a paper. Another possibility is to add food coloring to a container of liquid detergent, and beat the detergent with a beater until bubbles rise up over the edge of the shallow container. Quickly remove the beater and place a piece of white paper over these bubbles. The bubbles should burst against the surface of the paper, leaving delicate pastel rings.

SPATTER   Place a piece of paper underneath a piece of window screening or fine-mesh hardware cloth. Dip a toothbrush into thickened tempera paint and rub it over the screening, causing the paint to spatter onto the surface below. Place different stencils over the paper beforehand to make designs. Also, it is wise to do this art activity inside a cardboard box to prevent undue mess. Another kind of spatter instrument is a commercial pump-type fly sprayer, with a bottle that can be filled with thinned paint.

SQUIRTING   Fill a plastic squeeze bottle with thin tempera paint. Set up a large cardboard carton outdoors and tape a piece of paper to its interior wall. Show the children how to squirt this paint in streams onto the paper. A water pistol is handy for decorating the carton when the other painting is done. If you must do this type of activity indoors, give the children several eye droppers to fill with paint and squirt onto a surface.

STIPPLING   Cut a stencil to be used in the activity, then take a small sponge or a wad of paper toweling, dipping it into paint. Very gently press the sponge or paper wad around the edge of the stencil, leaving a feather design. Stippling can also be done with a paintbrush that is just barely touched to the paint, so only the ends of the hairs are wet. This approach can be used to produce effects like a snowfall, sand on a beach, stars in the sky, or similar dotted arrangements.

STRING PAINTING   A short length of string can give a variety of painting experiences. For one thing, string can be dunked into thick tempera and then held over a paper to dribble and drip randomly all over the surface. Another possibility is to place the string onto one half of a paper folded in the middle; then fold the other part of the paper over and press it down onto the paint-loaded string for a mirror image. A string pull is accomplished by having the string in the middle of the folded paper, as just described. However, instead of simply pressing the paper down on the string, press down and pull the string out from underneath your hand as you hold the one half of the paper down on the bottom half. This pulled string should produce an interesting double-image feathery design.

TWIRLING   Cut out a square of paper, and punch several holes in the very middle of it. Attach this paper to the bottom of a rotary egg beater, using string or plastic wires. Have one child hold the beater with one hand, and turn the crank with the other, while a second child dribbles paint onto the twirling paper. As the paint tends to fly off the paper, this process is best done down inside a cardboard box with the beater being held right side up and the paper at the bottom of it.

WATERCOLORS   For young children, watercolors are not espe cially useful. The pans of color are too small, and become too easily muddied. Also, the brushes appropriate for watercoloring are too small for easy handling. However, some paints are sold in large cakes which can be softened beforehand, and the children can use larger size brushes with these cakes of paint. One application of these watercolors is to make broad background washes for their pictures: when the backgrounds are dry, the children can paint over them, drawing figures of persons, houses, trees, or random designs.

WATER PAINTING   Just for fun with younger children, give them containers of water and large paint brushes purchased at a hardware store. When the weather is warm take the children outdoors and let them paint designs on the sidewalks or playground. Of course, these designs will evaporate rapidly, but the children will have a lot of fun. Try this same approach indoors on the chalk board when there is extra time.

What to Make with PAPER

ACCORDION FOLDS Show the children how to fold paper accordion-style for a variety of projects. (The easiest way to accordion fold is to fold the paper in half lengthwise, then in half again and again; finally open up the paper and refold it, alternating the creases, accordion style.) An obvious application is a simple fan, made by gathering the folds at one end, and stapling them to produce the fan shape. Or staple the folds in the center to make a hair bow or a bow tie. Also demonstrate how to cut paper doll type figures from larger accordion folds, remembering to keep a segment between each section so the multiple-folded images will not fall apart. Light paper, such as tissue paper or onion skin, is easier for children to cut when several figures are being produced at the same time. Accordion-folded strips can be used for spring-like elements that can serve as the arms and legs of creatures, as well.

ANIMALS Paper animals can be made in several simple ways. One approach is to draw original animals, or trace around pictures of animals, and cut them out. Then punch a hole in the top and bottom of each figure using a paper punch. Take a soda straw and run it through these two holes, and the effect will be an animal on a pole, like a carousel creature. Place a number of these figures between two paper plates, each of which has matching holes punched in its edge to accommodate the animal figures. The final product will be a clever merry-go-round.

Paper animals can be made by cutting folded pieces of construction paper. A piece of paper folded in half can become a stand-up animal, such as a bear or a rabbit, if it is placed on a surface vertically; it can represent a cow or a lion if it is used horizontally. Show the children how to cut into the fold to make a little slit that will accommodate other smaller pieces of paper that are to serve as tails, necks, etc. Each of these smaller pieces, in turn, can be folded, a slit cut into the fold, and still another piece of paper can be inserted as horns, heads, or ears.

ATTACHMENTS   Let the children experiment with a variety of ways of attaching one piece of paper to another piece. Paste and glue will be widely used, although some adhesives take too long to dry, and others tend to flake and lose their ability to adhere. Suggest a stapler for some activities, tape for others, and perhaps even string. On occasion, let them cut several pieces of paper and attach them with brass fasteners, allowing movement of the various parts. This latter approach is well adapted to making simple two-dimensional puppets.

BOX SCULPTURE   Empty cartons lend themselves to a wide variety of design experiences. For example, a very large box can be cut away with a large dull serrated knife or a keyhole saw. Each side of the box can be cut into a random shape, or it can be cut into a geometric design. Smaller cartons can be taped or stapled together to make surrealistic animals. A milk carton can be converted into an animal. Open boxes can become vehicles, houses, or other toys.

BRAIDING   Teach children the simple three-strand braiding process, letting them practice on large pieces of string or rope. Then apply this skill to papercraft by stretching out long strips of crepe paper and twisting them to make long, thin strings. Or, cut paper strips from construction paper, and let the children braid them by folding them in, onto each other.

CAGES   To hold the animals produced during a study of circuses or zoos, show the children how to use open-sided boxes, with notches cut in them, as cages. Wrap yarn or colored string around the box, fitting the strands into the appropriate notches to make the bars for the cage. Another approach is to give each child a piece of colored construction paper for the cage. Have him cut out his animals and paste them on this piece of paper. Then ask the child to cut strips of contrasting colored paper to serve as the bars of the cage, pasting them into place. A third idea is to fold a piece of construction paper in half lengthwise, and cut into the fold at about half-inch intervals, perpendicular to this fold, and almost to the outer edge of the paper. Then open up the paper, and interweave animals—that have been made to fit into cages of this size—between these cut strips. Add colorful wheels for a circus menagerie wagon.

CATERPILLARS A caterpillar can be made from sections of an egg carton, with the addition of pipe cleaners for antennae and legs. Or, cut a series of strips of paper and fasten them into loops, then tape or staple these loops together. A simple caterpillar can also be made from a long accordion-folded strip of paper to which eyes and feelers have been added.

CELLOPHANE SQUARES Cut a variety of cellophane squares from different colors, then combine several of these in an overlapped position, gluing them together with small dabs of liquid starch or clear glue. Before the adhesive dries, rotate these squares a partial turn. When the adhesive is thoroughly dry, hang these objects in a strong light source for an interesting and colorful effect. Cellophane squares can also be glued to the backs of black paper that has been cut away, producing a stained glass effect. Another use of cellophane squares is to glue them onto white paper in different arrangements and then draw on them with felt-tip pens of different colors.

COLLAGES A humorous collage is made as children cut out various animal pictures from magazines, and then cut these pictures apart, making a pile of heads, a pile of legs, a pile of bodies, and so on. Give each child a piece of paper as the background and have him select random body parts to construct his own animal. Then suggest that he glue pieces of fur, leather, or feathers onto the animal. Use this same general approach to parts of machines and foil paper, or adapt it to pictures of people and scraps of fabric.

CONES A cone of paper can be made into many kinds of things. To make a cone, cut out a circle of paper, and then cut into the center of this circle from the edge. A shallow cone of paper can be useful as a mask, or a hat. A deeper paper cone can serve as an Indian teepee, a Christmas ornament, a clown hat, or a May basket.

CORRUGATIONS Corrugated paper makes many interesting effects. Cut as it is, it can serve as a fence, a side of a log cabin, or it can give added texture to a collage. Or, cut strips of corrugated paper across its grain and glue these to make a sculpture arrangement that projects out from the surface of the background. Also, cut corrugations into small rectangles to make bricks for construction activities.

CRUMPLING Show the children how to add texture and variety to their paper experiences by crumpling the paper in their hands, and then smoothing it out again. Suggest that they look for creases in the paper that resemble figures and animals that they can outline with crayon or paint. Use these same lines to divide the paper into areas for painting or coloring in. As a paint activity, let the children paint over the paper with thinned paint, and the creases will absorb the paint. As another variation of this process, show the children how to randomly fold the paper, instead of crumpling it: again, open up the paper, smooth it down, and use these areas for color or design explorations.

CURLING The simple skill of curling paper strips opens many applications for the young child. First, show him how to hold a narrow strip of paper over the blade of an open scissors. Then instruct the student how to press against the blade and the strip, using his thumb, with just enough pressure to cause a little resistance. The paper will curl as it is pulled through. Use these curls for decorating masks, for making mobiles, for adding tails to animal figures, or just as added texture in a paper sculpture.

CYLINDERS Show the children how to roll large sections of paper into cylinders so they will stand up by themselves. Let them cut shapes into the cylinders before they are permanently fastened together; these can be random figures or geometric designs, or the features of a face. As a simple sculpture activity, instruct the children to choose rectangles of paper of different colors and different sizes, and roll each one into a rectangle, then stapling these cylinders together in a pleasant arrangement.

EXPLODED DESIGNS An interesting cut-and-paste involvement is the invention of an exploded design. To do this ask the children to draw and cut out an original picture, or cut out a picture of interest from a magazine or a newspaper. Then show them how to cut this same picture into thin strips, cutting either in a straight line or in curvy lines. Keeping these strips in their same relative positions that they occupied in the original picture, show the children how to paste them onto another paper surface of a contrasting color, allowing a fraction of an inch between each strip. The picture will retain its original impact, but will also have a somewhat fractured effect.

FADES Take advantage of the natural tendency of construction paper to fade. Ask the children to take a piece of paper and cut it into a shape that will serve as a stencil. Then have them take a dark colored piece of construction paper, and lay the stencil on top of it. Place these items in a sunny spot on a window sill, weighting them down to prevent their moving out of position. After two weeks of sunny weather, the stencil should be removed, and a design will appear on the larger piece of construction paper.

FRINGES Many young children need extra practice in handling a pair of scissors. One practical activity to provide this practice in an interesting way is to show the children how to cut fringes. To do this they need merely to hold the paper in one hand and cut simple cuts in series along the edge of the paper. Suggest that the children use these fringes as the whiskers for puppets, grass for their landscapes, edges of place mats, or as decorations on Indian items.

IMPALED DESIGNS All children like to punch holes in things. With paper this can be done constructively, and the paper can be used as an extra textural activity. One possibility is to give each child a piece of paper, and ask him to place the paper over a carton that has a sturdy piece of hardware cloth over it. Then, using a blunt instrument, such as a large nail, let the child push holes in the paper. When he is done, let him paste the paper onto another paper surface with the rough spots exposed to view. Another type of impaling is done by cutting a series of random shapes from colored paper, and punching a hole through the middle of every piece. Then draw yarn or string through each hole, using a looped wire needle.

INCISING Children sometimes want to be able to cut out an area inside the boundaries of a piece of paper. Although the quickest way to do this is to use a sharp instrument, for the sake of the safety of the younger child, a better alternative is to show the child how to punch a hole into the paper, using the point of his scissors, pushing against a piece of cardboard with the point instead of against his hand. Another safe way of cutting out an inside portion of a piece of paper is to cut into the area from the edge, cutting away the desired interior shape, then pasting this piece of paper onto another paper surface so the initial cut of the scissors will not show. A third approach to incising is to fold the paper in a crease at whatever point the interior cutting is needed, then cutting out the shape, and finally opening up the paper again and smoothing it out. This latter process can be used to decorate a rather large piece of paper with interesting shapes: the children can repeatedly fold portions of this paper and cut designs into these folds. Suggest that some of these folds can be done in double-folds and four-folds to multiply the images.

MOBILES   Bend coat hangers into different shapes, cover them with tissue paper or cellophane, and hang them in a strong light source. Use raffia loops covered with paper for the same general effect. Another possibility is to fold small geometric bits of paper and thread them on a string or a piece of yarn, suspending them from the ceiling. A third method is to press objects, such as bits of colored tissue paper, cellophane, or crayon scrapings, between waxed paper sandwiches. Suspend these from thin wires balanced in the middle: start a multi-level mobile from the bottom, balancing each element as it is added, and making a loop in the wire at this point of balance.

PAPIER MACHE   Many types of paper are appropriate for sculpturing with papier mache mix. However, since young children tend to be impatient with the long waiting required for this process, there are several shortcuts that may help. For one thing, although commercial wheat paste, or even flour, is sometimes used in the mixture, the mixing can take a lot of extra time. A simpler procedure is to use liquid starch reduced in strength with the addition of water. Also, the shredding paper activity is very time-consuming. A better plan is to use cleansing tissues or napkins, which take the mixture well and adhere to holding surfaces because they are not too thick.

For a solid molding experience, soak a roll of colored toilet tissue in water for several hours. Then tear it apart and add equal parts of salt and flour. Shape it into the desired form using the hands, or a pre-arranged mold. Since the molded products must be dried thoroughly before being painted, place them over a ventilator that has a steady air flow, or place them in an oven set on a low temperature. During hot, muggy weather, retard the possibility of molding and unpleasant odors by adding small amounts of oil of cloves or oil of wintergreen to the papier mache mixture.

POSITIVES AND NEGATIVES Ask the children to choose two contrasting colors of paper, rectangular in shape, one twice as large as the other. Show the children how to cut a shape out of the smaller piece of paper. Paste the smaller piece of paper onto the larger piece in such a way that it occupies one side or the other exactly. Then take the shape that was cut from the smaller piece of paper and paste it onto the larger sheet of paper at the same relative position that the opening occurs in the smaller paper.

PUNCH Give the children a paper punch and let them punch holes in scraps of paper. Use the pieces of paper that accumulate in the punch as confetti for mosaics. Show the children how to punch holes around the edges of a stiff piece of paper or cardboard, and then use a piece of yarn or string to weave in and around these holes. As an unusual variation of this activity, show the children how to use some pointed instrument, such as a kitchen skewer, or a large nail, to prick a design around a piece of paper, with the holes close enough together to allow the children to tear the design away, pulling carefully along the pricking marks. Demonstrate how to prick the paper as it rests on a pad of several thicknesses of corrugated cardboard.

SACKS A simple paper bag has almost unlimited possibilities for exploration. It can readily be turned into a puppet, using the folded portion as the mouth. As the child inserts his hand into this fold and moves his fingers, the mouth opens and closes. The sack can also be stuffed and decorated to resemble a jack-o-lantern, or a head of a puppet perched on the child's index finger. A sack can also be cut into along the folds to produce a random open sculpture. Parallel rings can be produced by cutting around the sack, and these rings can be combined into mobile hangings.

SCORING This is a technique that is useful for bending paper along a curved line. Show the children how to use the point of a pair of scissors, pressing this point or some similar instrument into the surface of a piece of stiff paper with just enough pressure to make a noticeable crease, without tearing the surface of the paper. Then pick up the piece of paper, and carefully bend the paper together at the crease.

SHOEBOXES Make a collection of shoeboxes and comparable cartons and involve them in your art program. A box can become a house for doll play. Several boxes placed vertically can represent a totem pole, as the children paint them and decorate them with ears and other facial features. Also use them for dioramas in which other paper and cardboard cutouts are pasted to the background or set up on the edge of the box facing the viewer.

STRIPS Cut a variety of paper strips on a paper cutter and encourage the children to use them in a variety of activities. For example, show the children how to lay them out in a starburst effect, and staple the assemblage in the center to keep them together. Or, using this same starburst, pull up the ends of each strip and staple them together at a second point to make a three-dimensional object. Too, you can show the children how to arrange strips in rows to make a rainbow stapled or pasted onto a second large piece of paper. Another possibility is folding and curling these strips, and arranging them in a random, three-dimensional construction.

STUFFING Make three-dimensional creatures by cutting out of sturdy paper two copies of the same figure: for example, a fish, a turtle, a face, or a jack-o-lantern. Ask the children to paint or color each of the two identical figures, and then staple them together, back to back, allowing just enough room to stuff the insides with crumpled tissue or paper scraps shredded on a paper cutter. When the figure has been stuffed, close the opening with more staples.

TAPE Use brown gummed paper tape in design experiences. One possibility is to fold the tape back onto itself, moistening it where it crosses itself, and make loops and whirls to decorate a random construction. Or, cut strips of this same type of tape and issue it to children to cut into interesting shapes to paste onto paper backgrounds. Masking tapes, fabric tapes, and other types of adhesive tapes can also be used in paper sculpture and paper design.

TISSUE PAPER Let the children use small pieces of colored tissue paper as painting devices. Dampen the tissue scraps thoroughly and lay them on a piece of white absorbent paper until the colors bleed off. Then remove the tissue scraps. Another use of these tissue squares is in making a fluffy surface on a large paper surface. Twist each piece of tissue around the eraser end of a pencil, dip it into glue and press it firmly onto the surface to which it is being attached.

TORN PAPER   Tearing paper is fun for children. It helps them to relieve tensions, and it gives them manipulative practice. Tearing paper also is useful for utilizing scraps of paper that otherwise might be discarded. Show the children how to tear random shapes and glue them randomly to a surface, side by side or overlapping to build up the surface. When the children need to tear paper along a line, show them how to hold their fingers close to the point of the tear. Also suggest that they crease the paper to further help them to tear the paper accurately.

part two

LANGUAGE ARTS:
Promoting
Expressive Abilities

COMPOSITION:
Writing and Telling Stories

ANIMALS Stimulate children's imaginations by reading them some of the *Just So* stories by Kipling, or other folk tales that account for the unique ways in which animals have developed their appearance or other characteristics. Then help the children to invent original stories about how the giraffe might have got his long neck, the zebra his stripes, the elephant his trunk, and the leopard his spots.

Another imaginative venture with the animal theme is the story that is told or written from the standpoint of the animal itself, such as "A Day in the Life of My Hamster," or, more imaginatively, "What It's Like to Be a Purple Elephant." Also suggest to the child that he invent an animal that would be a good friend, or ask the student to think of what animals would say about people, if animals could talk.

BOOKLETS Combine stories and pictures into booklets in a variety of ways. For example, lay several sheets of writing paper in a row on a tabletop and tape them together either at their sides or at their tops, using transparent tape. Then accordion-fold these sheets into a booklet after the child has written his story and illustrated it. Display these booklets in the open position, on a table or desk, or hanging from the ceiling or spread out on a bulletin board. Or, use them in the closed position as additional reading material in the book center.

Another booklet is made by using an attractive looseleaf notebook or scrapbook, and asking the children to add stories to the collection as they have time and interest. Or, reproduce original compositions, especially experience charts, on duplicating masters and staple the papers together to send home with the children.

CARTOONS Utilize the children's natural interest in comic characters by finding familiar cartoon strips and cutting away from them all the words that are a part of the panels. Let the children invent something that the persons in the pictures might be saying. Or, reverse this process and show the students how to draw a simple stick figure cartoon strip, adding the words after the pictures are done, illustrating several important happenings in the story.

CORRECTIONS Try to avoid inhibiting the children's creativity by overstressing accuracy of the mechanical details. Instead, try to make children aware of the more essential rules of spelling, usage, and punctuation, one or two elements at a time. Also, take special interest in these mechanical details during the more functional activities, such as writing "thank you" letters. It is also helpful to make children aware of their own errors by letting them check each other's papers from time to time.

DESCRIPTIONS Descriptive items help to sharpen powers of observation and organization. Begin with a task that the child can easily do, and ask him to describe it, such as how to ride a bicycle or how to play baseball. Or, ask him to describe himself, his pet, his family, or a special interest. Another idea is to give a pupil a commonplace object, such as an apple or a football, and let him describe as many details of this object as he can think of.

EXPERIENCE CHARTS Involve the children in composing group stories with large lined sheets of paper. In this way capture the thoughts of many children relating to activities and experiences in which they have all participated. When the children's attention is short-lived, take notes on their conversations in the group, and make the actual chart later. Where several children make contributions appropriate to the sentence being recorded, make a consensual statement incorporating as much of their content as possible. If a child's comment needs correction in the writing of it, say something like, "That's a good thought, Jimmy; another way to say it is . . ."

Use experience charts to record special topics and special events. For example, honor the birthday child by making a class birthday chart just for him; let him roll up the chart and take it home. Or, record on the chart the children's excitement about Christmas, spring, or a puppet show. Use the group composition technique also to serve as an invitation to another class to attend a party or a play.

FAVORITES Stimulate original composition by stressing the children's interests in special things. Help each child to complete a list of his favorites and then ask him to tell why they are so. Include favorite foods, hobbies, family activities, friends, school activities, stories, television programs, summer fun, days of the week, clothing, hero figures, and anything else that might encourage composition skills.

FEELINGS Allow the children to share their innermost feelings in story form. However, as they write about personal responses, respect their rights not to share them with other children if they prefer not to. This is especially true when the class is writing about things such as dreams, fears, worries, or family situations. Stress positive affective areas with settings like, "Happiness Is . . . ," "Comfortable Is . . . ," or "I'm Thankful for . . ."

FRAGMENTS Propose a series of sentence fragments that might either serve as the first part of an original story, or might be the conclusion of it. Where the child still lacks imagination to use these phrases, let him change some of the key words in them, or else have him connect several of them together to make an unusual type of a composition. Think of fragments such as these:

"The door squeaked open slowly . . ."

"Down the street came a circus . . ."

"I really didn't want a pet snake . . ."

GROUP WRITING Where certain students need help in their written composition, allow them to work together with other children having comparable ability or mutual interests. Encourage them to assist each other with their spelling and mechanical details, and suggest that they pool their imaginative powers. Or, ask a small group of children to sit in a circle and compose a story as each one, in turn, contributes a single sentence or one idea. Or further specialize the functions of several members in a group by asking one child to write a story, another child to illustrate it, and still another student to combine it into a booklet, complete with a jacket.

HEROES Read to the children an occasional story about a hero, such as historical figures like Lincoln or Columbus, contemporary persons of wide renown, or characters from fables or folklore, like Paul Bunyan or the Brave Little Tailor. After reading these stories discuss some of the qualities the children might admire in their heroes, and ask them to identify some of their present-day heroes from television or sports. Ask them also to think of themselves as a hero, and describe themselves in a story on topics such as, "If I Were a Giant," or "The Day I Saved the World."

IMAGINARY ROLES Have the children assume a variety of pretend roles, and then ask them to tell or write how they would act or feel in those situations. For example, ask them to choose an animal, bird, or insect they might like to be. Or, suggest that they take on the form of a toy animal or a mechanical toy, and tell about themselves. Or, tie into seasonal thinking with topics such as "My Life as a Jack-o-Lantern." Still another possibility is to stimulate discussion of some familiar object, and have the children write about "I Am a Grandfather Clock," or "The Sad Life of a Library Book."

LETTERS Young children are usually very excited about sending and receiving mail. As an application of composition skills to letters, suggest seasonal missives to Santa, to the Easter Bunny, or to St. Valentine. Enlist older children in the school or parents of your children to reply to these letters. Also encourage children to correspond with relatives in other geographical locations, sharing the important events of their lives. Letters for classmates in hospitals or for those who have moved to some other school are other opportunities for compositions. Also write notes of invitation and announcement to other classes in the school or in distant locations. Too, encourage the children to write letters to parents reporting special events in the classroom. Finally, suggest that the class write "thank you" notes to persons who have performed some special service or favor.

MAGIC Magic has always entranced children, for they love to pretend they have this strange power. Their oral or written compositions can thus take the form of magic carpets, magic lamps, magic wands, mirrors, or other paraphernalia of enchantment. Still another variation is to help the class think in magical terms expressed as "If I Had Three Wishes," "If I Were King," or "If I Had a Million Dollars." In these ways children not only show their composition skills but also frequently reveal their innermost thoughts and values.

MONSTERS Could there be anything more exciting for a young child than the shivery thought of a strange creature entertained in the security of a friendly classroom? One way to stimulate the thinking along these lines is to place huge footprints in the room before the class arrives some day. Arrange these ugly tracks on the floor, on the counters, and then run them up the wall. Challenge the students to imagine what kind of a creature might have visited their classroom overnight. Give the children long strips of adding machine tape, and have them write their stories vertically, one or two words per line, adding their own drawings of footprints and monsters to embellish their tales. Still another idea is to have them invent weird masks at Halloween time and then write or tell stories about their original characters.

NEWSPAPERS Children love to write for publication, and the mere mention that what they compose will be read by an audience is enough to motivate the most careful work. Make arrangements to have ditto masters for the children to use, one master per child, if possible—allow both stories and pictures to be included. Then duplicate these items, staple them together, and send copies home to parents, or exchange with other classes in the school. Suggest that the children choose a variety of different stories, such as new events, adventure or other imaginative tales, jokes and riddles, cartoons, as well as other kinds of writing representative of a community newspaper.

Also encourage the children to write stories and headlines based on their class-related reading, such as folk tales, fables, true stories, or nursery rhymes. Help them to think up original headlines for their writing. Encourage one or two children to sample the rest of the class in simple interview techniques, testing their thoughts on subjects, or favorite likes, as well as their dislikes.

PICTURES Sometimes children need some pump-priming before they are able to think of a good story. When this happens, let them choose two or three interesting pictures from your file and then ask them to write a story about all the elements included in the pictures. Or, if this is too confusing, give them just one picture, preferably an ambiguous one. Include adventure scenes, portraits, and landscapes.

Some students have personal pictures, particularly slides, photographs, postcards, or other reminders of travel fun. Ask them to bring a few into class. Too, have an instant-picture camera available and allow the children to take pictures of things that interest them in and around the classroom. Use the pictures and photographs to stimulate interest in creative writing or oral composition. If nothing else works, cut apart an exciting picture as a puzzle, and then ask the child to assemble the pieces as he would do to find a treasure, and then to describe the object of the search.

QUESTION CHART   Make a large chart and post it prominently in the classroom. On it paste a series of pockets, each with a different question label, such as: *Who? What? Where? When? How? Why?* In each pocket place word cards that qualify under the appropriate heading, or have the children collect small pictures that might be placed in these same pockets. (Glue these pictures to index cards for permanence.) Encourage the children to draw from these pockets different words or pictures and write or tell a story about them.

REMINDER CHART   Use a large poster to help the children to be aware of the need for accuracy in their written work. Include the most important suggestions for effective use of the language in oral and written form, phrasing them as self-checking lists for the children to examine after they have finished their work. On each chart have a special motif, such as an elephant, to attract their attention to a generalization. Or, include a series of small traffic signals, each one related to some aspect of composition skills—a comma might be written on a caution sign, a capital letter might be discussed on a green traffic light, a period might be related to a stop sign.

ROLLER STRIPS   Combine art and composition skills by having the children make a mural on a long roll of paper that they can attach to round sticks inside a box or carton, or adapt it to an empty television set. Assign each group of children a different portion of the paper strip, and stress with each group the importance of writing and illustrating the story in sequence. Or, assign each child in the class a different phrase of a group story to illustrate and record on the strip. When the story has been shown to all who want to see it, roll it up like a scroll for the children to use as reading material. Or, fold it accordion-style and file it for later use. Finally, let the children cut the panels apart and take them home to share with their families.

SENSORY SITUATIONS As one of the first composition activities of the school year, encourage the children to use their powers of observation and recall by having them itemize responses to some of these sensory stimulations:

Red is . . .	Slippery is . . .	A happy sound is . . .
Blue is . . .	Salty is . . .	Sour things are . . .
Hot is . . .	I like to smell . . .	A beautiful sight is . . .
Smooth is . . .	A special taste is . . .	

Provide actual pictures and objects to stimulate discussion in these areas. After the children have made one-word replies to each situation, ask them next to add descriptive words to each one to make a more specific word picture, with each extra word enhancing the meaning and color of the phrase or sentence.

SEQUELS The potential for original stories is increased if you ask children to recall the stories they have been reading in their readers or their library books and then write another version of the same story, or at least a different ending to it. Pose a question such as, "What happened after this story ended?" Or, treat the reader story as the sequel and ask, "What happened before the story you read happened?"

SHAPE BOOKS Ask the children to cut out shapes of paper on which they will write simple poems and stories, or even seasonal descriptive words. For example, have them cut writing paper, as well as construction paper, covers in the shapes of flowers, leaves, raindrops, a pumpkin, bell, star, ball, or top for their compositions. Gear these shapes to seasonal and holiday motifs, where possible. If the children are not yet proficient in drawing and cutting these shapes themselves, have cardboard templates for tracing available for the children.

SHOW AND TELL As an opportunity for oral composition, the traditional "Show and Tell" period in pre-school and primary grades is too often a waste of time. When it is handled routinely, the children lose interest. Where only those children who are outgoing are encouraged to participate, the shy child, who needs the oral exposure, does not get the practice. And even occasionally, the teacher uses this time to take care of her own business matters, a practice which tells the children that this oral activity is not important to her, either.

However, there are several good ways of handling this oral sharing activity to make it more meaningful to both the speakers and the listeners. Some of these suggestions are:

Scheduling: Re-evaluate the scheduling of the sharing period. Sometimes merely shifting it to a different part of the day is an effective way to renew the students' interest in it. A good approach is to have an end-of-session review and sharing experience, at which time the children are encouraged not only to explain to the class their own unique accomplishments, but also to help evaluate individual and group progress during the day. Also consider changing the frequency of the day or days devoted to oral sharing. Propose that each small group of children be assigned a specific day for their exclusive oral involvements. Be especially aware of the possibility of gearing sharing activities to topics of natural interest. For example, when the children are studying the ocean, it might be appropriate to ask the children to bring to school and to discuss only those items that have to do with boats, beaches, sand, shells, and driftwood.

Topics: At certain selected times have an enjoyable sharing experience by asking the children to bring in only funny things, such as riddles, cartoons, jokes and nonsense poems. Or, have them bring in their baby pictures or baby clothing. Also, suggest that some might explain how to play a new game. Or, correlate the sharing with topics of other study. For map study, ask the children to bring in and describe travel folders, flags, souvenirs, postcards, and other objects gathered during vacations.

Props and Prompters: To encourage the shy child in oral presentations, let him sit on a stool, for example, or use a low box as a platform. Or, let this reluctant child hold a familiar item out of sight and elicit from the group questions about it. If there is a child who has nothing to share, have a "Mystery Box" filled with high-interest items. Let this child reach into the box and pull something out and describe it. To make this approach even more attractive, wrap this show-and-tell box in gift paper, resembling a present, topped with a removable lid. As a variation of this idea, prepare a box with many miscellaneous objects in it. Ask the child to reach in, select several from the collection, and make up a simple story about the set he has selected.

Also use other simple props to stimulate sharing activities. One of the best of these is a discarded television set, from which the chassis has been removed. Label this piece the "Tell-A-Vision" and encourage the children to tell simple stories, and to illustrate them with captions. Another handy prop is a hand mirror with the glass removed. Each child can look into it and tell something about himself or his possessions. Or, use a pretend microphone to simulate a radio or television program. As the children gain confidence, use a real tape recorder to capture their comments.

Posters: Make a series of interesting charts to remind the children about good oral expression. Use comic pictures or pictures of animals to help them recall rules such as, "Stick to the *point,*" (illustrated by a porcupine), "Remember *whoooooo* is listening," (show a picture of an owl), or "Use your *ears*" (suggested by an elephant). Or, as another variation of the poster approach, show pictures that demonstrate how children might stand while speaking to the group, and likewise demonstrate how a good listener should behave.

SPACE STORIES Ask the children to pretend that a visitor has come to Earth from Mars or some other planet. Challenge them to explain some commonplace device or custom to this visitor, so that another child could draw a picture of this item, using the details supplied by the composer of the story. Another space trip opportunity is to make up a story about any space venture, real or imaginary, such as a visit to the moon or to another point in the universe.

STORY BALLOONS Give the children a huge piece of plain newsprint, one piece per child. Then ask each person to write any story he wants to anywhere on this large paper. When the story is done, ask the authors to draw a large balloon around each story, and then to draw a colorful picture of each person as a self-portrait. Show each child how to connect the balloon-enclosed words to a line going to the picture of that child's mouth to reinforce the notion that he has said that story by himself. Another variation of this idea is to cut out large comic characters and paste them onto large pieces of unlined paper. Then let the children write stories coming from the mouths of these characters.

STORY FOLDERS Make a pocketed folder for each commercial picture the children are going to use for inspiration in writing their stories. On the tab of each of these folders write the topic or the name of the picture. Inside each folder paste or staple the story picture and in the pocket put cards with words written on them that the children might need to use in composing their stories. On the second pocket in each folder have pieces of paper for children to use. Include a variety of types of paper so the students can have a choice in their writing materials.

SURPRISE BOX   Have a box with a good assortment of small objects, such as miniatures from the classroom toy collection. Ask each child to reach into the box and draw out several pieces, writing or telling a story about these randomly selected items. Or, have a "surprise story box" in which slips of paper are placed, each with a specific topic or the first sentence of a story on it. Each child is to withdraw his slip without looking at it beforehand and then he must write or tell a story based on the contents of the strip. Still another possibility is to have a collection of vocabulary cards in the box, especially nouns and verbs. Ask each student to take out several cards, read them, and then compose a story using this assortment of words as the main ideas in it.

TAPE RECORDERS   Where children lack imagination for making up their own stories, use a tape recorder to capture different sound effects, such as might be a part of a television show, a field trip experience, or produced in the classroom itself. Stimulate the children's discussion of these sounds and incorporate them into a narrative. Also use the tape recorder to register a child's dictated story if he is not capable of writing it down himself. In addition, be sure to use the tape recorder to play stories that have been prepared commercially for children's literary and dramatic activities.

TELEPHONE STORIES   Use the telephone to stimulate interest in composition by having the children tell or read their stories over the telephone to their parents. Or, identify some homebound child, or an invalid adult, and ask a child to tell or read this person his story. At other times, reverse the process by suggesting to homebound adults that they call various children in the classroom and read or tell these youngsters a story by telephone. A different type of activity is that which involves the children in thinking of some famous character they might like to talk with someday and tell or write what they might like to say to **that** important person.

TELEVISION STORIES   Where children lack imagination or where they need additional practice in composition, have the students recapitulate the best television programs they have seen recently.

Or, ask the students to write or tell their own television stories, particularly a sequel or another episode in a continuing series. To encourage this effort, find a console television set from which the chassis has been removed and use it as a broadcast instrument. Another related idea is to ask each child to invent a brief commercial for a television product, real or imaginary.

WHOPPERS   Give the children opportunities to stretch the truth as they compose exaggerations. See which child can think of the wildest story. For example, help them to think what might happen if cows gave chocolate milk, or if snow were colored red, or if rain fell upwards. Another idea is to help the children to make up stories about characters that are opposite from what might be otherwise expected of them. As examples, think of a story about a friendly witch, a super bug, a timid dragon, or a helpful bear.

Hints to Help
HANDWRITING

APPLICATIONS From their very first writing experiences, give the children opportunities to use their letter formations in actual words, helping them to see the relevance of their practice in useful applications. It is not effective to ask children to spend countless hours in reviewing basic strokes if this is being done in isolation from other subjects and other writing opportunities. It is far better to have the children practice only briefly and to apply each learned element immediately. Encourage the children, therefore, to use their letters in spelling words, correspondence, stories, directions, grocery lists, labels, invitations, and vocabulary words from their story reading.

CLEANLINESS Sometimes children become discouraged because their writing papers get dirty. When special writing is done, therefore, be sure everyone has clean hands, and be sure each child has a well-sharpened pencil or a ballpoint pen that does not smear. Demonstrate how to hold down the paper at the edge when writing to prevent smudging. When the children are erasing pencil marks, see that they have a soft rubber eraser of good quality to erase without blackening the paper. Show the group how to hold the edge of the paper while erasing, rubbing toward the edge of the paper to prevent tearing or wrinkling.

DEMONSTRATIONS Make the students more aware of proper handwriting techniques by letting them demonstrate for other members in the class. Even less able pupils will try harder when someone else is depending on their example or their explanation. Or, find low-achieving older students in the school who need added responsibility, and ask them to demonstrate letter formations for your own children, especially for those pupils with perceptual problems or others with the need for individual attention. Involving older children in this way also helps identify the special skills they may be able to share with others, and thereby enhance their own self concepts.

DISPLAY   Reserve a section of the bulletin board and label it, "My Best Writing." Let each child choose an example of his own best work and post it for all the class to see it. Challenge the class to improve its proficiency by allowing each student to decide when he has bettered his earlier performance, changing periodically his part of the display area. Similarly, when the children are working on individual letters only, let each child cut out only the one letter on his paper that he thinks is his very best, and paste it onto a collage arrangement on a colorful piece of construction paper.

EVALUATION   Use an opaque projector to evaluate individual items by involving the entire class in the discussion. Use items that are samples of handwriting submitted anonymously by members of the class. Or, make arrangements with another teacher to exchange children's work for evaluation. Similarly, ask another teacher in the school to make comments about the skill of the students in your room. A further possibility is to make contacts with commercial companies who sometimes offer this service for a nominal charge. To encourage self-evaluation, post a commercial evaluation instrument, such as the Ayres Scale. If you wish to appraise quickly all the individual letter forms, ask the children to write, "The quick brown fox jumps over the lazy dog." To enable the children to review the degree of slant, cut from a piece of acetate or tagboard a small section just large enough for the individual child to use to compare his own angle of slant with that suggested.

HIDDEN LETTERS   Motivate letter formations practice by inventing a series of pictures in which individual letters are incorporated as part of the drawings. Ask the children to trace over these hidden letters, or instruct them to make their own designs for practice. Suggest that they make a picture of something that begins with the particular letter being studied.

HISTORICAL HANDWRITING Find examples of historical handwriting styles, especially items written by famous people at important times in our nation's heritage. Let the children examine and rate each official document or letter for legibility. Also, find instances of Old English illuminated manuscripts and see if the children can read any of the individual letters. As an art experience, let the students make fancy decorated designs based on oversize capital letters. Allow them to use different colors of crayon, paper, or paint to embellish each letter.

IMPLEMENTS To help children appreciate the demands that handwriting used to place on the child, show them examples of old-time ink bottles, nib pens, or goose quills. Let the children experiment with these items and experience the resultant difficulty. Compare the speed and legibility of their products with the writing done while using modern instruments.

LEFTHANDEDNESS Be especially alert to the problems experienced by the lefthanded child. For one thing, help him to hold his writing implement far enough from the point to be able to see what he is doing: place a piece of tape at the appropriate spot on the pen or pencil as a reminder. Also ask the lefthander to rotate his paper toward the left at a fairly severe angle so his strokes are approximately parallel to the edge of the desk or table at which he is seated. This will further enable him to see what he is writing and will discourage the tendency to "hook" his hand. Be sure to give him a writing instrument that will not smudge as he draws his hand across his paper.

MODELS Try to present the very best model of handwriting that you can. This shows the children that you believe legibility is important. Take corrections from the class on how to improve your own handwriting skills. To acquire a better appreciation of the difficulties that many of the young children have in their own practice, work on letter formations yourself using your non-dominant hand. This should provide a realistic notion of the physical problems and the degree of concentration experienced by your class.

MOTIVATION Add extra interest to the writing program with a variety of activities. For example, cut out gigantic cardboard letters and let the children carry them about the room, post them on the display board, or walk on them on the floor. Ask each child to adopt one letter and be in charge of seeing that "his letter" is always correctly formed. Encourage each "letter captain" to cut out from magazines examples of his own letter and paste these letters in a notebook or a scrapbook to show children something of the different ways it may be formed. Cover some of these larger letters with adhesive transparent Contact paper and use them as tracing activities.

NAMES Practice writing names in a variety of ways. First, let the children practice their first, middle, and last names. Let them make their own name labels for desks, lockers, and storage areas. Cut some of these name tags from double-folded cardboard and tape them to the children's desks to allow the children to look 'at them and, if necessary, to trace them. Also, suggest that each child find magazine or newspaper letters to make a personal letter guide. Or, purchase a commercial letter stamper kit at a toy store and lend it to the students for this same purpose. Also, suggest that the children might want to use their monograms to make original stationery, stamping their names or letters at the top of each piece of paper.

PAPERS Give the children different kinds of paper to work on. Let them use both lined and unlined paper, large sheets and small ones. Add occasional color with pieces of construction paper, tissue paper, or other kinds. Where children are using lined paper and need help to know where to begin each letter, use different colors of crayons to indicate the top, middle, and bottom lines. Or label these three lines as the "first floor," "attic," and "basement," and make a list of the letters that use any of these spaces and lines. Another possibility for marking the starting places on lined papers is a commercial ink stamper.

PENCIL POSITIONS For the child who holds his writing implement too close to its end, use as a reminder a rubber band wound tightly around the pen or pencil at the spot where he should place his fingers. Or, purchase commercial pens or pencils shaped to the contours of the hand; some of the principal commercial suppliers of handwriting materials have these special items for sale. If there is a child who has trouble holding the pen or pencil, use tape to attach it loosely to his finger in the appropriate position. When you have a child who cramps his hand, let him hold a small rubber ball or a wad of paper in his closed palm as he is writing.

PROGRESS   Keep samples of each child's writing, beginning with the very first days of school in the fall. Make a display labeled, "Before" and "After" and post examples of work that show increased proficiency. Share these examples of growth by sending them home for parents to see. Include samples from each child's folder in a class booklet at the end of the year.

RELAXATION   To relieve the tension caused by concentration on handwriting, let the children practice letter formations to appropriate musical accompaniment, as, for instance, a march record for the straight strokes, waltz music for loops, or a lullaby for circles. Or, introduce some simple relaxing exercising, such as opening and closing their hands, standing up and sitting down, flopping arms, or rising on tiptoe. Do this to music, whenever it is possible.

RIDDLES   To add an element of fun to practice sessions, ask the children to make up simple riddles describing individual letters. Allow the class to guess these letters, and permit the correct guess to serve as entitlement to demonstrating that particular letter for the rest of the class. Where possible, make up riddles as part of simple poems, such as, "This letter has three humps, and it is found in words like *bumps*."

SEQUENCE   Show the order in which letter parts are made by using cardboard models that reveal the letter with first one part missing, then two parts, then three parts, and so on. The child is required to add one part, then two, then three. Otherwise use practice sheets where the directions and sequence of the letter formations are indicated with arrows, or use green dots to indicate the beginning of a letter and red dots to indicate its ending.

SIGNATURES   To help stimulate good writing, have each child make a signature card, including first name, middle name, and surname. Discuss the uniqueness of signatures and stress that individuality in signatures is not inconsistent with the need for legibility. Have the children post their signature cards on a display board, along with any other unsigned sample of handwriting, and challenge the class to match the pairs of related writing. Another application of signatures is the development of simple autograph books, in which the children can collect as many different names as they can in a designated time period.

SIMILARITIES Have the class examine letter formations to see which parts are alike. Then have them practice those elements that are the same. For instance, in manuscript printing, have the class work on all letters that include circles at the same time. In cursive writing, have them practice all letters that have loops above the baseline.

SPACING Show the importance of adequate spacing between letters and between words by writing a message to the children, using the chalkboard or a chart, and leaving no spaces whatever between letters or words. Challenge them to see if they can read the message. To help the children remember spacing, suggest a simple finger-spacer cut from cardboard as a replica of a human hand. Have the children trace their own hands on the cardboard, cutting off all the fingers except the index finger, which is painted vividly to attract their attention.

SURFACES Give the children many opportunities to practice their writing on surfaces other than paper. For example, make individual "slates" from pressed hardboard or from cardboard blackened with blackboard paint. Purchase the "magic slates" sold at toy stores, allowing the children to check and erase their work by lifting the plastic film over the slates. Use sheets of acetate placed on the stage of an overhead projector, and give the children waxed crayons or grease pencils to practice with. Still another idea is to let the children use wet brushes and water on a chalkboard, or have available shallow box lids filled with cornmeal, flour, or salt. Finger paints, a greased pan, or petroleum jelly on a cookie sheet are other possibilities.

TRACING Stimulate further interest in handwriting practice by providing different tracing activities. For instance, use discarded carbon paper or spirit master carbons—or use tissue paper or onion skin paper placed over dark letters. Change this activity into a game by asking individual children to trace letter forms on the hands or onto the backs of a partner, using just their fingers, and challenging the partners to guess which letters have been formed.

VISUAL AIDS Interpret letter formations with many different types of visual aids that the child can clearly understand. For example, make a series of individual letter cards that are folded in the middle horizontally in such a way that either the top half or the lower half can be folded out of sight. As a stimulus to the child's practice, show him just half of the letter and let him form the rest of the letter, or the entire letter, and then check his accuracy against the stimulus card.

Another series of letter charts can remind the children through simple sayings how each letter is made. For example, in manuscript printing, suggest that the letter ''p'' is made like a balloon on a stick, while a ''b'' is like a stick and a hoop. The letter ''h'' is a little chair, while a ''y'' hangs down its tail.

For children who are having perceptual problems, provide a series of letter cards that are vividly colored, or that have different types of surfaces, such as sandpaper, corduroy, satin, or fur. Or, let each child cut his own set of letters from cardboard to feel and to arrange whenever he needs the experience. Stencils that provide a negative image for the child to trace around with his pencil or pen are also possibilities.

Make handy slant checkers by lining a piece of acetate, which can be placed on top of a piece of handwriting, or by drawing the appropriate slanted lines with very dark lines to place underneath the child's own writing paper.

Strategies for Good SPELLING

ABSURDITIES   Show your children that you empathize with them in their struggles with the irregularities of many English words. Find examples of silly poems that point out the oddities of spellings, particularly irregular verbs and nouns, as well as silent letters or variations in representing one basic speech sound. Write words incorrectly at times in a deliberate way to point out these absurdities: "Shouldn't we write 'hamb' if we write 'lamb?' " "Do you own a knice knife?" Also encourage the children to find typographical errors in printed material that may make hilarious differences in meanings.

ANAGRAMS   This familiar parlor game is well-adapted to spelling skills. One possibility is to introduce new words in scrambled form to see if anyone can figure them out prior to practicing them. Or, give the children some longer spelling words and challenge them to see if they can find other smaller words in the larger one by simply rearranging the letters. Add further incentive by attributing to the different letters number equivalents so the children can acquire points for each word formed.

    Present anagrams in several different forms: let the children draw letter cards from a face-down pile, for one possibility, or let them wear letter cards on their clothing for a large-motor involvement in this game activity. Or, place letter cards on the floor and see if the children can step on them in correct sequence.

BATTLESHIP GAME Show the children how to adapt this well-known game to spelling skills. Ask the children to write their spelling words on large graph paper, both in vertical and horizontal arrangements. Label one axis of the graph paper with letters and label the other axis with numerals. Each child, in turn, suggests a coordinate point on the graph. If the opponent has a word that had a letter on the spot called, he must call out ''hit,'' and cross out that letter on the word. Each child who is calling should have a duplicate graph paper which he also marks to show where his shots have landed, in order not to call the same shot twice. A child is out of the game when all his letters of his words have been obliterated by the other player's guesses; or, with younger children, consider the word to be ''sunk'' when any letter is hit, rather than waiting for all the letters to be obliterated.

BEES The spelling bee has long been a favorite way of presenting spelling practice. Unfortunately, while the bees may be excellent exposure for the successful spellers and for those children who enjoy competition, spelling bees do little for the child who needs intensive practice or for the child who does not like to be put on the spot publicly. In addition, where the teacher asks children to select their own spelling teams, the members of the class are often under public pressure to choose or be chosen.

With some minor variations, however, the spelling bee can be helpful. For example, the teams can be chosen randomly, and the members of the various teams can be changed from time to time. In addition, allow the child who misses a word to sit down in place only until the next person on his side misses a word; then allow him to get back into the game. Furthermore, each child might be given a word to spell in keeping with his ability, or a word he has selected to spell. Let each student have a piece of paper cut out in the shape of a bee, and have him list all these words that he wants to be tested on during the bee. When a child has spelled all his words correctly, allow him to leave the contest, if he wants to, placing his spelling bee cut-out on a large beehive poster.

Still another problem sometimes develops because children so seldom are asked to spell aloud. Adjust the spelling bee to this situation by allowing children to spell the words with a pencil and paper, rather than orally.

BODY SPELLING Have the children use their bodies to transmit the letters in the words they are practicing. This can be in the form of a group or a pair of children, arranging their body parts to make letters; or instruct them to walk the letters on the playground, in snow, or in sand. Perhaps have them make the letters with yarn or rope and then walk the line of the letters. Still another body involvement is to have the children lying down and doing their letters with their feet.

COLOR CODING   Direct the children's attention to the more difficult elements in spelling words by color coding the individual letters that are bothering them. Each child can use a simple code as he records his own list, marking with a crayon that part of each word that is likely to give trouble. Or, as each student records his own spelling list, have him use red crayon to write the hard words; when these words have been mastered, suggest that he write over these words with a yellow or a blue crayon to change their color.

DEMONS   Make a list of the spelling words that are most frequently missed in the children's compositions and post these items as special challenges for the class as a whole. Head the list with the cartoon drawing of a monster or a devil to further attract interest. Stress the most difficult part of each of these words with a devil's arrow pointing to it. From time to time, when new words are introduced to the class as a whole, let them nominate the words they think will be missed by more of the children; then compare the test papers with the group's predictions.

DISPLAY   Although many teachers place on classroom display only those papers that are 100 percent correct, this constant exposure does very little to benefit the child whose spelling is consistently perfect, and it does even less for the children who are never able to attain this arbitrary standard. It is possible, however, to use display techniques to motivate children by, first, letting each child choose to spell as many words as he wants to work on each week, consistent with his ability and his interests. Then post those spelling papers for the pupils that show clear progress, regardless of the number or the percentage of correct answers. Instead of displaying only the very best papers of a few persons, designate a part of the bulletin board for "Much Improved Papers," or "This Is My Best Paper." Also suggest that each child keep a chart or graph record of his weekly progress.

GAME APPROACHES   Adapt spelling practice to a variety of familiar games, such as football and baseball, wherein each word spelled correctly permits the child to move his marker on the appropriately marked playing board. Or, use table games such as tic-tac-toe, checkers, Parcheesi, or other activities in which the child must spell a word before he moves, or moves to a designated place on the playing board which contains a stimulus word. Another possibility is to make a floor game using a large piece of oilcloth, paper, or plastic in the form of a target, a hopscotch board, a pathway, or a bowling lane. Let the child move on the board only if he can successfully spell the stimulus word. Or, in the instance of bowling, label the pins with words, and require him to spell the ones he knocks down.

HELPER CARDS Whenever a child asks for your assistance in spelling a word, particularly when the class is writing compositions, have the child write down the item on a word card as you spell it aloud for him. Let him use this word card as a reminder for his writing, filing it in a card box, arranged alphabetically. This should improve his spelling skills, writing skills, and reference skills. When the child masters these words he may shift them to another part of his word box labeled, "Words I Can Spell." If the child is too young to alphabetize the word cards, arrange a loose-leaf notebook in which he is to write the new words, using one page for words beginning with "A," another page for the "B" items, and so on.

HELPER CHART Make a spelling chart with a series of helpful hints to show the children how to spell a new word. Duplicate this list in miniature as a checklist for each child to have handy at his desk. The following steps might be suggested in learning how to spell a new word.

1. *Hear it:* Have someone say the word for you clearly.

2. *Say it:* Be sure you know what this word means. Use it in a sentence. Say carefully the parts you might not usually hear.

3. *See it:* Look at the word carefully. Note which letters are tall and which are short. Underline with a red crayon the tricky parts.

4. *Check it:* Look at the word for parts you already know. See if it has an ending you remember from other words. See if it has smaller words hidden inside.

5. *Trace it:* Take your pencil and write over the word. Then take your finger and write it in the air.

6. *Spell it:* Say each letter out loud as you spell it and trace it.

7. *Dream it:* Try to see the word only in your mind. Close your eyes for this. Does the word in your mind look the same as the word on the paper?

8. *Write it:* Without looking at the word, write it with a pencil, saying each letter out loud.

9. *Check it:* See if you made any mistakes, and if you did, make the changes.

10. *Erase it:* If the word is right, erase it letter by letter, saying each one out loud.

11. *Practice it:* Write the word two or three more times to be sure you know it. Write it in both printing and cursive writing to see how it looks both ways.

12. *Use it:* Show somebody else you know how to spell this word. Write it in your stories if you can.

13. *Review it:* Just for fun, have someone ask you next week if you can still spell the word.

INTRODUCING WORDS   Help motivate children's spelling by introducing new words in interesting ways. One way is to spell each word aloud and see which children can visualize the word and tell what it is. Or, where nouns and verbs are a part of the new word list, allow the children to draw pictures of each one. Introduce other words by spelling them backwards, or by developing a number code, one numeral for each letter. Enliven interest in hard words by enlisting the children in a cheerleading session in which one child spells the word aloud letter-by-letter, with the class responding in echo fashion. A crossword puzzle or a riddle can also be used for new words, complete with appropriate clues as required.

Still other possibilities include phonetic spellings of new words, with the children attempting to identify the correct orthography of each item. A special puzzle is that which hides the new words in a matrix of random letters arranged both horizontally and vertically. Finally, place just the first letter of each word on the chalkboard, with a blank space for each missing letter, then let the children guess which letters might also be in the word. Continue this guessing until all the blanks are filled and a child reads the word aloud.

LETTER DIAL   Make a simple letter device, a circular dial that has a vowel in the center and a series of other letters, including both vowels and consonants, around the perimeter. Let a child begin at one point on this wheel, and by moving in any direction either around the circumferences or along a radius to the center letter, see if he can spell some of the words on his list. As another variation of this wheel, the child can place a spinner in the middle of the wheel, and try to spell words by random spinning until the marker stops on the correct letters.

LETTER FORMS   Provide a variety of writing instruments and letter forms for the children's spelling practice. A toy printing set, for example, can encourage children to exercise care in their work. A second-hand typewriter is also helpful in spelling practice. Cardboard or wooden letters are other possibilities. Even something as commonplace as alphabet cereal can stimulate interest in spelling. Alphabet blocks are also useful in routine spelling practice.

LISTS   Many teachers use a standard grade-level spelling list as their source of words for practice. However, since children in any classroom represent a wide variety of interests, needs, and abilities, the teacher should also build spelling lists around the pupils' choices. Simple diagnostic tests can reveal which of the basic words are needed and which are already mastered by individual children. Seasons and situations can suggest other items in these lists. For example, holiday times generate interest in words relating to Halloween, Christmas, and Thanksgiving. Other words will be called for during activities involving written composition. In addition, let the children include personal items: the names of their friends and classmates, family members, street names, and labels of interesting pictures or objects in collections. Also suggest items from basic reading vocabularies for personal spelling lists.

MISSING LETTERS   Give spelling practice to children by listing a particularly difficult word as many times as there are letters in the word. Each time the word is listed, however, omit one additional letter from the word, leaving, instead, a blank for the children to fill in correctly. By the time an individual child has come to the end of the listings of each word, there should be only a series of blanks for him to fill in correctly. Another use of a missing letter approach is to spell a word but leave blank only the letter or letters that are troublesome, and challenge individual spellers to find and practice the missing items.

PARTNERS Let your children choose buddies with whom they may work at their various spelling tasks. One possibility is to have pairs of children who are allowed to pool their information about words, relieving you and other children of the responsibility of supplying correct spellings of words during the day. Another application of the buddy system is to encourage each pair to exchange papers for proofreading, or checking spelling tests, or to give each other the spelling tests.

PUZZLES Make a puzzle that includes configuration awareness as well as spelling skill. Make a series of blank cards, some single squares and some connected double squares. Using a playing board with one horizontal line across it, instruct the children to represent a word using only these blank cards, one for each letter of the word. For example, a letter the size of an "a," "e," or "c" would be represented by a one-square blank set on the baseline of the game board. A taller letter, such as "f," "t," or "l," would be suggested by two squares, one on top of the other, with the bottom of the card resting on the baseline. A letter that ordinarily falls below the baseline, such as "g," "p," and "q," would require a double square, one portion resting on the line, and the other part hanging down below it. Give clues where they are needed for the puzzle.

Crossword puzzles are other possibilities for spelling practice, along with cards that are cut apart like miniature jigsaw puzzles, requiring the children to reassemble them to see the words correctly spelled. Still another puzzle is a design made by writing the words in a variety of positions, sideways and upside down, for example, making an interesting abstraction which the child must figure out and spell the word correctly.

REPETITION One technique often used in spelling practice is the repetition of individual words ten or 20 times each. Serious questions about this practice have been raised since research suggests that children are inclined to forget the visual images of words practiced almost endlessly in isolation and out of context. It may be more helpful if the students write such words only a few times each, particularly in the framework of a dictated sentence or an original story. Wherever repetition is needed, let it be stressed in the elements of individual words that are usually difficult for the children.

RULES   In analyzing new words stress the rules of good spelling that are more regular, most consistent, and most helpful to the children. Integrate generalizations from phonics, composition, handwriting, and other language arts, showing the relevance of good spelling to all areas of expression. Emphasize the importance of good communication. Teach rules incidentally as well as systematically. Relate spelling errors to familiar rules. Make colorful charts and posters that remind the class of the most common spelling suggestions.

TESTS   Investigate the possibilities of varying the spelling tests so the individual children may take them when they are ready, rather than waiting for a weekly test. Encourage each child to correct his own test so he can see his mistakes. To give a visual reinforcement and to discourage cheating, ask the child to write the test in pencil and correct it with a crayon or ink. Give the child full credit for all the words he can spell, even without having them as test items.

WRITING VARIATIONS   Introduce variety to spelling practice by having the children write their words in vertical, as well as horizontal, arrangements of letters. Or, have them make an acrostic, in which a word is repeated both vertically and horizontally as many times as there are letters in the word itself. Get a commercial label maker for especially hard words. Also, give the children a variety of writing surfaces: individual slates; shallow boxes full of cornmeal, sand, or salt; cookie sheets dusted with flour; different colors and textures of paper; many different implements, such as paintbrushes, felt-tip markers, crayons, or pens.

part three

MUSIC:
Enjoying Songs
and Dances

Creative MOVEMENT Opportunities

BALANCE   Encourage the children, using their sense of balance, to see if they can stabilize with different body parts in a variety of positions. For example, ask the students to balance on tiptoe or on their heels. Or have them balance on two points, such as on knees and fingertips, or on toes and elbows. Then have them balance on any three points. In each of these activities encourage the children to suggest still other possibilities for the entire class to try. As a further movement experience, ask them to try different balance activities with one eye closed, and then with both eyes closed.

BODY CONTROL   Whenever certain children are reluctant to express themselves with their bodies because it might be considered "sissy," point out that rhythm, coordination, balance, and body control are essential to athletes and dancers, as well as to other vocations and avocations. Point out that athletes often study dancing to improve the qualities of body control. Find pictures of athletes in different graceful poses and challenge the class to assume these same positions, or ask a dance instructor to demonstrate certain moves and positions, and help the children to understand the practice and the discipline involved in mastering them.

BODY PARTS   To help the children understand the potential movement capabilities of the human body, obtain from a science department a replica of a human skeleton that can be moved into different positions. Point out where each joint allows motion.

Place the members of the skeleton into different positions and ask the children to imitate each pose. Challenge the class to see how many different movements they can perform with each body part, such as a hand, a foot, an elbow, or the head. If there is no skeleton to serve as a model for the group, use one left over from Halloween—or, make a simple jointed puppet from sturdy cardboard.

CURRICULUM CORRELATION Relate movement activities to other subjects in the curriculum wherever it may be appropriate to the children's study. Have the students respond with their bodies to situations such as these: in science, move like a volcano erupting, or like water flowing down a hill; in social studies, move like a boat crossing the ocean; in mathematics, form different geometric shapes; in language arts, react bodily to poetry and chants; in reading, represent characters described in the stories; in art, assume poses of figures depicted in masterpieces.

DANCE STEPS When introducing young children to different aspects of movement, it may be wise to avoid the term "dance" in order to surmount problems among children who may be wary of boy-girl relationships frequently associated with dancing. Instead, you may find it more useful to employ terms such as "games," "movement," "rhythms," or "action songs."

In teaching actual dance steps, one effective method is to do it through well-known game songs, such as "Looby Loo" or "Hokey Pokey." After the children have learned the original movements accompanying these songs, substitute some new steps for them to experiment with. Let the children do these simple steps as partners, facing each other, or side by side: try a stamp, bow, swing, dip, spin, slide, clap, hop, step, skip, or tap, or other possibilities. Where the children need a visual aid, tape footprints onto the floor to help them recall the sequence of footsteps. A chorus line, where the children can observe all the other children, is still another approach.

FILM STIMULUS Use a film or a film loop to stimulate the children's movement. Some excellent examples might include: a time-lapse film of a flower growing, trees changing their leaves, a bird hatching, the surf crashing on the beach. Examine all instructional motion pictures used in the classroom for movement possibilities. Where they exist, show the movie a second time without the soundtrack, and challenge the children to respond with their bodies to what they see on the screen.

FLUENCY   Encourage the children to move individually in one fluid, continuous line as you present in rapid succession a series of situations for the class to follow. These can involve a variety of positions, such as walking, lying down, rolling over, kneeling, or standing. The challenge can also include changes of direction, such as skipping left, then skipping right, or backwards, and then changing to forwards. Still another opportunity is a change in speed from fast to slow, a change in mode—such as gliding, then tiptoeing, or a change in level, from high to middle to low.

FOLLOWING LEADERS   As a rhythmic version of an old favorite activity, have the children perform different movements following a leader who is showing them what to do. Use a musical selection with a bouncy beat. Suggest that the leader demonstrate certain commonplace actions, such as combing hair, sweeping the floor, knocking on a door, keeping in time to the beat of the record. Let each child have a chance to be the leader, and where appropriate, have the children move freely about the room, either in a long line or randomly.

FOLLOWING LINES   When you have movement experiences in a play area where there are lines marked on the floor or on the playground, give the children practice in moving from place to place following these lines, as if they were a path. In this manner the children can frequently change their floor positions in relation to each other, but by staying on the lines and moving in the same general direction, they will avoid bumping into each other. When such position changes do occur, show the children how to use the floor lines as additional imaginative experiences, such as pretending they are tight wires for balancing, or icy sidewalks.

FOREIGN MUSIC   Obtain examples of music from other cultures and ask the children to interpret these pieces. Oriental music, African dances, or Middle East melodies are sufficiently different from the familiar to arouse children's interest. A similar activity is teaching the children a foreign dance. For this type of instruction, contact a foreign exchange student, a missionary, a service person, a dance studio instructor, or students' parents from an unusual cultural background.

HOLIDAY STIMULUS   Capitalize on seasonal and holiday themes to stimulate children's enthusiasm for movement activities. Channel the children's natural excitement into movements that might logically be associated with Halloween, Christmas, and Thanksgiving, for example, or with snow, falling leaves, growing flowers, or other signs of changing seasons.

INCREMENTAL MOTIONS   To the accompaniment of the folk song, "Make a Pretty Motion," show the children how to make motions one-by-one, then as partners two-by-two, and then as trios three-by-three. After a time the groups will become too large for them readily to decide what motion to make. When this happens, break up the groups and begin all over again, using completely different sets of motions. As another incremental movement activity, have one child suggest one movement for all children to imitate. Then have a second child suggest a second movement to be added incrementally to the first movement, and so on down the line of children until the task becomes too difficult for the children to remember.

INDIVIDUAL SITUATIONS   Elicit from the children a variety of movement problems that they must solve individually. To motivate their thinking, suggest possibilities such as these:

> Eat a bowl of hot soup when you are in a hurry.
>
> Hold an angry cat with a barking dog underfoot.
>
> Blow a bubble across the room.
>
> Put on a sweater that is too small.
>
> Move like a simple machine that is about to break.
>
> Be a robin that is pulling a worm from its hole.
>
> Go for a walk in some sticky mud, wearing your good clothes.
>
> Be an ugly statue with birds roosting on top.
>
> Climb over a fence and rip your clothing.
>
> Blow up a balloon until it bursts.
>
> Crawl inside a scarey cave.

INSTRUMENTAL STIMULUS   Challenge the children to respond to different musical instruments. For example, play an arpeggio on a piano, or trill the notes by pulling a finger down the piano keyboard. Or, perform a see-saw, high-low combination of notes on any instrument—sound the same notes over and over, both fast and slow. Still another idea is to have the children listen to different types of band or orchestra instruments, and move to their different timbres: a drum should stimulate one type of movement, while a triangle should stimulate another.

LETTER STIMULUS   Have the students move through individual letter formations, especially those letters in their own names, as they are learning to read and spell. See if they can spell a word by moving through space, or have them spell words by moving their feet in the air as they are lying on their backs. As other variations, ask the children to try the same letter formations with the head, arm, elbow, knee, or other body parts.

MANIPULATIVE OBJECTS   Children are more inclined to forget themselves in movement experiences and participate more wholeheartedly in the activity if they have access to objects they can handle as a part of the lesson. Appropriate to individual situations, have available props such as these:

Crepe streamers	Dowel rods, broomsticks
Elasticized rope	Filmy plastic
Masks, costumes	Mechanical toys
Strips of sheeting	Dress-up clothing
Crepe paper pom poms	Paper fans
Large beach towels	Large feathers
Umbrellas	Plastic hoops
Yarn streamers	Playground balls
Wrist and ankle bells	Batons
Large rag dolls	Puppets
Pinwheels on sticks	Canes
Cardboard tubes	Knit garments
Inner tubes	Mops, brooms
Tossed leaves	Rhythm instruments
Metronome	Sports equipment
Tissue paper	Foil paper

MECHANICAL STIMULUS   Find pictures of things that have a definite rhythm when they are operating. This might be something on an assembly line, the pendulum of a clock, a washing machine agitator, a flashing light, a dripping faucet, or a buck saw. Let each child select one picture and move to the rhythm of the object. Or, ask the children to bring to class actual mechanical objects to use in stimulating movement. Still another idea is to use a tape recorder to register the rhythmic sounds of mechanical things. Try to locate items such as a clanging railroad signal, a pneumatic drill, or a busy signal on a telephone.

MODELS   When children are first beginning their movement experiences, avoid using individual children as examples for the other pupils to imitate, and try not to demonstrate movements yourself. Modeling tends to close children's minds to new possibilities. Instead, when you, for example, use music to stimulate movement, do not tell the children the name of the piece, and do not show them how to move. Allow the class to do what the music suggests to them individually. Do not inhibit their thinking by pointing out models to follow. Instead, comment on the variety of their approaches and their effort.

MUSICAL STIMULUS   Show the children that the mood, pitch, and speed of music can suggest different kinds of movement. For example, take a piece of music and play it two or three octaves higher than it is normally played. Or, play a record at a different speed, faster or slower. As a variation, try to play the same music on different instruments to elicit different responses.

NAMES   Have the students experiment with moving to the rhythm of their names. Explore these names beforehand to see if they can be grouped by the number of syllables, or by the nature of the rhythm. After names have been discussed and grouped, let the children examine how they want to move. Say each name over many times to stimulate movement. Find all the names that have the same rhythm as "Peter, Peter, Peter; Raquelle, Raquelle, Raquelle; Anna Marie, Anna Marie, Anna Marie." Do this activity with surnames, as well as with names of pets, commercial products, or anything else with an interesting rhythm.

OCCUPATIONS   Identify jobs that have been discussed as a part of social studies experiences, and ask the children to move in ways that would tell the occupation being studied. Have the pupils identify the jobs their parents perform, or those occupations done in the school by specialized personnel, such as secretary, cook, bus driver, or custodian. Also, have the children identify and act out jobs they themselves might like to do some day, such as firefighter, circus performer, or astronaut.

OPEN SPACES Since adequate space is necessary for effective movement exploration, it may be appropriate to make arrangements to use settings outside the classroom. Investigate the accessibility of the gymnasium, the playground, the lawn, or the hallway for these purposes. Otherwise, if such spaces are not available, push all the furniture into a corner of the classroom, or stagger the types of involvement so some children are using some open parts of the classroom, others are moving while seated at their desks, and still others are seated on a rug planning their activities.

PARADES All children love a parade, and they are usually excited about planning one. Suggest that each child choose a circus animal to imitate, as one type of parade activity. Or, let the pupils select an imaginary instrument, playing the instrument in front, from side to side, high and low, as they strut along. Too, have an Indian parade with a war dance step. Still another version of a parade is a "ripple" accomplished by lining up the children, one behind another, facing the same direction. Have the leader at the head of the parade make a motion, and then require the second child to imitate it. Each child, in turn, must wait until the child ahead of him in line has performed the motion. This movement thus continues down the line of children in a ripple effect. The leader may choose a different motion as the first motion is rippling down the line. Some of these may be done as the children are holding on to each other, or as they are moving in a circular arrangement to better observe each other.

PARTNER ACTIVITIES Many movement experiences are perfectly suited to two-member units. Since children generally like to work with classmates, let them choose buddies and then ask them to propose situations such as these, appropriate to two participants:

> Play tennis or table tennis with an opponent.
>
> One person be a robin and the other be a worm.
>
> Be an inventor that has just made a monster.
>
> Act like you are in front of a mirror; imitate each other.
>
> Be a pair on a see-saw, going up and down.
>
> One person be a puppet and the other be the puppeteer.
>
> Hold hands and make up a folk game step to do together.
>
> Be your partner's shadow.
>
> One person be the kite and the other hold the string.

Pretend to hold objects between you.

Make different shapes or letters with both bodies.

Pose like two people in a picture.

Be a mechanical toy with a child to operate it.

PATTERN ACTIVITIES　Lay out on the floor a series of items to make interesting patterns for movement. Ropes, hoops, wands, beams, and other objects can be placed in positions to suggest this. Children can approach this experience as a rhythmic exercise: step in, step out; jump over, jump back. Or, let individual children perform several movements in and around these obstacles, and see if the other children can remember and repeat the same movements.

PERSONAL SPACE　Sometimes children involved in movement lose contact with the whereabouts of the other students in the group. To help solve this problem, tell each child beforehand that he has a personal space just like a bubble which must not be punctured by his running into someone else. Challenge the children to keep this personal bubble intact as they run to touch the sides of the room or the playground. Then ask each child to explore this personal space by touching each side of his bubble, by seeing how fast he can move different body parts without bursting the bubble or moving from one spot on the floor, and by seeing how tall or how small he can become inside the space.

POSING　Begin this experience by having the children moving freely to a musical stimulus, or to their own imaginations. Then, upon some pre-arranged signal, instruct them to freeze in position as if they were statues, then relaxing again and moving into still other poses. Another version of this idea is to have the class working in pairs, and asking one child to place his partner into a pose, and then try to imitate the very same position, face to face, or side by side. Encourage the children to move from pose to pose in slow motion, exaggerating their movements in the process.

REINFORCEMENT　Try to avoid responding to children's movement with comments such as, "That's good," or "That's the right way to do it." Remarks such as these tend to reinforce the children to do the same things, and to repeat them over and over in an effort to merit the same kind of praise. Instead, try to recognize individual pupil effort and inventiveness with more appropriate comments like, "That's one way to do it; can you think of other ways?", or, "I can see you're really thinking about how to move."

RESTRICTED SPACE   Although most movement experiences will be done in a gymnasium or on the playground, there may be occasions when the children will not have access to such large areas. In these situations, help the children think of ways to move while they are standing in one spot or when they are seated at desks or tables: stretching, bending, nodding, clapping, flapping, and flexing are some possibilities. Where the children are confined to small areas, keep small groups together with plastic hoops, short lengths of rope, or inner tubes. Have the children either stand inside these devices or hold onto the edges. Suggest small-group opportunities such as: "Pretend you are horses on a merry-go-round," or, "Imagine you are an animal in a zoo and you want to escape." If it is impossible to have all children moving at the same time in cramped quarters, have part of the group seated on the floor in other movement activities or ask them to be planning their own later experiences for the larger areas.

SELF-CONSCIOUSNESS   If you have children in the group that are uncertain about moving in the presence of their classmates, make arrangements for them to move in a special place, somewhat removed from the others. Or, have all the children close their eyes and move in just one stationary position. Or, give the shy child added security with a mask, encouraging him to become an imaginary character. Perhaps the best approach to the problem of self-consciousness is to participate in the activity yourself, lending it the dignity and respect it rightly deserves.

SIGNALS   Always have a signal to regain the attention of the group in movement exploration. This signal might be a hanclap, a musical tone, a whistle, or a drum. Point out the need to recapture their attention during these activities that tend to excite them and sometimes create a high noise level. Use such signals, particularly the drum, to gradually slow down such stimulating experiences, and finally settle the children to a position of quiet and rest.

SONG STIMULUS   Ask the children to contribute or lend to the classroom popular songs from their personal record collections. Have them interpret the beat or the rhythm or the melody of the record. If there are lyrics, help the children discuss the meanings of the words to further stimulate movement. As another variation of this idea, use the songs you are learning in class: if you are singing a song about boats, pretend to hoist the sails; a skating song should stimulate waltz-like movements; a song about elephants should elicit appropriate motor responses from the children.

SPORTS STIMULUS As a special appeal to your "athletes," present a variety of situations associated with athletic activities. For example, pretend to kick a football, swing a bat, dive from a diving board, or bounce on a trampoline. Help the children to see the relevance of graceful movement to skill in sports.

STATIONS To introduce variety into a large movement area, set up a series of learning stations around the perimeter of the room or the play space, each station equipped with different props and different tasks to perform. Organize the children in small groups to spend a specified period of time at each station. Then, on a pre-arranged signal, have them move to the next position in a clockwise direction. Or, number the stations with large numerals for identification and have the children follow a taped trail from one point to another as they individually complete the task presented to each station.

STORY STIMULUS Encourage the children to find cartoons, silly pictures, ambiguous photographs, newspaper pictures, or comic strips. Challenge the class to think up a story associated with these pictures and move appropriately. Or, have the group recall a story from a library book or a reader and move in interpreting that story and some central character in it.

SURFACES Help the children appreciate different kinds of surfaces through movement exploration. For example, have them take off their shoes and move in a variety of ways across a smooth floor, across a rough playground, through the grass, or on a thick shag rug. Challenge them to think of many different ways to use these surfaces with various parts of their bodies: push against the surface, move across the surface, make interesting footprints, touch the surface with different parts of the body.

VARIETY Demonstrate the wide variety of movement possibilities by asking the class to see in how many ways they can manipulate all the body parts, including the face. Also investigate the differences in directions, speeds, positions, levels, fluency, and mood. For separate lessons, take just one of these variables and examine it fully.

WORD STIMULUS Apply movement experiences to understandings of language in situations. For example, instruct the class to move to a phonetic clue, such as "Move like something that starts with the letter T." Or, discuss a series of verbs and see if they can move like something that tickles, scratches, pounds, floats, curls, or glides. Talk about descriptive words, and move in response to: sad, red, happy, slippery, sharp, angry. Too, let the children respond to voice level, as you speak or sing certain words at a low level, then change to a high pitch, or as you hum, whisper, shout, hiss, or shriek.

Teaching Basic MUSICOLOGY

ACCENT   Show the children that they can give variety to their music by accenting certain notes with a heavy beat on a drum—experiment with an Indian dance or a march. Later, introduce other ways of producing accents: clapping the hands, stepping and bending the knees, turning to change directions in a march, twirling, or lifting the arms.

CHORDS   Give the children experience in hearing chords that harmonize as contrasted with those that do not. Ask the children to identify notes that seem to belong together. Apply these discrimination skills to endings of songs—ask at a song's end which of several possible endings sounds like the most appropriate one. Refer to this correct chord as "home base" for the song. As another experience with chords, let the children play tone bells, rearranging the notes in different sequences. Or, have the children sing the notes of a harmonic chord, one group sustaining a note while the others chime in.

INTERVALS   Give the children an opportunity to experience intervals in music. Suggest special terms to indicate whether or not consecutive notes played on the piano change. ("Are they the 'same' or do they 'change'?") Or, for older primary pupils, use "step" to indicate an interval of one note. "Skip" can show that one note up or down the scale has been omitted, while "leap" might suggest that several notes are a part of the interval.

NOTE EXPLORATIONS   For children interested in music lessons, have on hand in the classroom examples of beginners' music books including simple songs for incidental practice. Duplicate these songs on a ditto master and send them home for supplementary piano exploration. Or, use these same songs to send home with children who have learned how to play them in class. Encourage the children to make booklets of these songs. One good way to help the children learn the location and names of the keys on a piano is to color-code or letter-code the keys with colored tape, giving the children a piece of music, the notes of which are similarly coded. When students have mastered an instrument, help them to make up simple songs. Write these songs down on a large music chart, and leave a set of tone bells or a xylophone conveniently in the room for other children to use in practicing these original songs.

NOTE NAMES   To help teach the children the names of the lines and spaces on the staff, give them simple words that can be spelled with music notes. Have the children locate each note on the staff as they spell each word, and then ask them to play the simple tunes thus represented. Some of the words used might include these:

bed	bad	cab	age	egg	fed	face
babe	cage	cafe	beg	cab	bag	fade

NOTE PICTURES   Enhance the children's interest in recognizing the various notes and other musical symbols by encouraging them to make simple pictures incorporating the notes. One possibility is to make a simple face, with the different notes as eyes, nose, mouth, and ears. Or, make a stick figure, with notes as arms, legs, and head. Another possibility is to invent a fantastic figure with a note as the central element.

NOTE VALUES   Assist the children in recognizing the different values and appearances of notes by cutting large, sturdy cardboard shapes representing them. Pass these around and have the children name each one. When the children have had success in differentiating them, place them in a box and have the children discriminate them by a sense of touch only. Another way to reinforce the group's knowledge of note values is to introduce simple mathematics problems such as this: "Add the number of counts of a quarter note in this song to the number of counts of a whole note." Or,

"Subtract the number of lines on the musical staff from the number of notes in an octave."

Still another visual aid for the time duration of different notes is a series of marks drawn on the chalkboard: a long mark represents a whole note, a line half that long stands for a half note, and a much shorter line indicates a quarter note. An accordion-folded piece of paper containing four panels can also show the note values in 4/4 time. For example: on one such four-fold panel, place a whole note on the first section, and leave the others blank. On another panel have two half notes, one on the first section and one on the third section. Adapt this same approach to different time signatures.

PHRASES   Show the children how to count the measures in a song by clapping in sets of three's, four's, or six's, in keeping with the time signatures of the songs. Help the children to identify the phrases of music by turning and changing directions at the end of each one. Have them also listen for phrases that are repeated in the same song, counting the number of occurrences.

PITCH   Show the "ups" and "downs" of a melody line by involving the entire body. For example, squat down close to the floor for the very lowest notes of a tune and rise to tiptoe for the highest ones. Utilize the other body positions for the pitches that occur in between the highest and lowest ones. Or, indicate pitch by raising and lowering the hands. A good song to begin with is "Taffy Was a Welshman," which is a simple ascending and descending scale. Still another device to show pitch is a line on chalkboard—an upward line indicates rising pitch, while a downward line shows a lower one. For added interest, make a series of horizontal lines on the chalkboard and challenge the children to look at both the length of the lines and their relative vertical positions to see if anyone can guess the tune being depicted.

SCALES   To show ascending and descending notes, use a xylophone held vertically to produce a ladder effect. Or, make a simple ladder from sturdy cardboard, each rung labeled with a note. Still another idea is to get a set of tone bells, mix them up, and then ask the children to put them back into the correct order to play a scale. A handy floor aid is a piece of cloth or oilcloth with notes taped to it in scale formation. Ask the children to use this floor item as a hopscotch board, jumping up and down the scale, stepping on or skipping certain notes as they go.

STAFF AIDS A handy way to make a musical staff for classroom use is to insert five pencils in a music liner and draw a series of staffs on a long piece of Kraft paper. Give the children plastic buttons, checkers, poker chips, and straws to make notes for replicating songs in visual form. Another way to make a staff is by attaching fabric tape to a large piece of plastic or vinyl materials. Add interest to the lines and spaces by making the lines wavy or zigzag, particularly if the children are learning songs about sledding, skiing, or other activities that might suggest interesting variations of the way in which these lines are drawn for staff exploration.

For this humorous approach to the staff, convert the note symbols into birds, flags, fish, or other symbols appropriate to the songs, especially those that are on a seasonal or holiday theme (Christmas stars, Halloween pumpkins, or Easter eggs), and further motivate the children's involvement with holiday songs. Or, spell out a seasonal message on the staff, using individual letters in place of the notes. For example, you might spell out "Merry Christmas" on the staff, positioning the notes in such a way that they make up the tune of "Jingle Bells." You might even make up a song about the staff, to suggest that Santa Claus has a house and the notes of the staff each has a separate floor to live on. Help the children locate the home line or space of each note on the staff.

TIMBRE Compare the timbre and tone of different instruments by playing the same note on as many of them as possible. Let the children examine the ways in which these different musical sounds are produced. Suggest that some instruments are struck, while others are blown into. Discuss the vibrations that create the music. Get a diagram of the human vocal mechanism to show how vocal music is made, as well.

Responding to RHYTHMS

BODY RHYTHMS Use different body parts to indicate both the rhythm (the movement of the melody line) as well as the beat (the basic underlying meter of the song). See if the children can tap their feet for the beat of a song, or clap their hands, nod their heads, or slap their thighs. When the children have had experience with indicating the beat of the music, see if part of the class can indicate the beat while another group demonstrates the rhythm of a familiar song. When this is mastered, challenge some of the more proficient children to clap the rhythm while they stamp the beat at the same time. To add further interest to body rhythms, introduce the notion of clicking, pounding, slapping, beckoning, waving, rubbing, snapping, or any other body motions that can be associated with the beat and the rhythm of a song.

BODY SOUNDS As a part of a rhythm band, or as a way to keep the beat of a song, encourage the children to see how many different sounds they can produce with different body parts. Help them to try some of these:

kissing	beeping	buzzing
heel beating	mouth clicking	finger snapping
slapping floor	whistling	snorting
tapping toes	heel clicking	shushing
squeaking	hiccuping	shuffling feet

CLAPPING Encourage the children to invent their own patterns of clapping rhythms to accompany familiar rhymes and songs they have learned. Teach them some of the more familiar clapping games, such as "Pease Porridge Hot." Another clapping activity involves the children in clapping just the rhythm of a song they have learned. Or, ask one child to clap the rhythm, and ask the class to guess which song is being clapped. Give the children a few clues beforehand to make the guessing easier, if help is needed.

ECHOES   Let the children take turns in beating different rhythms on a drum, and have the others in the group echo a reply by clapping the same way. Or, set up an antiphonal situation by arranging the class in two sections, one part on one side of the classroom and the other group on the opposite side. Have one cluster of children clap a rhythm, and then ask the other children to repeat it. Add interest to these echoes by interjecting shouts of "Hey" or "Ho" as punctuation.

GAMES   Adapt a variety of children's games to rhythmic experiences by having the children participate in jump rope activities, hopping games, ball bouncing, and similar experiences. Counting-out rhymes can also be adapted to rhythms. Or, take familiar game songs and adapt them to rhythmic actions. For example, a song about a baseball game might suggest that the children sing the song and act out batting, throwing, sliding, running, or other motions appropriate to the nature of the song.

HOMEMADE INSTRUMENTS   All children should have experience with a wide variety of rhythm instruments. Many of these are available from commercial sources. However, the children should be encouraged to make music with whatever is handy, and the experience of making their own items should contribute excitement and spontaneity to the activities with rhythms. Here are some simple devices that can be made by young children:

Banjo: Make a strummer from a shoe box over which different sizes of rubber bands have been stretched. A cigar box or an aluminum pie tin are other possibilities.

Chimes: Get a set of large steel spikes from a hardware store or a lumberyard. Suspend them from string tied to a piece of wood, allowing them to swing free for maximum vibrations. Use another nail or spike as a striker. Unpainted wire coat hangers, brass rods, brass tubes, unpainted can lids are some other materials to use for chimes.

Blocks: Find wooden cheese boxes, cigar boxes, or wooden chalk boxes, and strike them with a mallet. Or, salvage from a cabinet shop or a lumber mill hardwood blocks.

Drums: Use a variety of containers covered with rubber or leather laced top and bottom; ham tins, fruit drink cans, wooden salad bowls, nail kegs, drainage tiles, and carpet tubes are a few examples.

Gongs: Find metal trays of copper, brass, or aluminum and strike them with a spoon. Cast iron lids, hub caps, wheel covers, or stainless steel mixing bowls produce the same effects. An unpainted ceramic flower pot, suspended with rope, is also appropriate.

Rattles: For this use pill vials, pipe tobacco tins, bandage boxes, film cannisters, keys on a ring, spools on a wire, sea shells, cottage cheese cartons, or margarine tubs. Fill these containers with beans, gravel, or rice. Dried gourds are also useful for this purpose. Drill a small hole in the gourd and when it is completely dry, insert hard objects through the hole and plug it with clay. Still other possibilities are soda cans filled with bottle caps or pull-tabs. Papier mache can also be adapted to a maraca. Or, try a large balloon with several paper clips inside it, or a large tea strainer filled with rice.

Rhythm sticks: Salvage pieces of broomsticks, redwood, or dowel rods. Pieces of bamboo are also useful. Rib bones, clean and dried, and coconut shells are other ideas. To add variety to the dowel rods, cut notches in them and show the children how to rub them to make a clatter. Or use a rhythm stick on an old washboard or a piece of grooved plywood.

Tambourine: Staple together two sturdy paper plates, or aluminum pie tins, and add small jingle bells around the edge. Fill these instruments with beans, gravel, or rice, and then lace them together. Try pinching a piece of parchment between two embroidery hoops for a still different approach.

Xylophone: Make a simple xylophone by cutting different lengths of redwood from one inch by two inch stock. Lay these pieces on a pair of other pieces of redwood padded with fabric or rubber, or suspend them from strings. Strike these sticks with a hard object, such as a mallet, and hear distinct differences in pitch. Another type of xylophone is made from a series of soda bottles filled with water to premeasured and pre-marked depths. Color the water with food coloring for easier visibility, and when the bottles are not being used, cap them to prevent evaporation.

INSTRUMENT CHARACTERS Enhance the children's appreciation of all different kinds of instruments by making up stories about each of them. Ask the class to look at each instrument and think of what kind of character it might be. Think of the kind of music or rhythm each item produces. Then ask the students to make up a name for the instrument, such as "Tommy Trumpet," "Dummy Drum," or "Tubby Tuba." Have the children decorate pictures of each instrument, embellishing each one with a human face.

INSTRUMENT RESOURCES   Play musical records that have different instruments playing in a manner that they can be clearly identified. Show pictures of each instrument as its music is heard on the record and explain how the music is produced. Have several resource persons from the upper grades, from other schools, or from the community demonstrate the various instruments. After the demonstrations have been completed, give the children an opportunity to pantomime the playing of these instruments as accompaniment to the recorded music.

INSTRUMENT THEMES   Playing program music, such as "Peter and the Wolf" or "Danse Macabre," use one instrument to represent each character in the musical selection. Read or tell the story to the class and have several designated children play the instruments every time the appropriate motif is heard. Ask the other children to count the number of times each musical theme is heard in the record. Or, ask the children to make pictures of these fragments of melodies and hold up appropriate pictures for each theme.

KITCHEN BANDS   Set up a band made of instruments salvaged or borrowed from parents' kitchens. Think of table utensils, pot lids, metal graters, bottle brushes, pie tins, drumsticks, juice cans, dish mops, jugs, broom handles, thimbles.

NAME RHYTHMS   Experiment with the rhythms of people's names. Clap the names of the children in the class and see which ones have the same patterns. Try this same approach with the names of flowers, birds, states, cities, siblings, pets, cars, families, and anything else that might be both familiar and interesting to the class. After these patterns have been identified, let the children move around to these names, accompanying themselves with bells, drums, or other rhythm instruments.

POETRY RHYTHMS   Explore the rhythms of poetry by accompanying the oral reading or reciting of simple verse with drums or rhythm sticks. Use the words of songs, without musical accompaniment, as one such activity. Reinforce the children's sense of rhythm in poetry by stressing the heavy beats in each verse, syllable by syllable.

POP-UP ACTIVITY   Ask the children to stand in a circle, number them by three's, four's, or six's, and then play a piece of music appropriate to the numbering. Instruct the children to jump up from a stooped position only when their number is called. For example, all the children who are number one should jump up on the first beat of each measure; then the two's jump only on the second beat of the measure. In this way the circle of children should resemble a circle of popcorn all popping up at different times. Until the children catch on to the idea, it may be wise to count out loud to stress the numbered beat, and it may also be advisable to play a piece of music for them considerably slower than you ordinarily would, to help show them when they should pop up.

REPEATED RHYTHMS   Examine common songs for repeated rhythmic patterns and have the children count how many times the same ones recur. Show them how to clap each rhythmic arrangement and listen for similarities. To identify each repetition of the common pattern, ask individual children to raise a hand, or wave a small flag, or do some other obvious action to signal its appearance in the song.

RHYTHM STICKS   Get for each child a set of rhythm sticks and introduce simple exercises for them to practice. Instruct them to sit on the floor in pairs facing each other, for example, and after they have experimented with hitting their own sticks together, suggest routines in which they hit the sticks of their partners. Later, have the children practice routines with the sticks that involve them striking the sticks behind their backs, or with crossed hands.

SIT-DOWN RHYTHMS   Rhythmic activities can be done handily at the tables or desks when space is limited or when time is short. Let the children, for instance, tap their fingers on the edges of their desks, or on their lunch boxes or large wooden unit blocks, or cardboard boxes. Or, suggest that they take their shoes off and, holding the shoes in their hands, tap them on the desktops, or against each other, or against other children's shoes. Add spice to these activities by introducing some silly sit-down variations: wave goodbye, give the hitchhike sign, flap the ears, wiggle the nose—each motion in rhythmic accompaniment to a familiar song.

STEPPING RHYTHMS   Have the children step to the irregular rhythm of the melody of a song and compare it with the regular beat underlying the song. Or, vary the stepping accompanying the beat of a song by stepping it at the regular pace, then doing it twice as fast, and then four times as fast. Divide the class into small groups for these variations. Another suggestion is to teach the children how to march, changing directions after each phrase.

TOY BAND   Ask the children to bring to school as many different toy instruments as they can locate. Organize a room band using devices for making music such as harmonicas, whistles, bells, rachets, clickers, music boxes, xylophones, toy horns, song flutes, recorders, kazoos, squeakers, drums.

VISUAL RHYTHMS   Draw on the chalkboard visual representations of the beats of different types of music. A series of triangles or curlicues might suggest 3/4 time; a jagged line might indicate 2/4 time; squares might represent 4/4 time. Encourage the children to think of other ways to represent these beats and draw them on the chalkboard in time to the music being played. Then have the students draw these same designs in the air, before the entire group, using a baton, in the manner of an orchestra leader.

Simple SINGING Activities

COMMERCIALS   As a form of a solo singing experience, or as a small group song, let the children sing familiar radio or television commercials. Or, use a tape recorder to register some of the commercial tunes and let the children make up their own words to these familiar melodies.

ECHO SINGING   The echo approach is an excellent way to teach a new song. Divide the class into two groups, and prompt them to see which section will be the quickest to learn the new song. As each phrase of the song is introduced by one of the groups, let the other cluster of children sing that same phrase as an echo. When the children have learned a song thoroughly, let them sing parts of it as an echo, for added effect. Or, tape record the song and use the taped portion as an echo.

EMOTIONS   Show that singing can express a variety of emotions as you pose a series of situations for the children. Take a well-known song and ask the children to sing it as if they were feeling very sad. Point out that singing slowly, in a low pitch, and with a soft voice sometimes suggests sadness. Then ask the same children to use the same song and sing it as if they were mad, or happy. Subsequently, as new songs are attempted, discuss the name and nature of the song with the class to establish a mood that might be most appropriate to the singing of it.

FOREIGN SONGS Assist the children in learning songs from foreign cultures by obtaining the services of a person with experience in other countries. Try to locate parents from different ethnic and national backgrounds, missionaries, airline pilots, military personnel, or businessmen. Or, contact a teacher of foreign languages in a local school system. Try to obtain from commercial sources records of songs that the children might like to learn, especially those with strong seasonal and holiday connections.

GAME SONGS Find sources of some of the more familiar game songs and chants and teach them to the children as part of the long-term musical heritage of our culture. Then interject song-making and singing into children's routine physical activities such as jumping rope, playing on the see-saw, swinging on a swing, or bouncing on a board. Help the children to make up original words to these game tunes, or to make up original tunes to standard game chants.

HIDDEN SINGERS Stimulate children's singing and sharpen their discrimination skills by placing small groups of children outside the room. Then ask one member of a small group to sing a phrase or two and see if any listener in the room can identify the singer. As a simple solo experience, hide a number of individuals about the room, in closets, under tables, and in the coat room, for example, and have each one sing a short part of a song, following a pre-arranged signal, to add interest to a familiar song sung by the group as a whole.

INCIDENTAL SINGING Do not confine singing to music class alone. Singing can make other activities much more interesting. For example, let the children sing quietly while they work on special projects in the classroom, such as art work, or other informal group involvements. Or, use quiet music to sooth children when they become worried or fatigued: help them to sing a lullaby or some other quiet tune. A song is also a good activity when students are traveling in a vehicle, or when they are waiting for something to happen, or when they merit a break from a demanding task such as a test. Furthermore, a song can help calm down children who are overactive or too excited.

INCREMENTAL SONGS Children enjoy incremental songs where one more element is added with each repetition of the tune. "Old

MacDonald Had a Farm'' is perhaps one of the more familiar examples of this type of song. To help the class learn such songs, provide a series of simple picture cues for them to look at as a reminder of the words that occur in the prescribed sequence. As a variation of this idea, have the children make a picture booklet, with a drawing appropriate to each of the cumulative phrases, with the lyrics written underneath each picture. When the children come to the very end of the song, they must turn the pages in reverse order to review all the phrases that have been added during the entire song.

LEGENDARY SONGS Relate music to literature by reading stories about fabled characters and then teaching the children songs about these same characters. Johnny Appleseed, John Henry, Casey Jones, and Jesse James are some examples. Ask certain children to assume these heroic roles and act out the stories as the rest of the class sings the songs.

LISTENING As one listening experience, have the children cover one ear and listen to the music of their own singing. Or have them listen to themselves by cutting a simple telephone-like section from a small plastic bleach jug to enable each child to hear his own vocal productions. As another kind of listening activity, tape record the children's singing and have them evaluate it and compare it with prior efforts. Another type of listening involves playing a variety of vocal music for the children to appreciate: solos, ensembles, choruses, serious music, and nonsense songs.

MUSICAL DIRECTIONS Apply music to the daily routine in the classroom by using it to give directions during the course of the school day. For example, instead of telling pupils what to do, sing their instructions. Also, use singing as signals for different types of activities: find a fragment of a song appropriate to each one and sing it as a signal for the children to begin the activity to which it is cued.

MUSICAL RECALL Test children's ability to remember and reproduce vocal music by singing simple chants that involve easy intervals and basic melodies. These might include musical greetings, cheers for the athletic teams, and game calls. After the children have had experience in singing back musical phrases to you, encourage them to make up their own simple phrases and singing them to other pupils in the class, with the other children responding from memory.

NEW SONGS   Introduce new songs to the class by playing the melody several times. Encourage the pupils to hum the tune until it is familiar to them. Then sing every phrase of the song and have the children repeat it after you. If the song is unusually difficult or lengthy, provide a series of simple picture clues for each phrase to facilitate recall. Identify the better singers in your group and place them at the rear of the class to help carry along the less able singers until they, too, master each new song introduced.

NURSERY RHYMES   Play and learn the more familiar Mother Goose rhymes. Then conduct a guessing game in which the pictures of these nursery characters are displayed, and challenge the children to sing the first phrase of each matching song. Or, reverse the association process and ask the children to select the appropriate picture to accompany each tune. Another idea is to duplicate a series of key pictures for these songs, and let each child collect packets of pictures, one for each nursery song he can sing from memory.

OLD FAVORITES   Occasionally let the children review favorite songs they have learned in preceding years. Borrow from other teachers some of the books and records used in earlier grades by your children and let the children select some of the familiar melodies from past experiences. Also, encourage the class members to contribute well-liked songs they have learned at home, in church, or at camp.

ORIGINAL TUNES   Help the children write their own music. Let them experiment with the piano or with other instruments and encourage them to make up simple melodies. One possibility is to ask them to explore only the black notes on the piano to develop a song somewhat Oriental in nature. Use a tape recorder to register these songs and play them for the entire class.

ORIGINAL WORDS   Help the children to think of original lyrics for the songs they learn, at first substituting only a word or two in a familiar song, as, for example, the rhyming words at the end of each phrase. Eventually encourage them to expand their efforts into complete phrases and entire songs, using a familiar melody as their vehicle, or developing an original tune along with original words.

PERSONAL RECORDS   Encourage the children to bring to class some of their own personal recordings of music. As time permits, and as these songs are appropriate to the children's interests, play some of them and help the children to learn to sing them. Another possibility with these records is to set up a simple lending library, enabling the children to check them out for a specified period of time.

PROGRAMS   Children enjoy performing for others in public; however, sometimes the preparation for musical programs requires so much time and effort that the spontaneity and satisfaction of the children are minimized. One obvious solution to this problem is to teach, over a period of several weeks, a series of songs and other musical experiences on one theme, such as "Christmas Time," "Sing a Song of Seasons," or "Circus is Coming!" Develop a simple spontaneous narrative to join these songs together, and tape record it before the program begins. Add a few pieces of simple costuming, involve a few rhythm instruments, and the musical production will be ready for performance with very little advance preparation.

REHEARSALS   Take the children to a practice session involving a choral group, an ensemble, or a band or an orchestra. Let the children ask questions about different instruments and voices, and have the director tell them a little bit about the songs being played and sung. Try to identify members of the musical group that might be known to the children, such as brothers, sisters, or neighbors. As a part of this experience, point out to the class that practice is essential to making good music.

RESOURCE HELPERS   If you are not capable of playing your own musical accompaniment for the songs you want to use, seek help from persons who can assist you. One possibility is to locate a teacher who is using the same musical materials and ask him or her to record on tape the accompaniment for the songs. Parents are also able to provide this type of assistance, as well as older boys and girls in the school. Also, consider instruments that are relatively easy to use for accompaniment: autoharp, guitar, ukulele are some examples.

ROLL CALL   Musical attendance procedures are a good way to enliven the beginning of a music period. This can take the form of a roll call in which the child repeats his name in song just as you sing it, or, he can sing a musical phrase, such as "Good morning to you." Another variation is to have the child sing the musical syllables, as in the case of "mi-sol" used for "Deb-bie."

ROUNDS   Rounds are fun to sing, but they are sometimes difficult for young children to learn. To aid this situation, tape record a round. Then, start the tape recorder playing, and direct the children to begin singing at the appropriate times, first in unison, and then later, in smaller groups. Try to identify those pupils whose voices can help carry their part, and cluster them in one group. Another interesting activity with rounds is to have one group sing only the last phrase of a round while the other children sing the entire song; get this small group started first, and then have the other children join in. A further suggestion is to have the children perform a key movement for each important phrase in the song to help them remember the sequence of the various parts in the song.

SERENADING   Give your children a chance to share their songs with others by permitting them to serenade others in the school or in the nearby neighborhood. This is especially appropriate at holiday times. Also consider exchanging musical programs with other classes, or with other schools. Serenade in a local business area for even wider exposure, and consider the possibility of performing for shut-ins, people in nursing homes, orphans, and others who might enjoy the music.

SILENT SINGING   Check the children's ability to carry a melody and, at the same time, interject some fun into their singing by having them sing silently. This is done by pretending you are turning their sound on and off, just as you would do with a television set or a radio. Try this approach with a song that the group are well acquainted with: instruct them to sing out loud when you signal "On," and have them move only their lips, thinking about the melody when you signal "Off."

SOLO SINGING   Encourage the children to sing parts by themselves, but do not force them to do so. Where they are bashful about soloing, place two or three children in a cluster who can sing at least a few phrases by themselves. Or arrange the children in a line and tap individual students on the head to sing individual words or phrases.

SONG CHART   To remind the children of all the songs you have learned in your classroom, make a picture chart of the songs. Each song can be characterized by a photograph or a drawing appropriate to its theme. Use these charts as references when you give the pupils a chance to name the songs they would like to review. Use the titles of the songs as supplementary reading experiences.

SONG ILLUSTRATIONS   Find magazine pictures to illustrate the words of a song. Ask the children to make a booklet for a favorite song, allotting one page of the book for each phrase of the music. Include both the music of the song written on a staff, and the words of the lyrics. Use these song books as additional experiences in reading class.

VOCAL CONTROL   Help the children to control the loudness and softness of their singing, demonstrating that there is a difference, for instance, between loud singing and shouting. Ask the class to decide what volume would be suitable for putting a baby to sleep, or for singing in a parade. Then give them a piece of music, such as a lullaby or a martial selection to help them practice their vocal control.

VOCAL DICTION   To encourage better diction in children's singing, show them how to exaggerate lip and tongue movements, and help the children to exaggerate the words themselves. Let the children say the words aloud, whisper them, and shout them, as a preliminary experience to a diction lesson. Another suggestion is to introduce nonsense syllables to a tune that the children already know.

VOCAL LITERATURE   Vary the music your children learn by selecting songs that are easy to sing, relevant to their interests, and will satisfy the children's sense of accomplishment. Choose music that is well within their voical range. Include both silly songs and serious ones. Be sure to include street chants, folk songs, spirituals, game songs, seasonal songs, music from foreign cultures, and songs that develop a topic of study in other classes.

VOCAL RANGE   If some children find it difficult to sing high notes, use a story that incorporates high and low voices. "Goldilocks and the Three Bears" and "Three Billy Goats Gruff" are examples of these stories. This will give the children practice in talking in a very high voice. Use some of these same story phrases set to music for further experiences in vocal range.

part four

NUMBERS:
Beginning Mathematics
Experiences

Devices for Teaching
COMPUTATION

ADDING BOARD Make simple combinations by pounding different numbers of nails into several rectangular scraps of lumber. Give the children colored beads or metal washers to place over these nails and make different computation problems involving addition. Another adaptation is to use colored rubber bands to stretch over these nails as a manipulative device in experiencing subsets.

ADDING GRAPHS Use the largest graph paper you can find, preferably that with one-inch squares. Or, if this size is not available, make your own graph paper with a yardstick and a large sheet of newsprint, folding the yardstick over and over inside the paper to make creases in both directions. To show the different addition combinations, ask the children to take their crayons and color in the different squares to show varieties of ways of making their sums. When the children have finished coloring in the different combinations, ask them to cut them apart for further practice, using them like cuisenaire strips.

ADDING HANDS To help the children visualize the subsets in an addition problem, make a series of tracings on paper of a child's hands with his fingers in different positions so that some hands have no fingers showing. Write on the palm of each drawing the number of fingers showing. Then demonstrate how these hands can be arranged in a variety of computation problems. The children can count the fingers to check the accuracy of their answers.

ADDING MACHINES   Obtain an old adding machine and let the children use it to check the accuracy of their computations. Set up pairs of students to check each other. Another type of adding machine is one made by adapting a rectangle of cardboard to this purpose: cut slits in the cardboard so you can manipulate vertical strips of paper on which are written the numerals in their serial order. If the problem is 3 plus 4, for example, the child places the strip so that the 3 shows through the window in the card, then it pulls it four times, so the strip then shows 7 through the window. This kind of device is particularly useful in helping the children cope with the concept of regrouping into ten's and hundred's.

ADDRESS CARDS   Label each child with a different numeral card. Give one child a series of problems to perform as letters to deliver. Call this one child "Postman," and give him letters labeled, for instance, 9 plus 8; the Postman would deliver this letter to the child labeled 17. Still another approach with this same game is to set up a series of pigeon holes like a mail sorting box, and have the postman sort his address cards into them.

BEANBAG TOSS   Assist the children to perform several different operations involving two different numbers. Prepare sets of bean-bags for the students to toss onto a random assortment of numerals taped to the floor, or taped to a piece of paper or plastic. Let the child tell everything he can about the two numbers his beanbags hit: addition, subtraction, greater-lesser, and, if possible multiplication. Or, have a group of children standing in a circle, each person wearing a different numeral. One child stands in the middle of the circle holding three beanbags: one of them he throws to the child in the circle, the second to another child, and the third beanbag, which has a plus on one side and a minus on the other side, he throws to a third child. Then the leader calls upon still another child to put these three elements together and give the answer to the problem.

BINGO CARDS   Make a series of bingo cards on which the children write randomly-placed numerals. As the leader of the game shows or calls out different addition or subtraction problems, each child covers answers appropriate to them. Or, reverse the process, asking the child to randomly write on the card ten or 20 problems common to all players. Then the leader holds up numeral cards for the children to place correctly on their playing boards.

BOUNCE BOX   A device that adds interest to computation is a bounce box, made of an egg carton in which the sections are labeled with different numerals. Ask the children to bounce a table tennis ball into two or more sections and then perform the mathematical operation previously agreed upon. A large box with cardboard dividers can also be adapted to this game. As a variation of the game, ask the children to bounce the ball against the wall or a desk before it falls into the box.

BOWLING BOX   Make a miniature bowling alley from a long box. Set up small dowel pieces as the bowling pins and use marbles as the bowling balls. Mark a triangular field at one end of the box, and cut open the other end of the box. Label the dowels and their positions with numerals. Ask the children to add the numbers on the pins they knock down. Or, instruct them to count how many pins were knocked down and tell without looking how many are still standing. Adapt this same bowling game to milk cartons, toilet tissue tubes, or other discarded materials.

COMBINATION WHEELS   Construct a wheel with three concentric circles fastened together with a brass fastener. On the smallest inside circle write one or more addend or subtrahend. Then, dividing the other two concentric circles into pie pieces, place other addends on the sections of the middle circle, leaving the sections of the outer circle blank. Ask the children to add or subtract the sets of numbers and write the sums or differences on the blank spaces. As a slight variation of this wheel, make the middle circle merely an operational sign, and have the other two wheels covered with different numerals for computation practice.

   Another kind of combination wheel is made from a large cardboard circle, around the edge of which are written a series of computation problems. Make a series of spring-type wooden clothespins into answers by marking individual numerals on each one. Mix up these clothespins in a box, challenge the children to find one that matches a problem, and then clip the clothespin onto the edge of the wheel in the appropriate position.

CUISENAIRE STRIPS   Make individual cuisenaire strips by cutting pieces of colored construction paper into sections in exact multiples: the "2" strip is twice as long as the "1" strip, and so on. Label each strip with its appropriate numeral, and color code each strip so all the "1" strips are one color, the "2" strips are a different color, and the "3" strips are still another color .Encourage the children to assemble these strips to see if they can discover all the possible ways of making a combination or a set. When each child has explored fully all these possibilities, let him paste the strips down in rows in a number booklet.

DICE TOSSING   The simplest type of dice to use for computation practice are those borrowed from a children's game. Have the children count the dots and perform the addition, subtraction, or multiplication problems. Dominoes are also appropriate for this purpose, along with children's numeral blocks, or sponge blocks marked with numerals.

For jumbo dice, paint two or more large cardboard boxes with dots or numerals on four of the six sides. Cut away the bottom of each box, and in the sixth surface, cut a hole for a child to poke his head through. Each child can then put on a box, and the leader of the game can have experience in turning the sides of these large dice to make up different computation problems.

EQUIVALENCE BEAM   To show equivalent sets make a small balance beam using a wire coat hanger and two nut cups or plastic lids as the pans. After the beam has been balanced, add beans to each side to show that 7 is the same as 5 plus 2. Another application of this same idea is to balance building blocks on a piece of lumber or on a yardstick balanced on a fulcrum.

FISHING GAME   One type of fishing game involves three separate cans or boxes, two of them with different numeral cards in them, and the third can containing cards with plus and minus operations signs. Ask the child to reach in his hand, without looking, and pull out numerals and the sign card and arrange the cards in a number sentence to solve. Another approach to fishing is to have a series of fish-shaped combinations cards, each with a staple through its "nose." Let the child fish with a magnet, and allow him to keep any of the fish whose problems he can solve.

FLAP CARDS   Make a flap card from a rectangular piece of cardboard that is cut and folded in such a way that the right and left ends of the card flip over the center of the card, covering the center portion of the card exactly. On one of the flaps write one part of a computation problem and on the other flap write the other part. Directly underneath these two flaps, on the center portion of the strip, place sets of dots corresponding to the numerals on the flaps. This should enable the children to count the dots as a way of checking their accuracy in answering the problem on the flaps.

FLASHCARDS Children enjoy using flashcards to reinforce their skills in computation. These cards can be employed in timed exercises, and they can also be used in a two-child contest to see which child can accumulate the greatest number of correct answers. Be sure the answers are on the back of the cards for ready checking. To test all elements of these computation tasks, be sure the unknowns needed to solve them are presented in initial, medial, and final position in the number sentence. Assemble these flashcards in a fan connected at one point with a brass fastener for ease in handling.

JUMBO NUMERALS Construct a learning aid for combinations by cutting huge numerals from large sheets of newsprint or cardboard. Give each child a different jumbo numeral, and challenge him to recall all the possible number facts about that numeral and write them on the face of the cutout. For example, if the number "7" is one of them, the person holding it might write on it statements such as 4 plus 3, 9 minus 2, 1 times 7.

LADDERS Devise a combinations ladder for each sum, writing a numeral at the top of the ladder. Ask the child to place different sets of addends on each rung of the ladder in response to the other addend you have already placed there. As the child can identify the correct addend to match your addend, he may advance one rung upwards. Another version of a ladder involves the child answering random problems written on flash cards, and each correct response entitles him to move upward one more rung. Or, ask the children to write on each rung a different true statement involving two or more different operations.

LIFT-UP CARDS Fold in half lengthwise a stiff piece of paper. Then cut one edge of this paper perpendicularly from the edge toward the center fold in such a way that the paper has on one of the sections two separate flaps that lift up individually, with the center fold as the hinge. On each flap write a numeral as a part of an addition or subtraction problem. Ask the child to lift up each flap, in turn, and draw objects to match the numerals on the flaps, and then solve the problem. Or, reverse the process and have a child draw objects on the flaps to match the problem stated underneath them.

MAGIC SQUARES   Draw a series of squares, each of which is made of four equal, smaller squares. Write a numeral in each square and challenge the children to add the numerals in both the horizontal and vertical directions. When these four sums are found, add them, also. Add the vertical set and the horizontal set, and these two sums should produce the same number. Vary this activity by inserting some of the sums in position on the squares, and asking the child to identify the missing addends. Later, adapt these same squares to subtraction problems.

MATCHING LACES   Make cards of stiff cardboard on one side of which are listed in column form a series of problems. Directly across the page from these problems, list a series of answers to the same problems, randomly placed in their own column. Punch a hole beside each problem and beside each solution. Take long pieces of yarn or long shoelaces and tie a knot in one end of each piece in such a way that the child can grasp a string, and then thread it through the correct hole in the other column on the card. On the reverse face of each card, with colors or simple symbols, show which holes should match, so the child can check the accuracy of his responses. When the child is done with the lacing and checking, ask him to loosen the laces in preparation for the next child to use them.

OPERATOR GAME   Give each child in the group a different numeral as a label to wear. The leader in the center of the group pretends to be dialing a number on the telephone. He says something like, "Hello, I'm calling six plus three." Thereupon the child with 9 must reply, "Hello, I'm Mr. Nine." Adapt this same game to subtraction. Or, take one child's telephone number, and ask the operator to add the digits in it.

PATHWAYS GAME   Make a series of footprints of paper or cardboard and label each one with a different computation problem, one for each numeral in ascending order of counting. Mix these footprints up and let the children make a pathway, putting each footprint where it belongs in sequence. When the footprints are in order, let the child say the problem and then the solution as he steps along the pathway. Footprints might be labeled, in turn, as 0 plus 1, 8 minus 6, 6 minus 3, 2 plus 2, and so on.

A tabletop pathway game can be made by drawing a series of stepping stones on a large piece of cardboard or paper, and then having the child draw randomly from a stack of cards a series of problems: the addition problems correctly solved allow him to move forward the same number of spaces as the sum; if he draws a subtraction problem, however, he moves backwards the number of the difference. If he cannot answer the problem he loses his next turn, or else must return to his starting point on the game board.

PEGBOARD ADDER   Using a small piece of pegboard, label the holes with numerals, randomly arranged from 1 to 20. On another portion of the board leave several rows of unlabeled holes, also 20 in number. Place pegs of one color in the first set of holes, and pegs of another color in the second set of holes. Give the child a stimulus card with a numeral on it, as, for example, 16. Ask him to take colored rubber bands and stretch them around any set of addends that would suggest 16. He might think of several addends to combine. Suggest that the child use the second set of pegs to explore other possible combinations before stretching the rubber bands in place.

PRACTICE GRIDS   Mark large squares of tagboard into smaller squares of uniform size, like oversized graph paper. Along the horizontal axis at the top of the grid place the numerals in serial order, beginning with zero. Along the left axis, also in order, from top to bottom make another set of numerals. Cover the entire surface with a piece of clear adhesive Contact paper and let the children practice writing the sums, differences, or products on the grid, using a grease pencil or a felt-tip marker. Or, give them small numeral cards, exactly the same size as the squares, to place at the correct intersection on the grid. For instance, the 6 card would be put where the 4 and 2 lines intersect on the addition grid.

PROGRAMMED CARDS   Construct self-correcting combinations cards from rectangles of tagboard or cardboard. On the front face of this device write a series of problems involving addition or subtraction processes. Next to each row of problems cut away a part of the card allowing space for the child to slip a piece of paper the same size underneath the card and write on his paper the

answers to all the problems. On the back of this cardboard rectangle, write the answers to the problems, so the child can also
slip his answer sheet underneath it and compare his answers with
the correct ones.

PUZZLES Use ordinary playing cards as puzzles for helping in
adding and subtracting. One method is to take individual cards and
cut them apart with one irregular cut so there are a variety of sets
and combinations in each suit of cards. Let the child sort through
these cut pieces in each suit to reassemble the simple combinations. The numeral at the top of the card should tell him which
piece is missing. Ordinary flashcards can also be converted into
simple two-piece puzzles. Cut the answer from each one, in a
distinctive cut so only one answer will fit into each cut. In this way
the child can work the problem, and then fit the answer into its
place to check his accuracy.

YARN CARDS For each family of numbers, make a card of stiff
cardboard, attaching a piece of colorful yarn to the card at the
corner with a brass fastener. On the card have a series of dots
representing the number family—for example, nine dots in three
rows of three dots each, representing 9. Near these dots write a
series of computation problems relative to that number: for example, 3 plus 6, 4 plus 5, 1 plus 8. Give this card to the child who is
just beginning to learn his addition facts and let him demonstrate
the subsets of the number family by circling with the yarn one
portion of the array of dots. The student should see then that if four
dots are circled inside the yarn, there are five dots outside it. Use
this same kind of card to introduce subtraction facts.

Interesting Ways with COUNTING

ACTION COUNTING Have a small group of children stand in a circle or in a line. Label each child with a different numeral card. Present this situation to the group: "Do something with your body parts, making an action the same number of times as the number you are wearing." Each child must then think of something different to act out. The first child might stamp his foot once; the second child might sneeze twice; the third child might wave his hand three times. Then ask the children to hide their numerals and to mix themselves up in the circle or the line. Repeat the same instructions concerning the actions and challenge the students to watch and listen for the appropriate number of actions being performed. Help the group to reassemble in correct numerical order as they continue acting out numbers with their bodies.

CALENDAR COUNTING Use a calendar to reinforce the children's number skills. For example, ask them to count the number of days in each month and compare them to see which months have the greater number of days. Or, instruct the class to find the date on the second Sunday in the month, or find the date of the fourth Wednesday, for example. Placing all the months in their correct order, ask the child to locate the third month of the year. Or, have the group count the number of days in each week frequently to reinforce the notion that each week has seven days.

Make or purchase a calendar with movable dates to allow children to experiment with numerical order.

CARTON COUNTERS To assist the children in their counting, salvage an empty egg carton and mark the compartments from one to ten, with the other two compartments saved for storing the counting objects. Fill these ten compartments with lima beans, small buttons, nuts, seeds, or other similar items. Label each compartment with its correct numeral in order. Later, mix up these numeral labels to further challenge the children's recognition and counting awareness.

Another use of the egg carton is to cut apart the sections or compartments in such a way that there are single sections, double sections, triple sections, and so on up to a full 12-section box. Try to find several cartons of the same type for this purpose. When these different number-related sections have been cut apart, paint each one a different color to further serve as a visual cue to the child doing the counting and computation. As the child manipulates these cardboard or plastic sections, he can see graphically that 7 plus 5 is 12. And as he stacks them one on top of another, he can readily tell that 9 is 1 more than 8.

COUNTING CHAINS A simple chain is something unusual to count—and the child can mark every fifth link or every tenth link with a piece of colorful tape. Another chain is made from stringing beads—again, use a different colored bead to indicate five's and ten's. Still another counting chain is made of paper clips which can be combined in sections of ten's and 100's, wrapped around a cardboard tube to keep them out of the way; use bronzed paper clips to mark off sections of silver paper clips. Also, consider helping the class construct paper counting chains. Show them how to write the numeral on each paper link before it is pasted together.

COUNTING FIVE'S Help the children to count by five's by first showing them how to make the traditional tally marks in sets of five. Another method is to have all the children in the class hold up their hands so the person who is counting can see the sets of five fingers as he counts. Occasionally, as a part of attendance taking at the beginning of the session, ask a child to tell the class how many fingers are present in school today. Or, if the weather is favorable, have the children take off their shoes and stockings and instruct the counter to see how many fingers and toes are present. Still another way of counting by five's is to put a set of nickels on the table for counting, after the child is aware that a nickel represents five pennies. The face of a clock is also useful as an aid in teaching students to count by five's.

COUNTING FRAME   Make a simple counting frame by cutting out three rectangles of cardboard. Notch two smaller rectangles in the middle, and notch one larger rectangle at both ends so the larger one can stand up to hold wooden clothespins in a vertical position. Label each clothespin with a numeral, and ask the children to count them and place them in the correct order. Or, label the cardboard frame itself, and ask the children to match the clothespins with the labeled spaces, as a number recognition experience.

A frame like an abacus can be made by stringing colored beads or metal washers onto a wire cut from a coat hanger; or string spools on yarn for this same purpose. Another possibility is plastic spring-type clothespins clipped to a wire coat hanger, each pin labeled with a numeral. Stringing pieces of macaroni on wire is also helpful. When the children are studying the concepts of ten's and one's, cut small sections of wire just long enough to hold ten objects, then crimp the end of the wire, and use these items to demonstrate a group of ten.

COUNTING MAN   Make a large stand-up counting man of sturdy cardboard or poster board. Also make a notched holder for the man to stand in. Be sure that each hand of the counting man has five notches in it to hold other notched pieces of cardboard to represent the numbers from one to ten. Or, if the cardboard man is large enough to hold them, label spring-type clothespins with the numerals and clip them onto his hands for counting and computation practice.

COUNTING OBJECTS   For those children who are just beginning to count provide a wide variety of real objects to count. Discourage routine oral rote counting devoid of physical manipulation. For example, commercial cards of buttons are useful, along with other cards to which beans or buttons have been glued. Beads strung on yarn is another possibility. Still another idea is to make construction paper pictures, such as a ladybug with black spots or a clown with polka dots on his costume or spots on his face. Paper doll twins, one figure with the dots and the other with the matching numeral, are also useful. Blocks, especially those plastic ones that hold together, are particularly helpful in counting by sets of two, five, or ten. If additional reinforcement is needed in counting, add some auditory stimuli to the visual ones by having the children count pebbles, bottle caps, acorns, or other hard items, dropping them into a metal pail or onto some other hard surface.

COUNTING PAIRS   Assist the children who are learning to count by two's by using things that are familiar to them which come in pairs. Think of hands, mittens, feet, shoes, eyes, eyebrows, ears, twins, sleeves, socks, etc. Begin a chart titled "Pairs of Things" and encourage the children to cut out pictures of things that usually come in sets of two. As more items are added to the chart, let individual children have practice in counting the total number of objects pictured on it.

DOT-TO-DOT CARDS   An all-purpose counting aid is the dot-to-dot card which is familiar to the children and is usually a lot of fun. Make your own cards by tracing a picture from a coloring book onto a piece of cardboard; punch out the outline of the picture using the point of a nail, and label with numerals the key points along this outline. Give the children a long piece of colored twine or yarn and have them lace around the outline in correct sequence. Adapt this same type of card to a drawing experience by covering the card picture with clear adhesive Contact paper and giving the child a grease pencil, water-soluble felt-tip pen, or a soft wax crayon to use in drawing the outline of the picture.

FINGER COUNTERS   Have each child cut out from cardboard several tracings of his own hands. Label each finger with a numeral in its serial order, and let the child use this aid in counting and in simple computation activities. Another idea is to label the child's own fingers with washable colors. However, as soon as the student has mastered the abstract notion behind his finger manipulation, encourage him to put away these aids so he will not continue to rely on them.

GREATER AND LESSER   Help the children to compare the number of objects in different sets by matching them one-to-one, establishing that in fact some sets have more members than other ones. After the class has had experience in this type of correspondence, pose questions such as: "What number is one greater than this number?" "What number is one less than this number?" "What number is two greater or two less?'' Let them use manipulative items to confirm the accuracy of their answers. Give the children other practice in making comparisons of sets after they have removed equivalent sets from two collections of objects. For example, after the group has discovered that 8 is 3 greater than five, remove 2 items from each side of the table, and rediscover that 6 is 3 greater than 3. To add variety to this latter activity, have the children cover their eyes while the items are being removed, and challenge them to tell how many objects are missing from each set.

Since young children frequently have trouble in remembering the appropriate mathematical symbols representing ''greater than'' and ''less than,'' present the symbol as always representing a large bird's beak, pointing at the smaller number. Make up a simple story about how the larger number is wanting to eat up the smaller number, and that is why it has a beak. When discussing this concept of ''greater'' and ''lesser'' it is also important to avoid the term ''larger,'' because the child may mistakenly equate largeness of the actual figure cut from cardboard with the numerical value of the representation. Try to use ''greater,'' ''more,'' and ''most,'' but not ''larger.''

HUNDRED'S BOARD   Make a hundred's board by pounding a grid of nails into a wooden foot-square rectangle, ten nails in ten vertical lines. By placing these nails at one-inch intervals, the board may also be used as a geoboard and a perimeter board as well. Use a series of price tags or other labels that have holes already punched in them for the numerals—write a different numeral from one to 100 on each tag. Give the children experience in placing these tags on the board where they belong. Such a board may also be used as a simple counting device by giving the class members a box of metal washers to count and place on the nails. Pinning spring-type clothespins in a vertical position on these nails is still another idea.

A different version of the hundred's board is a hundred's graph made by labeling each of the squares on a large piece of graph paper, ten squares in one dimension by ten squares in the other. Unlabeled these squares can be counted. Or, label the squares, and the children can place other individual matching squares on the correct space on the hundred's graph. Too, the graph can be converted into a puzzle by cutting the paper grid apart into five or six irregular pieces. Ask each child to reassemble the puzzle correctly as he applies his knowledge of number sequence.

INCIDENTAL COUNTING Utilize natural situations for practicing counting skills. For example, have the pupils count the children in attendance each day, or count the number of times that they can perform some physical exercise, such as bouncing and catching a ball, or jumping rope. In addition, they can count the beat of a musical selection, count blocks and beads they are stacking or stringing, count toys in a set, count the days on a calendar until a special holiday, count the minutes until recess, or count the cookies needed for snack time. Children with birthdays like to count their age, and counting pennies or pieces of candy shared at birthdays is another possibility.

LARGE NUMBERS Young children are often curious about large numbers, and sometimes ask questions such as, "How many is a thousand?" or "What would a million things look like?" A relatively simple way to demonstrate 1000 is to get several sheets of graph paper and cut it into pieces that are ten squares in each direction. Lay ten pieces of this paper into an arrangement on the floor of the room.

Showing the children one million is also easy, although it may take a little more time. Using a typewriter and a ditto master, make a grid of dots covering the ditto master with 80 dots in the horizontal direction and 50 dots in the vertical direction. This grid will equal 4,000 on each sheet. Run this master onto 250 sheets of paper. Ask 25 children to each count out ten sheets of these dots and lay them out in a design on the floor of a large room to make a collection of one million dots.

NUMBER BOOKLETS Make a booklet that will introduce the children to all the numerals from 1 to 999. First find a spiral-bound notebook that has ten pages in it. With a pair of scissors, cut slits into each of these pages perpendicular to the spiral ring in such a way that there are three small notebook-like sets of pages, all of them attached to the same spiral wire, but in each of the three sets one can move the pages independently. Label each of the sets of small pages from 1 to 9, leaving the first page as a blank cover sheet. In this way, when the children are working with counting or with numeral recognition, they can flip over these small individual sheets to produce any combination of numerals from 1 to 999. Give special practice in making these numbers in the notebook as you present oral or written stimuli: "Show me the number 635," "Show me the number that is one less than 921," "Show me the number ten larger than 157."

Another type of number booklet, involving much smaller numbers, can be made by folding large sheets of newsprint and stapling them together. Instruct the class to label each page, in turn, with the correct numeral in sequence, and then tell them to draw or paste pictures appropriate to that specific numeral in each space. Add the number word to each page as the child learns to read them. For the beginning student, make a series of counting dots on each page of the booklet.

NUMBER CARTONS As a useful visual aid for the children in practicing counting, make a series of charts, each of which is keyed to a different numeral, and ask the children to collect pictures of things that are usually found only in sets indicated by that number. For example:

> One   is the number of heads we have
> Two   is the number of wheels on a bike
> Three is a triangle or a cloverleaf
> Four is the feet of a cat
> Five is the points on a star
> Six   is the legs of an insect
> Seven is the days of the week
> Eight is the arms of an octopus or legs of a spider
> Nine is the number of players on a baseball team
> Ten   is the number of toes we have

A simpler version of these charts is merely to label each chart with a different numeral and let the children find pictures in a magazine to cut out appropriate to each of the numerals.

NUMBER DIALS Facilitate the group's awareness of numerals used in counting by making a large cardboard replica of a combination padlock in which the inside dial is a pointer connected by a brass fastener to another larger dial on which the numerals are written. Give the children situations in which the class members, one at a time, work these imaginary combinations. For example, say, "Turn the pointer right three times and stop at 38. Then turn left two times and stop at 17. Turn left four times and stop at 49." If tne child performs the task correctly, let him open a small box of candy and get a special treat as a reward, along the order of a treasure box. As the children gain experience in following these directions, get a real combination lock and use it on the locked toy box. A child will have to open the lock correctly to take out a toy at play time.

NUMBER LABELS Number the lockers, cubby holes, and tote trays with number labels and encourage the children to use them to collect their own things in the classroom. Assign each child the same number designation that corresponds with his relative position in the alphabetical room list. Post this alphabetical-numerical list in the classroom and assign individual children additional tasks illustrated by instructions such as, "Give this paper to Number 22," or, "Ask the child who is 16 minus 9 to come to my desk, please."

NUMBER LINE Construct a number line to use in the classroom, making it large enough to walk on and sturdy enough to hang up vertically. A piece of oilcloth, vinyl, or plastic, with fabric tape numerals added, is a handy device. Lay this number line on the floor, and ask the children individually to move along the line in response to different kinds of counting questions: "Count the number of jumps you must make to move from 1 to 4." "Start at 9 and take away 5 steps and tell me where you are." "Stand on 7, then show me 2 more."

NUMBER POEMS Sharpen counting skills of young children by using a variety of seasonal poems that are about ten little pumpkins, or valentines, or Christmas trees. Cut from paper or flannel simple shapes that the children can manipulate as they count these holiday items. Also find poems that deal with the counting of numbers in reverse direction, decreasing the number of items involved: for instance, "Ten little pumpkins standing in a line; one became a pie and then there were nine . . ."

NUMBER TAPPING Enhance a child's listening skills as well as his counting and computation abilities by having another person tap on a hard surface, and asking a class member to count the taps. Or, have one child standing at the door tapping a designated number of times; a second child answers the knocks at the door, saying in response, "Come in Mister Eight." After the children have some computation practice, have one child tap two sets of sounds, and then ask another child to tell the problem and its answer. For example, eight taps plus four taps are 12 taps.

NUMBER WALK   Take a brief excursion in the neighborhood to look for things to count and numerals to read. Count the homes in a given block or count the number of cars passing a corner. Count the number of cracks in the sidewallk from the school door to the street. Find numerals to read on homes, on signs, or on license plates. Make a game of numeral recognition and counting by leaving simple clues as directions for the children to locate simple treats hidden on the playground. For example, "Take a right turn at the gate and count 12 fence posts for the treasure." Or, have different sets of directions at each of several different points in the area.

ODD AND EVEN   Make a series of number cards, each with a different numeral on it. Distribute these randomly to the class, one to each child. At a signal, have the children sort themselves into two groups: Odds and Evens. Then, as a follow-up activity, at another signal, have the children try to arrange themselves in serial order: 1,3,5,7,9 in one group, for instance, and 2,4,6,8,10 in another.

As a visual aid for odd and even numbers, cut from graph paper sections of squares representing the different numbers. To illustrate, the number 2 is represented by two squares side by side, attached in the middle; the number 3 is shown by two squares side by side, plus one other square extending down, also attached to the other two. Using these aids, the child will see that every odd number is represented by an irregular shape and the even numbers are shown as pairs of squares. Demonstrate also that the sets of odd number squares can be fit together to make regular sets of squares representing even numbers.

PAGE NUMBERS   As an experience in counting and recognizing numerals, direct the attention of the class to their textbooks and have them count the pages without looking at the numerals on them. To add interest to numeral recognition, have each child hold a copy of the same textbook and hold it shut as it stands upright on his desk. At a given signal, give a page number for all the children to find. The first child to find the correct page stands up and reads the first word on that particular page. Make this race into a contest, where teams of children are competing against each other for speed.

PERSONAL NUMBERS   Introduce a variety of personal numbers for children to practice. Make a "My Own Numbers" booklet, and on separate pages let the child draw a picture of his home and write the address below it. On another page have the child draw or paste a picture of a telephone and write the telephone number underneath it. Then connect a piece of yarn or string between these two pictures. Other pictures might include the license numbers of family vehicles, birthdates, and any other personal data that might be recorded.

PLACE HOLDERS   To help children visualize the use of numerals as place holders in concepts related to hundred's, ten's, and units, make a series of house-like cardboard envelopes labeled "Hundred's House," "Ten's House," and "One's House." Have different colors of construction paper cards, each color coded to a specific house. For example, the one's cards could be blue, the ten's cards yellow, and the hundred's cards red. Each one's card should have only one black dot on it, each ten's card should have ten dots, while each hundred's card should have 100 dots. As the child counts, when he accumulates ten of the units markers, tell him that these ten one's must move over to the "Ten's House" to become a part of that family. Put the one's cards out of sight and show the child that the dots are now on one ten's card. Use a similar analogy when the child has counted ten ten's.

SERIATION CARDS   When children are learning the serial order of numbers, make a set of cards on which all their numerals are written. For each successive numeral of greater quantity, make the card of a slightly larger size so the children can have this added visual clue, as well as the numerals themselves. Another type of card might use shades of paint that gradually increase in intensity as the numbers increase in size.

SERIATION LABELS   Have the members of the class cut price labels from newspaper advertisements or from food containers and practice placing them in order. Or ask them to cut from magazines pictures of racing cars, sailboats, airplanes, or similar vehicles. To each picture attach a numeral and ask the children to place them in correct order. Or, collect address labels from discarded envelopes and packages and have the children place them in order.

SERIATION RODS Make a set of seriation rods by pounding large nails into a pine board and then obtaining large metal machined nuts or washers and stack them on the nails in the order indicated by the numerals painted at the base of each nail. Or, find a series of long bolts and insert them through holes in a piece of wood, and ask the children to thread the machined nuts onto the bolts according to the numeral cues on the wood. Still another idea is to impale empty spools on dowel sticks that are inserted into the wheels from Tinker Toys.

SERIATION SONGS Develop the notion of the serial order of numbers as you sing songs familiar to the children. For example, with the song "Ten Little Indians," have the children assemble themselves or arrange pictures of Indians in an order appropriate to the words of the song. Try to find a book containing counting out rhymes, game songs, as other possibilities. Adapt some of these familiar tunes to counting out and numeral recognition and seriation, by adding or changing words: for example, "Farmer in the Dell" could easily become, "The One Takes a Two . . ."

STORY NUMBERS Find examples of stories that have counting experiences for children. This might include something as commonplace as the "Three Little Pigs," the "Four Musicians" or the "Billy Goats Gruff." Use these stories for simple computation problems, as well as counting activities. Make up other elements to these familiar stories, inventing imaginary situations for the other seven little pigs, or the rest of the dozen billy goats. Also, when the children are solving other number problems, encourage them to make up their own stories to help make the solutions more promising for them.

MEASURING
Time, Money, Distance

ACTUAL SALES   To stimulate interest in learning about money in the classroom, use the "sale" technique to "sell" items to the children. For each child, prepare the same amount of pretend coins and currency. Make a series of posters and signs advertising a variety of simple privileges, snacks, or toys for the children, and sell each item at a fixed price. Make each of these transactions an exercise in recognizing money and making change. At the end of the day let each child decide if he wants to save the money he has left, or spend it for other special treats still "on sale" in the classroom store.

CALENDAR CLOCKS   Add variety to calendar skills by making a clock in the shape of a circular clock, placing January where 1:00 would ordinarily be, adding the other months around the face of the clock, ending with December in the position of 12:00. Give the children experience in associating time with the months, asking questions such as, "What is the month at 3:00?" or "At what time on the clock would you find June?"

CALENDAR MATCHING   As you discuss the different months, assist the group in identifying principal holidays and other special observances appropriate to each one. Cut out pictures that are suitable and paste them to cards. Ask the class to match these picture cards with cards naming the months. As another calendar matching activity, request the students to match the cards labeled 28, 30, and 31 to the names of the months on other cards. Also, have the group find examples of things that are dated, or make their own dates on cards using a library dating device. Match these dates with the dates on the calendar. Still another matching idea involves color coding the numeral cards on the calendar, so each day is represented by only one color. For example, all Mondays might be blue, Tuesdays purple, Wednesdays red, and so on. The child can see at a glance if the numerals are in proper order.

CLOCK ADDITION   Combine practice in computation with clock reading skills by making a large clock face on a cardboard circle, omitting the numerals around the clock perimeter. Instead of these numerals, leave small blank circles. Then label a series of small cardboard circles, each with a different addition or subtraction problem. Challenge the children to find an appropriate small marker card and place it in its proper position around the clock face. For example, if the child is looking for a marker to place on the spot ordinarily occupied by 4:00, he might use the circle problem that states, "12 minus 8." Still another computation activity involves spinning the hands of the clock, and adding or subtracting the two numbers that the hands point to.

CLOCK GAMES   Make a human clock by placing pairs of children around a large circle drawn on the floor or playground. Locate pairs of children at each hour's position, with the child standing inside the circle at each point representing the hour, and the child standing on the outside representing the minutes. The leader of the game taps any two children standing at a numeral, and calls out a time for them to demonstrate. For example, if the leader taps the two children who are standing at the numeral for 3:00, and calls out "6:45," the hour-child runs to the 6 and points with outstretched arms from the center of the clock to a spot partway between 6 and 7; meantime the minute-child runs to the far side of the circle and points from the center of the clock toward the 9:00. Place colored labels on the children's hands to remind them that they are either hours or minutes. Colored streamers of crepe paper might also be helpful, particularly if one child stood in the center of the clock holding the ends of the streamers which represent the hands of the clock.

CLOCK MANIPULABLES Cut out a large clock using a large piece of paper several feet in diameter. Add the numerals at the appropriate places around the edge of the clock, but omit the clock hands. Have one child lie down with his shoulders at about the center of the clock. Give other students the task of manipulating this child's feet and arms to represent different times.

Another type of manipulation involves old clocks that are beyond repair. Let the children practice setting the hands of these clocks for different times written on stimulus cards. If such discarded clocks are not available, make them from cardboard for this type of practice.

CLOCK MIX-UPS Make a series of activity cards on one side of which are pictured certain types of routine daily occurrences. On the other side of each card, make a clock that tells at what time these are customarily done. Each child can make his own set. Suggest such commonplace things as:

getting out of bed	having a rest
eating breakfast	getting home after school
going to school	eating the evening meal
having lunch	going to bed at night

Ask each child to mix up his own set of cards, and then instruct him to put the cards back in their correct order. Use picture cues to remind the child of each activity. Or, make a set of matching cards, one set with clock faces indicating times, and the other set indicating the activities routinely done during the day.

ESTIMATION Compare the approximate measurements of different containers and guess which one will hold the most. To make the task easier, have a box collection which includes items that vary in only one dimension. Later, add others that vary in two or three dimensions. Test the accuracy of the children's guesses by pouring dry cornmeal or rice into a clear glass measuring pitcher. Let the class also explore estimation of weights, linear distances, as well as other forms of measurement.

FRACTIONS Make the measurement of fractions graphic for the children by making a clock divided into fractional parts, especially quarters and halves. Color-code each section for further visual stimulus. Another good suggestion is to introduce fractions in the preparation of foods, such as might be done by cutting fruit into sections, cutting pieces of pie and cake, dividing sandwiches, and measuring foods by half cups, quarter cups, and third cups. If real foods are not readily available for this purpose, find colorful pictures to illustrate the same concepts. Take care to point out to children that items can be divided in a variety of ways: a piece of paper, for example, can be cut into half vertically, horizontally, or diagonally.

GRAPH GAMES   Using a number grid on a large rectangle of tagboard that has been divided into a graph of squares, play a game that involves the children in identifying coordinates on the graph. Along one axis of this graph paste a series of pictures, one for each row of squares. Find another set of pictures to paste along the other axis, also. Give the children a variety of situations such as, "Trace the paths where the lion would walk to meet the policeman." Or, reverse the procedure, asking the child to place a marker on one of the squares on the graph, and then telling which two persons or animals pictured along the axes of the graph would meet at that particular intersection occupied by the marker. When the children have had experience in locating these coordinates, make a similar graph with numerals on one axis, and letters along the other axis.

GRAPHING   As a preliminary activity for graphing, get a series of inch-square ceramic tiles. Prepare a chart with one-inch squares on it, and as sets of objects are compared, lay these tiles on the axes of the chart. Comparisons might be made, for example, among numbers of siblings, number of buttons on shirts or blouses, the types of household pets represented in the children in attendance, or the color of clothing. When the comparisons have been completed, remove the tiles from the chart and color in the graph with crayons as a permanent reminder of the discussion.

If graphing is done frequently in the class, make an all-purpose chart for graphing by cutting slits at the top of a large posterboard that has been marked into different axes. Make different labels that fit into the slits, appropriate to the different elements being compared. If the lines on the poster are about three-fourths of an inch or an inch apart, the children can use spring-type clothespins along the edge of each chart to show the comparisons in a dramatic way: the children will be able to see and count the number of clothespins representing each criterion.

LINEAR MEASUREMENTS Demonstrate the importance of standard units of linear measurement by suggesting that, without such units, many different ways of measuring would lead to confusion. For example, try using a shoe, a thumb, a handspan, or a pace for determining the dimensions of objects and places. Point out, after several children have tried measuring with informal means, that shoes, paces, and handspans differ. Make models of some of the measurements that are standard. For example, draw a picture of a foot that is exactly twelve inches long; or draw a thumb that is exactly one inch; use these standard models to measure things in the classroom. Point out that historically these units were standardized to make measuring more uniform.

MEASUREMENT DEVICES Make a display using a variety of measuring devices and implements. Consider odometers, reel tapes, scales and balances, counters, timers, clocks, markers, measuring cups and spoons, thermometers. Discuss how each item is used and stress the importance of number skills in using each one accurately. Collect pictures of other implements. Have the children bring empty containers of things that are sold by standard units of measurement. Suggest commodities such as sugar, butter, margarine, flour, or potatoes. Consider liquid measurement also: juice, cream, or milk. Also ask for things sold by the pound, such as apples and oranges, as well as items that are sold by the foot and the yard.

MEASURING TAPES Help the children to make their own personal measuring tapes using strips of ribbon, oilcloth, vinyl, or heavy paper. Attach these tapes to empty spools for convenient storage. To add variety, give each child a long piece of stiff paper or thin cardboard and show him how to measure it into inches, marking it like an inchworm. (Green paper is appropriate for this activity.) When the inchworm is completed, show the child how to accordion-fold it for storage. Add a funny face to the worm to give it further appeal. Still another kind of measuring tape is made from masking tape that adheres to the top of a desk or a table—mark this off in inch units and let the children measure books, papers, pencils and other commonplace objects.

MEASUREMENT TERMS In discussing measurement, point out that some terms are specific, while others are general. Make two charts to illustrate the point: one chart should have exact terms, such as : hour, dozen, quart, pound, foot, minute. The other chart might have terms such as: few, some, bunch, heavy, many, tall, several. Demonstrate the inexactness of these latter terms by asking two or more different children to bring you, for example, "a few" crayons, and then count them out to see the variation in numbers. Or, give each child large pieces of paper and a pair of scissors. Present a series of oral directions, such as, "Cut this paper so you have one long piece and one short piece." Compare these "long" pieces of paper. Then help the children to change these strips: "Find a wide piece and make it narrower. Take the long piece and make it shorter." To further illustrate the relative nature of the indefinite terms, have the children arrange the books in the shelves by height, then in terms of their width, and finally, in order of their thickness. Or, line the children before a mirror and compare how tall they are. Then compare them with an outlined figure of an adult.

MEASURING THINGS   Children who have learned to measure enjoy trying their skill with a variety of objects. In addition to the commonplace items they would ordinarily think of, suggest that they bring in food items for weighing. Use these same items at snack time. Measure large items, such as a truck or a car. Or, mark a point on the wall that shows how tall a giraffe is, or how long an elephant might be. On the playground, measure off the size of the "Mayflower" or Columbus' three ships, or the length of a dinosaur, or the diameter of a giant sequoia tree. Tape or paint some of these dimensions on the floor or playground for added play value.

MILEAGE   Using a map of your nearby area, give the children tasks in which they must find the distance to nearby towns, adding together subtotals. If the map is too complicated for them to follow, make a simplified version, adding a grid for them to use in finding coordinates. Compare distances to various large cities with which the class might be familiar and estimate how many hours would be required to get to each point on foot, in a car, on a bicycle, or in an airplane.

MONEY COUNTING   To provide practice in counting money without losing the coins, attach them with epoxy glue in varying combinations on pieces of cardboard or wood. Explore the relative value of each panel of coins. Another related approach is to make small cards or panels: on the face of each card have a combination of coins totaling a given sum, and on the other face of the card have another set of coins that also totals that same sum. Still other arrangements can be suggested by the students themselves.

Adapt money cards to a game by making replicas of money in a series of cards to be shuffled and compared. Let each child choose pairs of coin cards from a pile and tell which one would purchase the most items. Have the sum written on the back of each card for self-checking. Use these same cards to purchase pretend items for sale at a classroom store, matching each card to a price posted. Or, ask the children to arrange the coin cards in order of their face value.

MONEY REPLICAS To make play money for children to use in their money counting, from magazines cut pictures of coins and currency and paste them onto stiff cardboard. Also, contact parents for discarded play money from children's playthings. Or, show the class how to make coin rubbings with a soft lead pencil, cutting these out and pasting them to cardboard, and covering them with clear adhesive Contact paper to prevent smearing. Still another idea is to use small squares of aluminum foil, pressed down over coins to make temporary impressions.

PERSONAL MEASUREMENTS Measure a variety of dimensions of each child and have him record them in a personal booklet, or compare them on a chart. For example, measure body height and weight, as well as waist distances, lengths of shoes, handspans, foot lengths, or circumferences of heads. Also measure a variety of physical feats: how high they can reach, how high they can jump and touch, how far they can jump across, how far they can step with a giant pace. Repeat some of these personal measurements from time to time to show the group graphically the growth that is occurring.

PRICES Add motivation to money manipulation by presenting as many real situations as you can. For instance, give each child a chance to itemize an ideal menu for just one meal. Let him choose from the prices indicated in newspaper ads, or let him use an actual menu from a local eating establishment. To illustrate his own special meal, let the child look for pictures of the items selected, paste these pictures onto a piece of paper, and label each item with an appropriate price. A similar approach is to give the child an order pad and have him order from a toy catalog, or make a shopping list from a grocery advertisement.

RECIPE MEASUREMENTS   Find several simple recipes for making food items for snack times. Engage the children in measuring and mixing the ingredients. Point out the importance of exactness in measuring, especially in the addition of spices and flavorings. Give the group experience with a variety of instruments used in these kitchen processes: thermometers, measuring cups and spoons, scales, and timers.

STORY CLOCKS   To help visualize the relative functions of the hands of the clock, make a large circle from cardboard, and place the numerals in their appropriate positions .On the hour hand place a picture of a turtle and put a picture of a rabbit on the minute hand. Or, label the hands with pictures of two cars, one an old-fashioned car and the other a racing car. Too, make a story of these two hands by having two children holding streamers that are held at the other end by a third child. Instruct the "hour-hand" child to take baby steps, and the "minute-hand" child to take giant steps.

TALLY MARKS   As an introductory activity to graphing, show the children how to make tally marks when they are counting. One interesting application of this is to set up several observation posts on the street corners near the school. Give different children the responsibility for counting and marking the types of vehicles that pass each point in each direction; sub-divide the categories by types of cars and trucks, colors of vehicles, add bicycles and pedestrians, if appropriate. Make miniature pictures representing each thing counted and convert these into a bar graph to compare the data collected.

TELEVISION TIMES   Relate the children's ability to tell time with television schedules by making pairs of cards. On one card of each pair write the name of a favorite television program, and on the other card of each pair make a clock face that indicates the time at which that program is seen locally. Picture clues pasted to these cards might assist the recognition skills. Add calendar skills to this game, as the children must read the day of the week as well as the time the program is viewed. Later, poll the class to identify the favorite programs at each time slot, and make up a master schedule to be posted prominently in the classroom.

TIMING PRACTICE   Help the children with their clock skills by bringing an inexpensive kitchen timer to class. On the face of the timer tape small numerals in the relative positions of the hours and assign different students the tasks of setting time for various activities in the classroom. This can be done as you tell the pupil, ''Set the timer for fifteen minutes,'' or, ''Set the timer so the hand points to 9:00.'' Let the children also practice in estimating how long a minute is, or how long five minutes is. Another suggestion is to get a stopwatch from an athletic department and time accurately how long it takes for children to run from one point to another on the playground or in the gymnasium.

WEIGHING   Use a kitchen scale for weighing different objects in the classroom. Or, set up a simple balance beam made from a coat hanger with a plastic coffee can lid as the balance pan. Too, use a yardstick balanced in the middle for the same types of comparisons. A bathroom scale is appropriate for reading numerals and comparing the weights of larger items. Adapt these weighing experiences to addition and subtraction problems as two objects or persons are weighed individually or together.

part five

PHYSICAL EDUCATION:
Training Safe and Sound Bodies

FITNESS Equipment and Activities

ANIMAL STUNTS Young children enjoy imitating animals, especially in connection with their study of animals as a part of a unit on the zoo, the circus, or the farm. It is important that the students have an opportunity to imitate these animals freely, suggesting their own appropriate movements as they might imagine them. This kind of free movement experience is somewhat different from general fitness activities that are a part of a physical education program in which repeated movements are required to develop adequate muscle tone. With that in mind, suggest some of these basic animal behaviors:

Bear: Walk on all fours, ambling along as fast as you can.

Crab: Place your legs and arms both underneath your body, raising it with your back towards the floor.

Duck: In a squat position, walk, keeping your feet close underneath you.

Elephant: Bend over with your arms serving as a trunk, swaying from side to side as you move.

Frog: On all fours in a squatting position, hop as far forward as you can with each leap.

Inchworm: Stretch yourself out flat on the floor, face down. Move your feet up to your hands; then move your hands forward, away from your feet, until you are flat on the floor again.

Lame Dog: Walk on three points, dragging one leg behind.

Kangaroo: Hop upright with your arms held in front of you.

Mule: On all fours, kick out straight behind you with one foot at a time.

Seal: Pull yourself along by your arms, your torso raised from the floor, and your legs straight out behind you.

Snake: On your stomach on the floor, move along wiggling and pushing with your hands.

Stork: Stand on one leg, flap your arms, and hop to the other leg.

BALANCE BEAM Make an inexpensive balance beam from any piece of lumber that measures 4 inches by 4 inches, cut to the desired length. Preschool children will find this width of board just about right, although older primary children will probably be more challenged with a piece of lumber that is only 2 inches wide. In using the narrow beam, attach a pair of metal shelf brackets to each end to prevent the beam from falling over when children are on it. Also, be sure both ends of the beam are flat on the floor so it will not tip up when a child steps on it. Sanded and painted, this beam will be appropriate for bare feet and for outdoor as well as indoor use. Here are some stunts for children to try on the beam:

Hold your arms in different positions.

Tiptoe across the beam.

Change positions or speeds in the middle of the beam.

Do a one-foot balance on the beam.

Pick up an object from the beam.

Do a kneeling knee-dip.

Step under or over a wand.

Bounce a ball as you walk along the beam.

Walk backwards along the beam.

Walk with your eyes closed, holding someone's hand.

Walk on the beam with your eyes focused on the wall, not on the beam.

Carry something balanced on your hand.

Carry something balanced on your head.

Step through a hoop.

Do a four-footed animal walk on the beam.

Walk along the beam sideways.

Toss and catch an object.

Lean to the left and right as far as you can without falling.

Move along the beam with your arms folded or behind your back.

> Walk with bent knees.
>
> Walk on tiptoe.
>
> Walk with a partner, face to face.
>
> Push an object along the beam with your feet.
>
> Bend over, hold on to the beam, and raise one leg.
>
> Use a bamboo pole like a tightrope walker.

BALANCE BENCH Any ordinary wooden bench can be built or adapted to balancing experiences. Care should be taken to be sure that it is sufficiently stable not to tip over when the children are using it, low enough not to be dangerous in case of a fall, and having no ends that project over the base. If two or more of these benches are used, place them in a zigzag pattern for added interest. Where such a bench is not possible, produce the same general effect with a smooth plank that is placed across sturdy, flat-bottomed chairs. Here are some suggested stunts for the children to perform:

> Vault from one side of the bench to another.
>
> Scoot along the bench, pulling yourself along on your seat.
>
> Pull yourself along the bench as you lie down.
>
> Straddle and walk along the bench, one leg on each side.
>
> Balance on your seat; feet and torso are at a sharp angle.
>
> Balance on any three parts of your body.
>
> Perform some animal stunts.
>
> Do any of the stunts suggested for the balance beam.

BALANCE SQUARE Make a balance platform from a square of plywood that is about 18 inches on a side. A short piece of 4 by 4 inch lumber is attached underneath the square. The child mounts the square by stepping directly onto its center and moving his feet outward from that point. As a child gains proficiency at this task, substitute smaller center points to challenge his sense of balance. Or, round the center post to make it more difficult to balance. Suggested stunts might include:

> Toss a ball to someone and catch it again.
>
> Bounce and catch a ball.
>
> Balance a beanbag on your head.
>
> Support yourself on any three points.
>
> Rock the board back and forth.

Rock the board side to side.

Balance a stick upright in your palm.

BALLS   Choose balls of a variety of sizes for many different kinds of applications. Sometimes balls are available as discards from families. Ask the children to try these activities:

Balancing

Balance a ball on a paddle as you stand still.

Balance a ball on a paddle as you move around.

Balance a ball on your head.

Balance a ball on your hands.

Bouncing and Catching

Bounce it as high as you can, counting the times it bounces.

Clap your hands and catch it again after the bounce.

Bounce it with another body part, such as a foot or elbow.

Bounce it between someone's legs, or between your own.

Bounce it and step your leg over it.

Bounce, catch, and toss it in a pattern.

Bounce it to a partner, then use two balls.

Bounce it over a hurdle.

Bounce it to hit a target.

Bounce it against a wall.

Bounce it with one hand, then alternate hands.

Bounce it once, turn around, and catch it.

Dribble it while you are walking, with one hand and both hands.

Bounce it and chase it before it reaches a distant point.

Bounce it and hit it with your fist or with a bat.

See how many balls you can keep bouncing at one time.

Bounce it while you are sitting down.

Throwing

Throw it as far as you can.

Throw it to hit a target.

Throw it over a rope or a net.

Throw it through a rolling or swinging hoop or tire.

Throw it with one hand, two hands, overhanded, underhanded, or toss it over your head.

Throw it straight up in the air and see how many times you can move under it before it stops bouncing.

Throw it straight up while you are on your back.

Hitting

See how far you can hit the ball.

Hit it with your fist as it is suspended from a string.

Hit it as it is swinging or bouncing.

Hit it over a rope or a net.

Hit it with a paddle or a bat.

Hit it at a target.

Kicking

See how far you can kick the ball.

Catch it and kick it back to another person.

Stop it with your foot as it rolls to you.

Roll the ball with your foot.

Bounce and then kick the ball.

Dribble the ball around some markers in an irregular path.

BALLOONS Inexpensive but sturdy balloons can be used in place of balls for a variety of hitting and bouncing activities. In addition to these ball stunts, a balloon can be used in these ways:

Bat it up high and do a stunt before it lands.

Toss it in a sheet, with a partner, trying to get it over your opponent who is holding the other end of the sheet.

Bat it over a net as a lead-up activity to volleyball.

See how long you can keep it from hitting the ground.

Sweep it along the floor with a broom.

Blow it along the edge of a table toward a goal.

Catch it in a funnel or a cut-down bleach jug.

BARRELS Fiber drums or barrels are sometimes available from commercial laundries, bakeries, or other places where materials are stored or shipped in bulk. After they have been thoroughly cleaned out they lend themselves to some interesting explorations:

Crawl through it.

Ride on it, rolling back and forth from side to side, like a cowboy.

Lie on it on your stomach and roll back and forth.

Lie inside the barrel while someone rolls it slowly.

Stand it on end and crawl inside it.

Roll the barrel around with your hands.

BEANBAGS   These simple play objects are made by sewing squares of sturdy cloth together, leaving a small opening after the squares have been turned inside out. Use a funnel to fill the opening with beans, shelled corn, rice, or other bulk grains. Then sew the opening shut. If you make a separate cover with a drawstring to go over each bag, the problem of washing them is simplified. For the younger child, add interest with beanbags in the shape of animals. For a quick beanbag, fill an old mitten or sock with beans, or sew two washcloths together and fill them. Beside the more usual tossing and catching activities, ask the children to try these:

Toss it to a partner, back and forth.

Toss it between your legs.

Juggle two bags by yourself.

Balance one on your head, shoulder, arm, hand, or foot.

Toss it up and clap your hands between your knees, or behind your back before catching it.

Toss it up and touch something and then catch it.

Pick it up with your toes, knees, elbows, or wrists.

Use it in bowling or in shuffleboard or in hopscotch.

Flip it from the back of your hand and catch it.

Place it on your instep and toss it to a target.

Place it on your back and try to shake it off as you crawl.

Pass it around your body in many different ways.

Toss it over your head, from hand to hand.

BOUNCING BOARD   Let the children explore jumping and bouncing on a resilient surface by making a board of a piece of plywood ¾ of an inch thick, about 2 feet wide by 6 feet long. Screw each end of this board to a 2 foot length of lumber that is 4 inches square. Pad each of the wooden feet with carpeting or rubber padding. Assign to the children some of the same activities used for the balance apparatus. In addition, suggest some of these:

Bounce on one foot, and on both feet, then alternate feet.

Bounce and turn part way around.

Bounce and touch some other part of your body.

Bounce and kick your heels together.

Bounce and jump over a rope.

Bounce and toss and catch a ball.

CALISTHENICS Repetitions of the same exercises that are needed for good muscle tone can become very tiring and boring for young children. However, there are several ways in which calisthenics can be adapted to motivate the participants. One idea is to allow the children to exercise to music. Suggest that they provide records from their own collections, either traditional children's songs, or popular items. This can be as much a rhythmic experience as a strengthening one. Similarly, have the exercises done to the beat of a drum, a triangle, or a tone bell. Another approach is to have the exercising done with pieces of physical education equipment; it is more fun to jump if there is a rope in hand to jump over, for example. Variety is also introduced if you give a series of directions, so the children do not tire of the same activities. Challenge the children to respond as quickly as they can to a sequence of activities: "Sit up; run in place; do a jumping jack; do a half push-up." Or, as the children are doing their exercises, surprise them with an occasional command to "freeze." On other occasions, phrase your directions as simple poems, such as, "Now lie down on your back/ Pretend to do a jumping jack." Also, encourage interest in fitness experiences by allowing the children to perform them in self-selected partner groups. Begin the calisthenics with:

Do a jumping-jack, slapping your hands against your thighs.

Bend down and touch your toes on a count.

Lie down on your back and lift your head enough to see over your toes.

Lie on your stomach and lift with your arms just enough to raise your chest.

Lie on your back and drum your heels on the floor.

Jump in place, swinging your arms and reversing foot positions.

Jog until the whistle blows, then do a simple exercise.

Jog slow and then jog fast.

Hop in place with one foot, then both feet.

CLIMBING APPARATUS A simple climbing unit can be made from portions of extension ladders that are fastened securely to a piece of lumber attached to the wall. A climbing rope can be made from knotted rope run through the ends of hardwood dowels. A cargo net can be adapted from lengths of chains run through plastic or rubber garden hose. Fasten these lengths of chain with S-hooks available from a hardware store. Under any of these climbing items that are indoors place a discarded mattress or a mat for added protection. Some activities for climbing are:

Climb up to a certain rung and sit on the rung.

Pull yourself up by holding onto the rope or the bar.

Crawl through the rungs in the climber.

Use a cargo net in a tug-of-war.

Suspend a cargo net horizontally and use it as an obstacle course.

Hang from the climber by both hands.

Hook your knees over a rung and hang upside down.

HOOPS   A plastic hoop can be purchased for very little money from a physical education supply house. Or, use and inflated bicycle tube or the tire casing from a bicycle for some of these hoop activities:

Twirl it in one spot and run around it until it falls to earth.

Roll it to a partner.

Roll it along a pre-marked tape pathway.

Twirl it around your arm, waist, leg, or neck.

Use several hoops as an obstacle course.

Throw it like a quoit toward a target.

Use it like a jump rope, swinging it back and forth.

Try to run through a rolling or a standing hoop.

Roll it alongside you with a stick.

See which child can roll it the farthest.

Jump in and out of it while it is held horizontally.

JUMPING   This is a simple, enjoyable activity that works off a lot of energy and develops wind and leg muscles at the same time. Children can jump on the floor or from a jumping box, a platform made from a sturdy wooden box or crate about 12 to 18 inches in height. Brace this box against a wall or some other permanent object. Cushion the bottom of it with carpeting, and provide a mat for the children to land on. Propose these jumping explorations:

Jumping Box

Jump from the box and dismount with a turn.

Jump with legs and hands spread apart.

Jump and roll on a mat.

Jump into a hoop.

Jump over a rope.

Jump into a shallow box and then jump out again.

Floor Jumping

Jump over an object in different ways, different directions.

Jump over a partner, as in leapfrog.

Jump on alternate sides of a line or a rope.

Hop in a circle around a target.

Jump with small and large steps, alternately.

Gallop like a horse.

Skip by stepping, then hopping on the same foot.

Hop along a taped pattern.

Jump and see how far around you can turn in the air.

Jump sideways, feet together, feet apart.

Jump to see how far horizontally you can jump.

Jump to touch a mark on the chart on the wall.

Jump backwards.

Jump with a partner, holding hands.

LADDERS A loose section of an extension ladder can be used for many different activities. It is also easy to store and easy to move. One application is to suspend the ladder horizontally and flat on low wooden blocks or sturdy primary chairs, and ask the children to walk along the rungs. Suspend it between two low tables and the children can crawl along underneath it, hanging on to the sides or rungs. Another idea is to place the ladder flat on the floor, and ask the children to walk along the edges of the ladder, like a balance beam. Or, they might hop along the ladder, from space to space between the rungs. Another activity is to have two children prop the ladder on one of its edges, and ask the others in the class to crawl through the spaces between the rungs. Or, ask the children to carry the ladder, one child in each of the between-rungs spaces.

MATS In addition to serving as protection for climbers, mats can be useful as instructional aids. A plastic-covered mattress will serve as a temporary mat, especially if the children are instructed to take off their shoes when they are using it. Some of the ways to involve the mat in physical education might be:

Fall forward and catch yourself with your hands.

Roll like a log from one end of the mat to the other.

Roll a forward somersault by tucking your chin to your chest first and then pushing with your feet.

Lie on your back, grip your knees tightly to your chest and rock back and forth like a rocker.

Do a partial headstand by forming a triangle of your arms and your head, and pushing up gently with your feet.

Lie on your back, raise your feet, and ride a bicycle.

Crawl on your hands and knees as fast as you can.

OBSTACLE COURSE   When the weather is bad, making it impossible for the children to have their physical education outdoors, enliven the class with an obstacle course made in the classroom itself by rearranging the furniture so the children must climb into areas, climb over tables, crawl through tunnels, hop along a series of footprints laid on the floor, and perform any other activities that are appropriate to the children and the area and its equipment. As another exciting version of this activity, have the children make a human obstacle course in which children must step over, crawl under, and leapfrog over their classmates.

PARACHUTES   One of the best investments for physical training is a parachute, which, with luck, may be purchased at a reduced price from a surplus store. Some of the following activities can be done with a light tarpaulin or a double bed sheet held by a small group of children. However, the parachute best serves these activities:

Shake the parachute to make waves.

Toss objects, such as a balloon or a ball, into the air.

Roll a small ball all around the parachute.

Carry and toss a doll in the parachute.

Sit on the floor and pull yourself up as you hold on.

Raise the parachute into the air, and let several children exchange places before it falls to the floor again.

Raise the parachute into the air, and try to pull it down as fast as you can.

Raise the parachute into the air and let it go when it has reached its apex.

Raise the parachute and lower it as you move in an undulating way around the circle.

Holding the parachute, move around the circle skipping, gliding, marching, hopping.

Try to shake off a short rope that is a "poison snake" without letting yourself be touched by it.

With everyone holding to the edge and jogging around in a circle, one of you run ahead and take the place of a child in front of you around the edge of the parachute.

PRE-SPORTS With the current interest in sports, it is not uncommon for even the preschool child to be an avid enthusiast. While it is not the responsibility of the classroom teacher to encourage participation of preschool and primary children in organized sports, you can provide activities which will lead up to later understandings of the game and skills that may be utilized in them. Here are some lead-up possibilities:

Baseball: Play a simple version of kickball, running around a set of bases in a prescribed sequence. Throw a ball at a target that is shaped like homebase. Hit at a ball on a tee, or one suspended from a string, using either the hand or a plastic bat.

Basketball: Dribble a ball around an obstacle course. Toss it into a basket or a box, or through a hoop, that is about head-high.

Football: Catch a ball thrown through the air. Kick a ball on the ground. Kick a ball dropped from the hands. Chase and tag someone who is carrying the ball.

Golf: Hit a small ball with a plastic stick into a series of cups or cans set into the ground in the play yard.

Hockey: Using plastic hockey sticks and a plastic ball, hit the ball into a goal.

Gymnastics: Participate in free movement activities on a mat or on the floor surface. Roll across the mat in several different ways. Do simple tricks on a low chinning bar. Jump and dismount, with assistance, from a mini-trampoline like those used by cheerleaders.

Soccer: Control the ball with the foot moving from one point in the play area to another. Kick the ball between goal posts.

Skating: Practice on roller skates on a rug area until a good sense of balance is developed.

Tennis: Using badminton rackets with cut-down handles, hit small balls across a net or rope.

Track: Run a race to see who wins; jump over a wand laid on large wooden blocks; Jump across two ropes laid on the ground. Throw a small ball for distance.

Volleyball: Hit a light beachball over a net. Catch the ball and then hit it back.

RELAYS Young children sometimes have problems in the relay situation. For one thing, the very young child generally doesn't understand the rules, and sometimes there is disagreement about the conditions and the fairness of the participation. Another problem is that the older primary children tend to understand the rules, but in the desire to win they sometimes sacrifice the physical skill being developed for the sake of winning. Still another difficulty with relays is that some teams are more proficient at the skill than the other teams, and the teacher must take care to control this so all children have a fair chance to compete and at least some chance of winning, if that is one of the goals of the exercise. It is wise to assign children randomly to their relay teams, as one idea, or, as one team turns out to be superior, rotate the members of the other teams into the stronger team. Try some of these relay situations:

With two children inside an elastic rope, drive them like a team of horses to a goal and come back.

Put clothespins or pin clothing onto a clothesline.

Sweep a balloon to a point and carry it back.

Shuffle with your feet in shoeboxes to a point and return; or use large shoes or boots for the same activity.

Push a ball or a balloon with your head, on hands and knees.

Pass a ball between the legs of a line or children, or over their heads.

Race with a partner with two middle legs tied together.

Put on a jacket and take it off again.

Build a simple structure with blocks and dismantle it.

Crawl through a tunnel made by the legs of a line of children.

Hold on to the waist of a child in front of you and race like a centipede.

Race around an obstacle course.

Ride a broomstick to a point and return.

Hold on to your ankles and run to a point and return.

Pass a hat from one index finger to another down a line of children.

ROPES Jumping ropes are easily made from heavy-duty cotton clothesline, with knots on either side of spools that serve as the handles. Add extra weight to the rope by winding adhesive tape around the part that hits the floor. Young children are usually very anxious to learn to jump rope. The best way to introduce rope jumping is with a two-person rope, with a child holding one end tight, and the adult in charge of the twirling. Some basic steps in using this rope in instruction are these:

1. The child first jumps up and down in place to a set rhythm, without using the rope.

2. Then the child jumps over a stationary rope that is raised slightly off the floor.

3. The child jumps over a slightly swinging rope; show him how to anticipate the rope as it begins to swing toward his knees.

4. Throw the rope over the child's head and drag is slowly toward him so he can see it as he jumps over it. Be sure to hit the floor or ground with enough force to produce a definite noise, suggesting the rhythm of the rope.

After the children have mastered the long rope, assign some of these activities:

Pick up an object while you are jumping.

Jump in and run out.

Run through without jumping.

Jump with a partner facing you.

Jump on one foot, swinging the other one.

Jump while the rope is being twirled backwards.

Jump with your feet alternately together and apart, alternately front and back.

Jump with a partner side by side.

Jump and click your heels.

Jump on heels and then on toes.

Jump and twirl your own small rope at the same time.

Decorate your rope with pretty yarn or ribbons.

Jump in a pattern marked on the floor.

Jump and cross and uncross your feet.

SCOOTERS Floor scooters can be made inexpensively from squares of plywood, with the corners rounded to minimize injury. Attach ball-bearing casters underneath, far enough recessed under the edge to avoid running over the fingers. Another safety feature is a plastic strip tacked around the edge to serve as a skirt to keep fingers out. Pad the scooters with scraps of carpeting to make them more comfortable. Some ways to move with the scooters:

Place your feet against a wall, push real hard, and see how far you can roll before you stop.

Push yourself around an obstacle course.

Chase a ball and move it from place to place.

Push yourself as you are lying on the board.

Push yourself as you are kneeling on the scooter.

Push yourself as you are sitting on the scooter.

TIRES AND TUBES   Contact automotive centers and bicycle shops for discarded tires and tubes. Farm implement dealers sometimes have tractor tires and tubes for physical education activities. There are some interesting things to do with tires and tubes:

Bounce a tube with you astride it, like a bucking horse.

Use a tire or tube as an obstacle course: go around, crawl through, jump over it, or jump into it.

Use a bike tire like a hoop, using a stick or your hand.

Walk around the edge of a large tire.

Roll a tube or tire to a partner and catch the tire when it is returned.

Bounce a ball into or through a tube or tire.

Toss the tube at a target like you would throw a quoit.

Place a tube over two children for a race or a dance.

Toss a beanbag through the tube or tire as it is rolled.

Use it in a relay race, putting it on over your head.

Use a tube in a tug-of-war with several children.

Bounce on a large tube as you sit on its rim, with two other children at the same time.

Stand on the edge of a large tube as it lies on the floor and bounce on it; have another child on the other side of the tube and hold onto each other as you bounce alternately.

WANDS   Short lengths of dowel sticks can be used for a variety of exercises in flexibility and balance. One good suggestion for the sake of safety is to put crutch tips on the end of each of these wands. Where the wooden wands are not available or appropriate, give the children the long cardboard tubes that are found inside gift wrapping paper sold at department stores. Or, use sections of discarded broomsticks. Suggest explorations such as:

Twirl the wand in your hands like a baton.

Jump over the wand laid across two low standards.

Bend and stretch with the wand in your hands.

Crawl underneath the wand as someone else holds it.

Toss it up, flipping it, so you catch the end opposite the end you were holding at first.

Hold the wand vertically and toss it to a partner to catch.

Step over the wand and back while you are holding it in both hands.

Balance the wand across your palm, your arm, your ankle, your thigh.

Stand the wand on its end, then turn yourself completely around quick to catch the wand before it falls to the floor.

HEALTH:
How the Human Mechanism Works

BALANCED DIET   Make a large chart and divide it into the several basic food groups. Ask the children to cut out pictures from magazines and paste them in the appropriate categories. Or, ask them to make up an ideal menu, remembering to include foods from each of the appropriate groups listed. Another activity is to set up a big box, and paint on it a face of a person, cutting out the mouth to allow things to be inserted. Ask the children to cut out pictures of foods by categories and paste these pictures to small pieces of cardboard. When you are discussing a certain type of food required in a balanced diet, have the children sort through all their pictures to "feed" the box the right foods. Another idea is to paste a picture, preferably a large one, on the front of a paper sack. Cut eye holes and a mouth hole in this sack. Ask a child to don this mask and talk as if he were the vegetable or other food item, telling why it belongs in each child's diet.

BODY MACHINES   Help the children appreciate the versatility of the body by asking them to think of all the things they can do with their hands, their feet, or their heads. Or, ask them to think of the things they could not do without one of these parts. Point out that most body systems operate without conscious thought, as nearly automatic machinery that requires fuel in the form of food and modest health care. Draw a figure of a person on the display board.

Then look through magazines to find pictures of machines that do jobs similar to those accomplished by different parts of the body. Attach yarn from each picture to the corresponding body part in the diagram. Here are some suggested analogies:

A camera	as the eye
A pump	as the heart
A food processing plant	as the stomach and digestion
A cutting blade	as the teeth
A lever	as an arm or leg
A mechanical claw	as the fingers

BODY PARTS To acquaint the children with the names of all the parts of the body, ask one child to draw a picture of a person as each element is named. Or, draw a complete person on the chalk-board and ask individual students to erase body parts as they are named. Another activity is to play, "Simon Says," in which the children are asked to touch their own body parts as they are named in the game. After the children have mastered each name, just for fun introduce to the children some of the more technical names of body members.

Other activities might include asking one child to lie down on a large piece of paper, and then tracing around him in duplicate and cutting out a full-body image. Stuff this double image with paper, then staple it together, label the body parts and use it for instruction. Or, similarly, have the child lie on a piece of cardboard for the tracing of his body; then cut apart the members to be reassembled as a puzzle experience. Make riddles about body parts, write them on cards, and have the child responding to the query place the card on the correct spot of the large human model. Also ask the children to make collections of pictures of body parts, so they begin to appreciate the almost limitless variety of skin colors, shapes of hands, heads, sizes of people, and other characteristics.

BONES Discuss the nature and the purpose of the different bones in the human body. Illustrate bone action by bringing to class bones from chickens, and ham joints. Bones from round steak can illustrate that bones have marrow inside. Get a picture of an animal or a fowl and show where each bone came from. Salvage a Halloween skeleton to study the general structure of the body. Show the importance of the spine by threading a series of spools onto a sturdy string making a simple arrangement that is both strong and flexible. Display a rag doll to suggest what we might be like without our bones. As an example of the strength of bones, soak some chicken bones in vinegar for several days. Compare their more flexible nature with the brittleness of dried bones that were not soaked. Discuss the fact that baby bones are more flexible than those of adults, particularly elderly people.

CIRCULATION   Increase appreciation for the bloodstream by filling seven or eight pints with water tinted with red paint or with red food coloring to show visually how much blood is in the average young child's body. Make a simple stethoscope to listen to the heartbeat: connect a section of garden hose or other plastic hose to two funnels. Or, borrow a regular stethoscope from a doctor, or ask him to explain its use. Compare pulse rates by counting the number of heartbeats before exercise and then after strenuous activity. Show the children how to feel the pulse with the tips of their fingers pressed against the artery in the wrist. Demonstrate other pulse points: inside the upper arm near the elbow, just above the collar bone, etc.

CLOTHING   Stress with the children the notion that dress must be appropriate to the weather. Make a series of boy and girl cutouts large enough to be handled readily. Then cut out clothing from a mail order catalog that might represent different types of garments for different weather. Let the children take turns dressing these toy children appropriate for the weather each day.

DICTIONARY   Ask the children to help you compile a "Good Health Dictionary," complete with pictures and words and statements appropriate for sanitation, nutrition and good grooming. A few suggestions might include:

> **A** is for Apple. It is Nature's toothbrush.
>
> **B** is for Babies. They need food to grow.
>
> **C** is for Clothing. It keeps us warm in winter.
>
> **D** is for Dentist. He helps us take care of our teeth.

EYES   Help the children understand the importance of vision by asking a few at a time to be blindfolded to experience what it might be like without sight. Encourage them to feel their way around, taking care that no real harm might come to them in the process. Ask them to rely more fully on their other senses to tell where they are and who is nearby. Give them an opportunity to feel different objects to try to tell what they are, or have some person who knows braille script demonstrate it for the class.

Demonstrate the need for stereoscopic sight involving both eyes by having a child first cover one eye with a blindfold, and then try to put the cap on the end of a pen held at arm's length on the very first try. This will be more of a challenge if you instruct the child to bend his arms slightly before he attempts it.

GROOMING   Avoid a spirit of nagging when you remind the children about the need for good grooming, good sanitation, and good nutrition. Encourage them to take this responsibility because of its inherent value. Also, try to avoid having a routine morning inspection of fingernails, breakfasts, handkerchiefs, and the like. Children will invent answers rather than admit they are not prepared foi these inspections. Rather, motivate the children to do their own inspection. One way to do this is to have a series of reminder charts, each with an animal as the friendly helper. For example, a walrus could remind the children about brushing their teeth, a giraffe might help children remember to wash their necks, and an elephant would remind children to cover noses when they sneeze. Set up a classroom inspection station, complete with a three-sided mirror, plus actual elements of good grooming, such as a comb, toothbrush, hairbrush, washcloth. Tie each of these objects into a large chart that reminds the class about their correct and needed use. One further suggestion is to parody songs to arouse interest in grooming. (For example, "This is the way we brush our hair . . .")

GROWTH   Study the growth and development of humans by taking measurements of children of different ages and making charts and graphs of these statistics. Also, suggest that the children cut out pictures of different sizes and ages of people, and attempt to put these pictures into some type of general sequence such as: babies, small children, teenagers, adults, old people. Ask the children to find appropriate pictures that might represent some of the activities common to each of these stages of growth.

HAIR   Compare the differences in hair color and texture. Have the children cut out pictures of the heads of different people, and try to categorize these, in terms of either texture or color. Collect from a barbershop or beauty salon small samples of different hairs that can be attached to strips of cellophane tape. Look at each sample under a microscope. Discuss proper care of hair and find examples of historical difference in styles and length.

MICROORGANISM   Look at small organisms under a microscope to show the children that there are agents of infection that cannot be readily seen. Make a simple culture for growing microorganisms by placing several spoonfuls of tomato soup in a custard cup. Touch the surface with unwashed fingers. Then cover the top with plastic wrap and put it in a warm dark place until mold grows. Examine some of the mold under a microscope. Use an agar culture for the same type of experiment. Make a collection of different foods in the process of decay. Compare the appearance of these items with those that are fresh and wholesome.

Discuss the germ theory in the discussion of prevention of disease. Ask the children to think of reasons for using hot water, soap, antiseptics. Identify diseases that are now controlled by vaccines. Make up little puppet characters who characterize the nature and danger of germs in the body.

NERVES   Discuss the different nerves that control the sensory reactions: tickling, involuntary reflexes, the tactile sense, for example. Ask the children to try to tickle themselves; then let someone else try it. List the different parts of the body that are generally ticklish. Check the knee and elbow reflexes with a child's mallet. Point out the value of the nerves in protecting the body against cold and heat extremes.

POSTURE   Perfect posture is not possible, but children should be aware of the ways in which different postures cause their bodies to form. Make large jointed human figures from sturdy paper or tagboard—one figure should be from the front view and the other should be from the side view. Show the children some of the different positions you have observed during the day, and then suggest the proper position for good growth and less body fatigue. Be aware of the need for changing postures and allow the children to sit, stand, or move about the room as often as possible, consistent with the general classroom routine.

RESPIRATION   Compare the lungs to a giant pair of bellows that brings air into the body and expels the air that is low in oxygen. Get pictures of damage done to lungs by industrial diseases or by tobacco to suggest the need for clean air. Measure the air capacity in lungs by filling a clean jar or bottle with water, submerging it in an aquarium. Then invert the jar, and, using a rubber or plastic tube, have each child blow into the jar, seeing how much water is expelled. If small marks are placed on the side of the jar beforehand, a comparison of lung capacities can be made. Another interesting experience is to see how long each child can hold his breath. Use a stopwatch for this activity. Similarly, count the number of breaths in normal activity, and then ask each child to perform some mild exercise, counting the number of breaths required each minute afterwards.

SCENTS Test the children's sense of smell by placing small containers of different materials in baby food jars. Place these jars inside bread wrappers to prevent their being seen. Put them inside a shoebox that has a series of holes poked in it for the bread wrappers to stick through. Keep the wrappers closed with rubber bands when they are not being used. Let each child sniff each substance and try to identify it. Or, place these scents in numbered pairs of small jars and ask the children to match them by smell alone. Some possible aromas might include:

shaving lotion	onions	garlic	mothballs
perfume	lemons	bleach	ginger
soap	vanilla	mint	cloves
tobacco	vinegar	ammonia	cinnamon
coffee	cedar	citrus	chocolate

Instruct the children to sniff cautiously.

SENSES Encourage the children to discuss and value all their senses. Ask them to consider which of their senses is the most important. Ask them also to think of ways in which their lives would be different if any of their senses were missing. Demonstrate that all senses are vital: in a commonplace activity such as eating a piece of candy all the senses are involved. Engage the children in an activity of appreciation for their senses by asking them to list, or write or talk about, some of their favorite sensations. These topics might be useful to get the thinking started:

Sounds I Like to Hear	Things I Think Are Pretty
Some Special Smells	An Outdoors Walk
My Favorite Foods	This Weather Makes Me Feel . . .

SPEECH MECHANISM Refer to the vocal mechanism as the "Talking Machine" and discuss its importance in the child's normal life. Get charts that demonstrate the various parts of speech production. Compare each element with some mechanical apparatus: the lungs are the bellows, the cords are the vibrating strings, the tongue is the vane that directs the airflow, and the mouth is the window that lets the sound out. Try to talk with various parts of the machine not in operation: the nose pinched shut, the vocal cords not vibrating, the teeth clenched, or the lips closed.

TASTING   Pass a mirror around the class to let each child examine his taste buds. Point out that different parts of the tongue respond to things that are sour, salty, bitter, or sweet. With a medicine dropper, drop small amounts of substances on the children's tongues, and see if they can identify them: use lemon juice, saltwater, vinegar, fruit juice, mint water. Another activity is to blindfold the children and have a tasting party, seeing how many substances in the foods categories can be identified by taste alone. Then check the changes in taste and the probable lowering of the children's accuracy in identification of foods, as you pinch the noses of the children who are blindfolded. Apples, cucumbers, onions, and potatoes may taste quite a bit alike without the use of the nose to check the aroma.

TEETH   Several activities focus attention on the importance of teeth and stimulate children to take care of their own. A visit from a dentist or a dental technician is one obvious possibility. Or, get plaster casts from a local orthodontist illustrating malocclusion. Too, show a set of normal teeth in cast form. Compare the size and number of adult teeth with a child's model. Identify the job of each type of tooth. Borrow some X-rays from a dentist to show what cavities look like. Give the children a simple formula for brushing their teeth, using commonplace materials: one teaspoon of salt, two teaspoons of baking soda, a few drops of flavoring, such as wintergreen or vanilla. As a final idea, have some fun while showing the importance of tooth care by finding a picture of a happy smile, and then blackening some of the teeth with a pen.

TOUCHING   Give the children experience in using the tactile sense as they are blindfolded for some exploration of commonplace objects. Ask them to judge the relative size and weights of wooden blocks, for example, or match regular geometric shapes. Match them or place them in sequence, as appropriate. Have the child place sheets of sandpaper in order by the coarseness of the grains. Provide different fabrics and let the child describe the feeling of velvet, fur, feathers, satin, corduroy, burlap. Also let each student examine, by feeling, unusual items. Include wet spaghetti, peeled grapes, hardware cloth, dish scrubbers, bread dough, wigs, bark, pine cones, corrugated paper, bricks, sawdust, seeds. Each of these items can be placed inside a mystery box, instead of having the child use a blindfold; or, use a discarded sock to contain these objects, and let the child guess them by feel as well as by the general shape of each item.

Instructing Students in SAFETY

BICYCLES   Explain to the children that riders of bicycles and tricycles are really drivers, just as are adults who operate automobiles. This means that they must also know the rules of the road, just as the grown-ups. In addition, a driver is responsible for the mechanical repair of the vehicle. To make more vivid both of these considerations, issue to the children licenses to operate their ride-on toys outdoors on the playground. However, if they are negligent in the operation of these vehicles, suspend the privilege by taking their licenses for a brief period. As a graphic reminder of the importance of mechanical maintenance, have the local police inspect the bikes, trikes, and wagons for good condition, and issue approved stickers made of colored tape that will adhere to each vehicle.

BUSES   After discussing good bus behavior with children, consolidate their learnings by having them make colorful posters that can be placed overhead inside the bus as further reminders. Change these from time to time to maintain interest. As a practice experience for bus safety construct a large bus from a discarded shipping carton for a refrigerator or a freezer. Cut out a door and a window, and add another smaller box on the front for the engine. Place blocks or chairs inside the bus for the passengers. Have the children act out good safety practices and poor safety practices.

ELECTRICAL HAZARDS   Commission each child to make a list of all the electrical appliances in his own home. Suggest adult help in this, if it is needed. Find pictures of these electrical items and paste them into a book, each page with a special notation about proper use of electricity: "Check each cord," "Keep electricity away from water," "Don't overload the outlet," are examples. Suggest that each child use a checklist to have his parents inspect each appliance.

EMERGENCY DRILLS   At the very beginning of the school year explain to the children the procedures for disaster drills. Since young children are easily upset by fire alarms and tornado watches, for example, make a point to walk through the procedure at least several times before the first drill is scheduled. If possible, ask the person in charge of the drills to give at least a few minutes' warning the first time or two that the drills are called for. After the children are at ease with these practices, take them around the building and show them all the exits in the building; help them locate a telephone for emergencies, and show them where the fire alarm boxes are located.

FIRE PREVENTION   The first week in October is usually a time for special emphasis on fire prevention. The more obvious activities include field trips to the fire station, or the use of resource people in showing the children at school how to prevent fires. Such a resource person might demonstrate how to put out a fire, how to generate carbon dioxide that can extinguish a candle. Show the children handy ways of putting out a small fire, such as pouring on tablesalt, covering the fire with a blanket, tossing on sand, or pouring on water.

FIRST AID   Post in the classroom in a prominent place a chart which shows simply the basic procedures. Set up occasional hypothetical situations as a way of quizzing the children from time to time. Make it clear that their first responsibility, however, is to call for adult aid—they should use first aid only when no one else is available. Also train each child in calling for this adult assistance: dialing the fire department, the police, or a local hospital. Schedule some pretend practice sessions for these calls, with children as the "victims."

HELPERS   Identify the safety helpers in the school and the community and suggest specific ways in which they help us to be safe. List and picture personnel such as a doctor, an electrician, a nurse, a repairman, a policeman, a fireman. In addition, schedule regular helpers in the classroom to be "inspectors" to check the safety and the cleanliness of the immediate environment. Suggest that they issue citations to children for either good safety practices on the playground or in the classroom, or for improper safety habits.

NURSERY RHYMES Examine the better-known nursery rhymes which involve an accident and discuss them from the angle of accident prevention. Some possibilities might include: "Humpty Dumpty," "Jack and Jill," "Three Blind Mice," "Ding Dong Bell," or "Who Shot Cock Robin?" Have the children pantomime these rhymes and discuss how the accidents might have been prevented.

PEDESTRIAN SAFETY As a part of the first school experiences review with the children how to cross the street and where to cross it safely. Discuss with them the jobs of the crossing guards. Demonstrate in a dark room the added visibility of light clothing for those who must walk along the streets or highways. Obtain from your local American Automobile Association free posters and teacher materials for pedestrian and bicycle safety.

PLANTS Caution children about poisonous plants, especially those that might be eaten by a curious child such as a younger sibling. Children should be aware that many parts of common foods are poisonous, as, for instance, the seeds of apples, the leaves of rhubarb, the sprouts of potatoes, and the leaves of certain edible berry plants. In addition, all or part of these ornamental plants are toxic when eaten:

Laburnum	Castor beans	Delphinium
Chinaberry	Hyacinth bulbs	Lily-of-the-valley
Oak trees	Crocus bulbs	Nicotiana
Wild black cherry	Narcissus bulbs	Privet
Holly	Daffodil bulbs	English ivy
Mistletoe	Iris	Rhododendron
Poinsettia	Larkspur	Oleander
Wisteria	Yew	Lantana

PLAYGROUND At the beginning of the school year discuss with the children the safe way of using each of the items on the playground. Instead of posting lists, however, help the children to think of situations that might arise for them to cope with. Have at the exterior doorway a large poster reminding them to play safely. Change this poster from time to time to keep their interest up.

POISONS   Make a collection of empty boxes and other containers of poisons and show them to the class so they can be aware of the danger poisons pose to younger brothers and sisters. Show the class the current symbols that are being used to indicate poisons, and ask the group to check their own homes to be sure such elements are not readily available to younger siblings. Also, train the children to recognize some of the poisonous plants they might encounter in the woods: ivy, oak, and sumac.

SAFETY ALPHABET   Help the children to collect and illustrate an original book of ABC's about safety. On each page place a letter and a picture and an appropriate word. Some possibilities might include:

> **A** is for Automobile. We use seat belts when we ride in one.
>
> **B** is for Bus. We do not talk to the driver.
>
> **C** is for Closet. It must be uncluttered.
>
> **D** is for Door. Close it when the lights are out.
>
> **E** is for Electricity. Treat it with care.
>
> **F** is for Fire. Put it out when you are done.

SAFETY BELTS   Give the children practice in fastening and unfastening a restraining belt by fastening one permanently to an old wooden chair. Each child can have a turn with the buckling process. Demonstrate graphically the need for these restraining belts by placing a large wooden block in a wagon, pulling it rapidly, and then stopping suddenly. The block will pitch forward. An even better idea is to use a large doll as the passenger. As a contrast, in a second experiment, tie down the figure that is riding in the wagon, and repeat the former procedure. The figure should stay in its original position.

SEASONAL HAZARDS   At the beginning of each new season of the year, or each special holiday, stress with the children the unique dangers of that particular time. Ask the children to think of special reminders appropriate to each discussion and combine them into different booklets, each generalization illustrated with a student's picture. Here are some samples:

Be careful with sleds in the winter.

Leaves must be burned in containers.

Kite strings sometimes get tangled in the powerlines.

Halloween costumes should not trip the wearer.

Fireworks can burn and injure.

Christmas trees should not be allowed to dry out.

SIGNS AND SIGNALS   Give the children practice in recognizing the standard signs and signals regulating vehicles and pedestrians. These can be included as cards in an "Old Maid" game, or they can be adapted to a "Lotto" game, matching shape with shape. Or, make a traffic signal series including a traffic signal, stop signs, and other cautionary items. Use these signs or verbal commands in outdoor games in which the colors or commands can give each player addressed the right to move rapidly (on green), move slowly (on yellow), or stand still (on red). Where children are not yet old enough to read the words on signs, train them to recognize the shapes of the signs and the picture legends on them. Another activity is to have each child make his own traffic light from an empty, rinsed cardboard milk carton into which holes have been cut for the lights. Cover the openings with red, yellow, and green cellophane, and let the children use a flashlight inside it. One other adaptation to other areas of safety is to use the signs and signals in other contexts. On a poster have a picture of the traffic signal, but add other safety rules such as these:

STOP . . . putting your toys on steps

SLOW . . . when you come to a crossing

ONE WAY . . . to be safe in water is to learn to swim

CAUTION . . . others not to ride with strangers

SITUATIONS   Let the children practice their thinking skills regarding safety practices as you provide imaginary situations for them to respond to. These can come as a result of newspaper stories dealing with accidents, or they can be strictly imaginary. The more a child considers different alternatives, the more likely he should be to respond well to a real emergency situation:

What would you do if you were lost in the woods?

What would you do if you saw a young child run into the street?

What would you do if the neighbor's house caught on fire?

What would you do if someone dropped some glass on the sidewalk?

SNOW PLAY   Channel children's natural interest in snowballs into more constructive lines than throwing them at each other. Set up an old tire or a box as a target, for example. Or involve the children in building a snow fort, packing snow into boxes and then turning these upside down to make snow bricks. Encourage the children also to get involved in snow sculpture, adding small amounts of tempera paint to the snow for an added effect.

TRAFFIC   Give the children experience as vehicles moving about on roadways taped or painted on the playground. If actual vehicles are not available, make them out of boxes cut to shape and hung over the children's shoulders. Another activity in traffic-experience is to check the local newspaper for reports of vehicular accidents. Make simple bar graphs as a permanent record of the frequency of these occurrences.

part six

READING:
Introducing Children
to Books

Fun with Reading
GAMES and AIDS

ACCORDION FOLDS   Accordion-fold a long piece of paper, allowing 26 different panels on it. On one side of the strip list all the letters of the alphabet, one letter to a panel. Underneath each letter list words that begin with that letter. On the reverse side of each panel have the children draw or paste pictures of objects that begin with that letter. Stand the panels upright on a table for the class to examine. Use this same approach for other reading generalizations, such as for word families that rhyme, families that begin or end with the same sounds, or families of synonyms, or front-and-back antonym sets.

BINGO   Adapt this familiar game to a variety of reading situations, such as antonyms, homonyms, letter identification, initial consonant sounds, discrimination skills with shapes, vocabulary words, consonant blends, digraphs, and any other element or reading skill that involves simple auditory or visual recall. Prepare a ditto master by which you can produce many blank copies. Let the children randomly fill in the blanks on the playing surface, depending on the stimulus being reviewed at any given time. For more permanent playing cards to suit all purposes, prepare a sheet of acetate with lines, and let the child slip his own playing paper underneath it, marking the acetate with a grease pencil.

BLOCKS   Utilize ordinary children's letter blocks for reviewing reading skills. Collect several sets from parents' donations or purchase

162

them at rummage sales or at second-hand stores. Use these blocks to introduce and review new vocabulary words, and to help the children in the spelling of new words. The most obvious use is, of course, matching upper and lower case letters, or selecting the letter to answer a stimulus like, "Find the letter that begins like the word 'baby.' " Blocks can also be adapted to other purposes by attaching masking tape to each side of the blocks and writing words on the tape. Challenge the child to spill the blocks onto the carpet or rug and see if he can make up an original sentence. Or, mark these taped pieces with phonic elements for the children to identify.

BROADCASTER   Make the front of a television set from a fairly small cardboard box, including in it a number of openings corresponding to the number of letters in the longest word in the vocabulary list being studied. Then make a series of flashcards containing these words, writing them in such a way that the letters are positioned to show through these openings in the box, one letter per opening. Using this simple device, have the children pretend to announce, placing the word cards in the holder, and calling on children in the "audience" to identify the words on the cards. Make it seem more like a quiz broadcast by offering small rewards for successful answers.

CARD GAMES   Apply any element of reading instruction to card games such as "Old Maid." Challenge the children to see if they can get rid of the odd cards as they exchange cards with the other children or as they draw next cards from the face-down deck on the table. Or, let the children take turns drawing cards from a pile and permit the child whose card matches the one drawn by his predecessor to collect it in his own pile; the largest pile of cards wins the game. Attach to each recognition card an appropriate skills-related task so the child cannot proceed with the game if he cannot answer the question correctly.

CIRCLE GAMES   Many elementary circle games can be used in developing reading skills. For example, attach a letter or a word to pairs of children and then randomly draw a stimulus card matching one of the several cards attached to the children in the game. When the stimulus card is flashed, the two children whose cards match it must try to exchange places while the child who is "It" tries to get into their places in the circle.

A circle game with a ball involves bouncing the ball from "It" in the center to a child on the circle, giving ten seconds to respond to any predetermined type of question. The child on the circle must bounce the ball back to the center before his time expires. The ball may also be tossed up, and the child on the circle must catch it or fetch it, and answer a question that has been asked by the leader of the game.

CONCENTRATION   Lay out an array of pairs of word cards or other reading cards on a flat surface. On the back of each card have different numerals. With the cards face down on the playing surface, ask the players to take turns calling the numbers of cards in pairs to see if they can match the stimulus pictures on the fronts of the cards. When a child calls two cards, he turns them over to see if the pictures or other stimuli match. If they do match, he may keep those two cards; if they do not match, however, he must turn them over again and the next child in the group gets his turn to play.

Another way to test visual recall is to line up reading cards on a chalk rail. Give all the players a short time to look at the cards. Then remove one card from the group and challenge the class to identify the missing card after they uncover their eyes. Or, change the order of two or more items while the children have their eyes covered.

DOMINOES   At the simplest level, the children can make their own domino cards using stickers or seals for easy discrimination practice. Letter recognition, word recognition, and other skills can also be adapted to dominoes. Adapt domino cards to matching purposes by making large ones from cardboard. Ask the children to draw or paste pictures at one end of the card, and then write the matching vocabulary words at the other end of each card. Cut each of these cards apart in an irregular way, so no two cards are cut exactly the same way. Use these as self-checking experiences for young children. The card pieces will not fit together unless they actually do match because the cut pieces will have to match also at the point of the cut.

FISHING   Very young children like to fish for answers. Use this simple game for recognition practice by making fish, each with a letter, a word, or some other element of reading practice on it. Tie a magnet to a string, tie the string to a stick or a short pole, and let the child fish for his "catch." Allow him to keep only those stimulus items that he can respond to correctly. Since paper clips on the nose of each fish often get tangled up or lost, it may be wiser to punch several staples into the nose of each one instead.

HOPSCOTCH Use the favorite game "Hopscotch" with a number of reading skills, employing a game board labeled with stimuli that the child must respond to correctly before proceeding further. Use a large rectangle of oilcloth, plastic, paper, or vinyl to make a permanent hopscotch board that can be rolled up and put away when it is not being used. Vary the shape of the board by placing the individual spaces in circular, triangular or other arrangements. Add further interest by labeling the beanbags that are used to toss into the spaces on the playing surface.

INTEREST CARDS Make vocabulary cards that appeal to children's natural interests. For example, to appeal especially to the boys, make cards which have on one side the picture of a car, a sports figure, an adventure hero, and on the other side have the name of the automobile or the person pictured. Or, for simple matching experience, cut out from identical issues of current magazines pictures of racing cars, sailboats, or people, and have the children make sets of them that match.

In addition, as a part of the child's overall reading experience, let him make word cards that list the names of children, their friends, their siblings, their favorite toys, holidays, foods, street signs, or hobbies.

LABELS Children do much of their early reading with labels of food products, signs on the street, and names of places familiar to them. Capitalize on this natural curiosity by encouraging them to bring to school objects and materials for sharing experiences. Place these items on a table in the classroom and label each one with a piece of paper folded so it will stand by itself. Give the group a chance to examine these objects and their labels; then remove the objects and see which children can read some of the labels.

Another idea is to make a large jointed human figure, each body part labeled with removable name cards. Help the children learn to read these word cards. Use this same jointed figure and cover it with articles of clothing for a similar reading experience.

A scale drawing of the typical classroom or of the child's home or personal room (or bedroom) can also be labeled with names of items of furniture.

Still another idea is to make a label board with hooks or clips where any child can place pictures pasted onto small cards and labels to match. Let the children remove the pictures and see if they can read the labels.

A further possibility is to cut out a large, interesting picture and paste it inside the lid of a shallow box. On individual cards write the names of all the important aspects of the picture, each of which may be color-coded or symbol-coded so the child can check his accuracy as he compares the code on the back of the word cards with the markings on the picture itself.

Finally, cut labels from food boxes and other commercial containers and small signs. Let the children match the labels to the remainder of the containers or signs. Later, print them on cards.

MATCH RACE   Separate the class into two teams in a large play area. Randomly give the members of one team, one by one, the cards for a reading review experience, then give matching cards to the members of the second team. An example might be lower case letters to one team and capital letters to the second team. At the signal "Flash" the children must show their cards to all the other players in the group, whereupon the pairs that match try to get together with their partners before anyone else can find theirs. Adapt this same approach to rhyme words, compound words, synonyms, and any other appropriate skill.

MONEY   Obtain some play money at a rummage sale or from a toystore. On each piece of pretend currency write with a felt-tip pen one basic vocabulary word being studied. If some of the words are more difficult than others, put them on currency that has higher face value. Play a simple game where the children can earn dollars for their skill in reading the words on each piece of money. If such currency is not available, make it yourself from colored construction paper, or use the coupons that are often a part of bulk mailings.

MUSICAL SQUARES   Place any number of cards on the floor, each one with a different reading stimulus on it, such as a letter or a vocabulary word. Play a selection of music and ask the children in the group to step from card to card as if they were crossing a brook on stepping stones. When the music stops, selected children must identify the squares on which they are standing. If they are not able to do so, they must "swim" in the water until some other child loses his turn.

PASS-AROUND   When the class members are in a reading circle, give each child a cut-out animal figure of his own choosing, and write his name on it. As a group member performs well in response to stimulus situations, let him pass his animal one place to his right. As soon as his animal makes it all the way around the reading circle, allow him to leave the group and return to his own work space. As a similar variation of this game, make on the top of a reading table a merry-go-round, a car race track, or some other similar multi-lane raceway. Give each child a marker and let him take turns responding to stimulus cards, contending to see which one can complete the circuit first.

PATHWAYS   Use any simple pathway, highway, stepping stones, or ladder for the children to move on as they draw stimulus cards and respond correctly to them, or as they spin a spinner to point to a question. Adapt these games to tabletops by giving children markers or miniature cars or figures to move down pathways drawn on posters. Suggest that when they mistakenly respond to a stimulus situation they must take a detour, move in reverse, or lose a turn.

PINNED TAGS   On the back of each child in the game pin a word from a vocabulary list, an individual letter, or any other stimulus that lends itself to guessing. Ask each person to guess the item he has on his own back by clues presented by the other children in the room. Or, using these same pinned tags, challenge each of several children to identify the items pinned on the backs of the other participants while he himself tries to protect from their view the item pinned to his own back. The last person with his label not read is the winner of the competition.

POSTMAN   Let one child in the room pretend to be delivering mail with a pack of vocabulary cards. If the recipient of each "letter" can read it, he may keep it; otherwise the postman sends it to another house, or back to the dead letter office. To add greater interest, let the children make mailboxes from shoeboxes, in the form of post office "pigeon holes." Label each mailbox with a different criterion, and let the "postman" sort the cards into the appropriate receptacles.

PROGRAMMER   Make a simple programmed reading device by cutting a piece of thin cardboard just as wide as an envelope but about twice as long. Cut out the ends of the envelope and cut a small slot like a window in the face of the envelope. On the strip of cardboard write the vocabulary words from a lesson. When the child using this device is ready for a word review, he can place the cardboard inside the envelope and pull it through, passing each word in front of the window. On the back of the envelope a similar window can be cut with a picture or symbol drawn on the back of the cardboard strip. The child can turn the envelope over to check the accuracy of his responses.

PUZZLES   Make a simple puzzle or series of puzzles by having the child write each vocabulary word on an index card, and add a picture cue at one end of each card. Cut these cards apart in the middle in an irregular way, and then mix up the pieces in a pile. See if a child can reassemble the matching pieces, as a discrimination skill. Or, have the child read the words, checking his accuracy by putting the picture clues back together with the matching word. Also, make a larger puzzle by writing all the words from a given vocabulary lesson on one large piece of cardboard or paper. Cut this puzzle apart, allowing one word per irregularly shaped puzzle piece. Challenge the children to put the puzzle back together as they are required to read the word on each piece before putting it into its proper position.

SCRAPBOOKS   Allow each child in the class to make a scrapbook on a topic of special interest to him. (Suggest areas such as sports, space exploration, mechanical objects, or animals for the reluctant reader.) Encourage the children to collect pictures appropriate to each topic, and write simple textual material, or important words on each page. Other pages in the scrapbook might include newspaper headlines of important local events, greeting cards, original stories, mementoes of trips and special occasions, as well as seasonal and holiday words. Adapt these items to reading practice.

SHIFTY CARDS   Have some fun with reading review by taking from the vocabulary lists all the noun cards and all the verb cards. Place the former items on a flat surface in a column on the left side, and place the latter items in a column on the right. Instruct the children to interchange the positions of the different word cards in each column to see what different combinations they can invent. Some of these two-word expressions are bound to be humorous. Adapt this same approach to a wider variety of word cards of sufficient number to make fairly long sentences. For example, experiment with substituting face-down noun cards in noun positions to make unusual expressions. To help the children exchange nouns for nouns and verbs for verbs, color-code the cards to give added visual cues.

SIGNS   As high-interest reading materials use any kind of a sign about which the children might be curious. Begin with the safety signals they may see every day. Make replicas of these signs, complete with words such as, "Stop," "Walk," "Slow," "Children Playing," "No Parking," "Danger." At first give the children opportunities to relate these words to the shapes of signs, and then see if they can read the words printed on cards without the visual or color cues. As the child matures, introduce informational highway signs and simple directions.

SNATCH   Adapt the game "Steal the Bacon" to reading practice by labeling the pairs of opponents on each of the two teams with different vocabulary cards, letter cards, discrimination shapes, or any other useful set of two items. The leader of the game, instead of calling the children out to snatch the beanbag according to numerical order, calls their stimulus card, whereupon the children must rush to the center of the play space and try to get the beanbag back to the safety of their line without being tagged by the opponent.

TARGET TOSS   Make a simple target with string, chalk, or paper. Write vocabulary words or any other reading stimulus items on pieces of tissue paper, for example, and have a child drop them towards the goal. Those items that land in the target must be responded to correctly to be kept or to be tallied in an individual's score. Or, ask the child to combine words he reads into sentences, or to make up original compositions using these same words.

TOY CATALOG   Make original toy catalogs for the children by having them cut from discarded catalogs pictures of things they might like to own or to receive for Christmas presents. Label each toy with a word card, and give the children practice in reading them with and without the picture stimulus. Later, have the children write a letter to Santa Claus or a birthday list including these same items.

TRAINS   A simple train game involves asking a child to draw a card from a pile, responding to it correctly, then placing it upright on the chalk rail. The second child draws a second card from the pile, places it next to the first card, then answers both questions. A third child draws still another card and responds to all three of the cards in a row. This continues until there is a child who cannot continue correctly, whereupon the train "derails" and a new game begins.

Another version of "train" requires the leader to move about the classroom, stopping at individual students to flash stimulus cards at them. If that child so approached can answer correctly, he may get up and hold onto the "engine" to make the train longer. Each successful child joins the train until stimulus questions are exhausted, or until some other child cannot respond accurately. When this happens the children can return to their seats for a new game and a new leader.

A third version of "train" designates one child as a conductor who is equipped with a paper punch. Each child in a row of desks or chairs is a passenger. As the conductor moves down the row, he flashes a stimulus card at the passenger beside him. If that child can answer the question correctly, the conductor punches his ticket. The object of the game is to see how many punches each child can collect during the playing.

TREASURE BOX   Place the unusually difficult reading items inside a small box decorated like a treasure chest, along with small pieces of candy, dry cereal, or small privilege cards. Let the children reach into the box, respond to the stimulus task, and if they are successful, allow them to select the "reward" they would like to have. As another idea, have each child make his own treasure box, placing inside it the special word cards he would like to collect and keep for a time, incorporating them in original stories.

TREASURE HUNT   This game takes the form of hidden cards spread about the classroom for the children to find. Require each child to respond correctly to his discovery before he can keep it. Another type of Treasure Hunt involves the children reading a series of simple directions cards, one by one, following a set of clues until they reach a goal, finding a "treasure" planted somewhere in the classroom or on the playground.

WORD WORMS   Make a simple worm-like creature, the head of which is labeled with a specific generalization, and let the children add segments to the worm as they discover additional words that qualify. See which worm can attract the most student contributions. Or, make an ugly worm that has a mouth to gobble up all the stimulus cards that the children cannot answer correctly.

MANAGEMENT: Organizing and Stimulating Reading

AUCTIONS An auction is a useful method to pique children's interest in books. One application of the auction approach is to allot to each child at the beginning of each week a certain number of pretend dollars with which he may bid on new books as they are introduced to the class. A child may thus decide to spend his money on one or two high-value books, or he may choose to spend his credits on more books of lesser appeal to the group as a whole.

AUTHOR TALK To acquaint children with actual writers, contact publishers of popular children's books to arrange for a book talk by a local author or illustrator. Many parents write or illustrate books or stories for children's magazines, and a careful survey of the community might reveal some of these professionals. Sometimes book company sales representatives know of such contacts. Ask these resource authors and artists to read some of their stories to your children or to draw an original illustration for your group. Where such people are not locally available, tape record book-related conversations conducted among your own children and ask the resource person to respond to your children's comments and questions about the book. Or, conduct a long-distance telephone conversation with an author or illustrator.

BAD READING HABITS Many young children develop habits that slow their reading development. One of these habits is finger-pointing in following a line of print. Since this pointing may become a crutch, suggest that this child use an index card or a piece of cardboard with a slot cut in it to guide his eye movements along a line of print. Another problem is that of vocalizing words during silent reading: the child moves his lips, forming each word individually, rather than relying on his eye sweep to incorporate several words in each phrase. Since this habit also slows reading speed, ask the child to hold a pencil or a soda straw between his lips, or stick his tongue out when he is reading silently. This will not only make him aware of the habit, but may also amuse him as he tries to remedy it.

BOOK CARE Develop responsibility and respect for books as you stress the proper use of reading materials, especially library books. Help the children to show consideration for other children who will be using the same items as they generate a list of suggestions that can be posted prominently on the wall. Decorate such a list of rules with humorous cartoons. Further consolidate this concern for books as you ask the children to make up an original story in which the library book becomes a person and tells all the good and bad things that happen to him during the course of a week. Where appropriate, ask the children to dramatize these stories.

BOOK CLUBS An adult-sponsored book club for young children is well worth the investment of time and energy. Some of the more useful clubs are those that offer inexpensive paperback materials for purchase six or eight times each school year. In this way even the youngest children can purchase from their own funds high-quality literature at a nominal cost. In addition, some of these book clubs offer bonus materials to help the adult in charge of the class. Furthermore, children are always thrilled to have their very own books, especially when they are able to read them to the class or to their parents, and when the teacher takes time to meet with them a few minutes each week to share their literary experiences.

BOOK CRITERIA Hundreds of new books are published each year for the young reader. While it is impossible to personally review all of them, it is wise to maintain contact with reputable periodicals and professionals who do make it their business to advise on the best purchases. Generally, it is wise to include in your collection books that meet all or most of these criteria:

1. Realism: Choose some stories that, as in real life, have happy endings, as well as unhappy or ambiguous endings. Children need not be always protected against an occasional uncertainty.

2. Relevance: Find books that compare favorably with your children's own experiences. Before ordering a new supply, canvass your children's interests.

3. Attractiveness: Illustrations that are visually appealing and that help advance the story are essential. For group work, find stories that have large enough pictures for all the members to see.

4. Therapeutic value: Select some stories that deal with the same types of problems facing your children. Help your students to relate vicariously to the solutions of these situations. Provide the class books that also permit a healthy release of tensions, as well as excitement and adventure.

5. Imagination: Appeal to the children's creativity with books that have elements of the unreal and fantastic. Be careful, however, not to frighten or overstimulate the readers.

6. Simplicity: Be sure the vocabulary is in keeping with the children's abilities to understand the words in the narrative. The plots should be uncomplicated, with few characters.

BOOK DAY Schedule an occasional "Book Day" when the children are permitted to read as much or as often as they want to, completing their other assignments only if they care to. During "Book Day" encourage children to bring to school their own books from home, and suggest that they plan a variety of activities based on books, such as puppet shows, dramatizations, stories for television, or posters advertising specific books or the special day itself. Arrange to share these book activities with parents or with other children in the school.

BOOK FAIRS Conduct an occasional festival of books to coincide with weeks of special emphasis, such as National Book Week or National Library Week. Use different approaches for selling books: one possibility is to contact a publishing company to send basic collections of books on consignment. This permits the sponsor of the sale to sell books from the collection, to take orders for others, and to return to the supplier only those books that were not sold. Enlist the aid of several older children or parents to help with setting up the display, taking orders, collecting money, sending out the publicity, and distributing the books to the purchasers.

Another idea is to have a sale of second-hand books for a few pennies on the dollar, or a white elephant sale, where the proceeds are used to purchase new books. Or, sponsor a book exchange where children can swap their own used books for others of comparable value.

BOOK RACKS   Maintain in the classroom a book rack to hold a variety of reading materials. Slant each shelf slightly so some of the books can be displayed vertically facing the children. Prepare a special place for paperback books—have some of these for sale at cost to the children. Or encourage the students to donate their own paperback books when they are done reading them.

Change these books on display rather frequently, so some books are put out of sight as soon as the children lose interest in them, and new books are constantly added to the collection. For ease in identification, color-code the books included in the permanent group as you classify them by subject or by difficulty. Color-code the shelves of the racks to match the books.

BOOK STORE   Set up a display of inexpensive paperback books and designate a specific time each day or each week when children may purchase them. Maintain a small inventory of the most popular selections in the collection. Contact a book wholesaler who may be able to provide these books on consignment. Set aside an area with a sales booth made of a large cardboard carton, for example, complete with pennants, flags, and a clever sign, such as "Tale Sale" or "Story Store" or "Book Nook."

COMPETITION   Because children's personal reading choices reflect different interests and different abilities, minimize the competition that is too often fostered among young readers. The teacher who, for example, uses charts that stress the numbers of books each child reads turns reading into a race rather than a savoring of good story material. One way to modify this competition is to develop a popularity contest for books: instead of using a poster that lists children's names (each with a star for a book the child has read), make a chart listing the names of books in the classroom collection. As the children read these books, have them add a star after the names of the books read. Encourage the class to see which books accumulate the most stars as the year progresses. Also suggest that the children lobby for their own favorites listed on the poster.

DIFFICULT BOOKS   Allow each child to choose his own books for recreational reading and for reinforcing the skills and concepts stressed during the reading instruction. Avoid telling anyone that a book is too hard for him and that he should not attempt it. Slow readers particularly often need a big book or an acknowledged hard book as a security item to help convince themselves and their peers that they, too, are capable of reading demanding material. A child will soon enough discover that a book is too difficult, particularly if he is given adequate time to investigate a wide selection of possible reading items, and if you give no greater credit or notice to students who read hard books than you give to those who choose easy ones. Stress books that suit personal interests and do not always expect children to read up to grade level expectations, even if they are capable of it.

EXCHANGE READERS   Many times slow readers from the middle and upper grades are in need of strengthening their self-concepts. Sometimes it is possible to have these older students come to your classroom to share stories with the younger ones by reading aloud to a group, or to listen to younger children in oral reading. Also suggest that the older students ask simple questions about your pupils' reading experiences. As another type of exchange activity, make arrangements with your colleagues to have your students visit the other classrooms and share their reading with children of their own ages.

FIELD TRIPS   Visit your local public library and ask the librarian to show your children how to use the facilities. Ask that a special story be read to your group. Provide information about how to get library cards for withdrawing books. As another field experience, make arrangements at a local bookstore or department store for the children to examine the new juvenile acquisitions. Suggest that the store manager set up a "Junior Jury" of selected children to evaluate new children's books.

FLASHCARDS   Children have long used flashcards to learn new vocabulary items. Flashcards are handy to use and can be changed to meet new requirements. Some children like to keep their vocabulary cards on a key ring for handy review. Another idea is to make the flashcards on seasonal motifs: at Halloween, make them in the shape of pumpkins with orange paper, for example. Or, if the words are on a specific story theme, make the flashcards appropriate to the theme. For *The Happy Egg*, for example, make egg-shaped cards for the vocabulary words. When children have mastered certain cards, ask them to post the cards or file them for later use in spelling and handwriting activities, as well as in original compositions.

GROUPING   During the course of a school year children should be grouped in a variety of ways. Unhappily, most teachers group children only according to ability, and the child who is stuck in the "slow group" all too often is stigmatized in ways that are not intended. As other ways of grouping, consider: arranging the children by common interest; with classmates of their own choosing; on the basis of a special project; or in terms of a specific skill they all require. Change groups often and avoid naming them after individuals, such as "Jimmy's group"; rather, let children name their own long-term groups, if they are interested in being identified as a group.

HOME HELP   Maintain with each child's family a relationship in which reading is recognized as an essential communication skill. Keep each family well-informed concerning the child's reading progress. Let the children demonstrate their growth by taking books home to read to brothers and sisters. Also, ask parents to commit a certain time each day, such as bedtime, to listening to their children read. Also encourage them to provide regular library visits, to subscribe to children's magazines, and to give the child opportunities to enrich his personal background in experiences and ideas.

MODELING   The model behavior of a teacher who is an avid reader can do much to encourage reading among the students in a classroom. From time to time share some of your own personal reading experiences with the children, making a point to do reading yourself while the children are doing theirs. Also schedule time every morning, before you get involved in the business of the day, when you can read at least a few pages of a high-interest story. Make a comparable effort at the close of the day's session to read a poem or tell a story. Use these settings to introduce new books to the class, reading only a few pages, just enough to stimulate the children to read the books themselves.

ORAL READING Many children are uncomfortable reading aloud before their peers. When such is the case, try to provide the shy child a private hearing, with no other students present. Give the students practice with a tape recorder, allowing them to hear themselves as a means of self-evaluation. Be sure not to require any child to read aloud anything he has not read silently first. Also, at the primary level use oral reading only to check a child's word identification skills, and leave the matter of fluency in oral reading until the later grades. If there are able students who enjoy oral reading, permit them to serve as narrators for original dramatic activities; or suggest choral situations in which they might want to read in unison.

PARTNER READING Allow the children to choose partners of comparable ability with whom they can read a book as a joint venture. These might be buddies who belong to the same reading group, or two children with the same interests. Suggest that these pairs read aloud to each other to check word identification, to ask each other questions to check comprehension, or to share reading experiences with each other, rather than reporting to the class as a whole.

READING CIRCLE When children are grouped by ability for oral reading, the most common procedure used is "reading around" in which each child takes his turn according to his position in the group. All too often the children who are not reading do not follow the text, lose their place, or worse, become bored and lose interest. Since this kind of reading slows down every member of the group to the speed of the child reading, you might consider changing the function of your reading circle by changing it into a "listening circle." As one child reads aloud, have the other children close their books and listen to the story. Ask them to be ready to pose questions for the reader, or ask questions of each other, based on the story being read aloud. Another suggestion for situations in which all children need to be reading aloud in turn is to call on them randomly so individual children are never quite sure when to expect being called on. Allow children to return to their desks after their individual turns have come, in order to minimize the amount of time they would otherwise have to spend waiting for other readers.

READING MATERIALS Too many teachers are bound in their

reading programs to basal readers, supplementary readers, and workbooks as their materials. Children respond to a wide variety of reading matter as they review and apply their reading skills. Consider, for example, student newspapers, either commercial or class-made versions. Also include original stories written by the children themselves or by older students in school. Posters, banners, signs, and labels provide other reading experiences, along with advertisements and children's magazines. Where children need to be reading controlled vocabularies at specified grade levels, arrange to exchange certain books with teachers of other grades. Or, salvage discarded books and textbooks, cut them apart, and reassemble them in attractive bindings.

RELUCTANT READERS   Children with low reading abilities, or those with reading problems, are often difficult to motivate. Help your slow readers by allowing them to use and perhaps keep permanently inexpensive paperback books that often arrive as bonus items in classroom book orders. Let them use small booklets, homemade booklets, or other materials that give them the sense of being able to finish their assignments. Be particularly aware of their needs and interests: use an interest sheet to discover the types of books they most prefer. Arrange to spend more time with them individually than with the able children who can work more independently. When your reluctant readers are hesitant about locating books to read recreationally, give several children a set of books within their reading capabilities and allow them five minutes only to examine each book. At the end of the time limit, ask them to exchange books with another child. In this way, in a short time they can be introduced to a wide variety of books they might like to read someday.

SCHEDULING   Schedule reading activities for different times of day. Plan to have skills development at one hour, and then much later in the day schedule recreational reading to apply those skills. Do not get bogged down in a page-by-page use of a reader or a workbook. Inject some variety into the routine by having the children themselves decide which materials they would like to use, when to do it, and what individual follow-up activities they would like to get involved in.

SHOW CARDS   For specific reading skills, give the children in the group a series of small cards, each with a different potential answer on it. To make these cards easier to use, color code them so the child has one answer on a blue card, a different response on a yellow card, a third one on a pink card, and so on. Then, when you need to pose a question to the entire group to respond to individually, upon a signal the children can hold up the answer cards they think are the correct ones. The color of the card each child chooses will itself enable you to see at a glance if there are children in error on each point posed. Caution the children to keep their hands in their laps just prior to picking up the show cards, so other students will not be tempted to look around the class to see which card the other students are selecting.

TESTING   There are several kinds of tests for reading: readiness tests, achievement tests, and diagnostic tests. All of these serve a specific purpose. It is important to remember, however, that the principal purpose of reading instruction is steady progress in keeping with the child's own potential. If the teacher takes a grade level expectation and compares it with the child's test scores, and attempts to make them necessarily coincide, she does both herself and the child a disservice. Tests are no better than the value of the data they produce; and they are useless unless this information is helpful in developing a meaningful instructional program. The far more effective type of testing is that daily experience and recording of growth that comes as the teacher observes what every child accomplishes in each skill area.

VOTING FAVORITES   From time to time let the children vote for the most interesting story they have read, or for the best illustrated book, or the book from which they learned the most. Set up a "Hall of Fame" or a "Hit Parade." Make simple foil medallions and attach them with tape to the books selected in this way.

Ideas for Developing
Reading SKILLS

COMPREHENSION ACTIVITIES To help develop children's abilities to understand their reading material, pose a variety of situations that will test their comprehension. Ask them to attempt some of these tasks:

1. Answer a series of questions about a story, using "True" or "False" answers, "Fact" or "Fancy" answers, or "Before" or "After" answers.

2. Make up a good title for a story read silently or read aloud by someone else. Think of the main point of a paragraph and record it.

3. Draw a picture of what a story told about; draw a picture of the main character or place described in the story.

4. Fill in the correct words in blanks in a set of sentences after having read the story.

5. Retell a story in original sentences, or retell the story by rearranging a set of printed sentences cut apart for manipulation.

6. Match some statements made in the story with the names of the persons who said them.

7. Read a set of directions carefully and then do or write whatever is required in them.

8. Draw a verb card from a pile of new vocabulary cards and act out what it says to do; or, draw a noun card from the same pile and act out that person or thing.

9. Circle all the names of people in a story; underline all the words that show people doing something; mark with red all the words that tell what kind of person, place, or thing is being described.

10. Listen to a story, or read it, and tell how these characters felt. Explain your personal feelings if you had been in that place.

11. Read a part of a story, then guess how the story might end. Compare your guess with the way the story actually did end. Or, write a different ending to the story.

12. Fold a large sheet of paper into quarters and unfold it. On each of the four parts draw a picture of the most important happenings in the story. Be sure they are on the paper in the order in which they occurred in the story.

13. Look at a series of cartoon drawings on the left side of a work paper and then look at the statements in the balloons on the right side of the paper. Draw a line between each person and what he said in the story.

14. Look at the statements written at the top of each of the several panels on a work paper; then draw a picture in the open space underneath each statement to show that you understand what it means.

15. After reading a story make a list of ten things remembered. Or, make up a riddle about a character in the story and ask it of someone else who read the same story.

16. Look at a series of vocabulary cards and match the correct one to each picture card in the same array.

PHONICS AIDS Young children enjoy manipulating learning materials and they are easily motivated by visual presentations. There are many useful learning aids appropriate to phonics skills development. Here are several:

Charts: One type of phonics chart is a large alphabet poster, with one letter in large print on the face of each oversize piece of paper or cardboard. Add a key word and a key picture at the top of the chart. Ask the children in the class to find other pictures of objects, or to make word cards from their reading, that belong on these different charts, appropriate to the phonics generalizations they represent. Another type of chart is made from a large piece of cardboard and has a sturdy arrow attached to the center of the poster with a brass fastener. Around the edges of the chart make slots where the children can insert pictures they have cut from magazines and have pasted onto index cards. Instruct the children to move the arrow to point to any of the picture cards that represent the generalization indicated at the top of the chart.

Faces: Humorous faces are appealing to children in applying their phonics learnings. A cardboard clown face with a movable wheel behind its open mouth is one good example. Effective also is a funny face with a tongue that pulls out; or, have the children cut out large posterboard comic "Letter Animals," each with a distinctive name, such as, "Sister Super Snake" or "Mr. Mighty Mouse." Decorate each figure with colored paper, and add pockets for children to display pictures or words that belong to each figure. A clock face can be made from a pizza round. Mark the 12 spaces on the face with phonics elements rather than with the usual numerals. The children must answer questions such as, "What did you buy at 10:00?" The child looks at that space on the clock and responds with an appropriate item, as for example, "Bottle," if the stimulus letter as initial consonant was the letter "B." Two children can play the game if the clock hands are replaced with a spinner.

Labels: Using cereal boxes, or other food boxes and cans, cut apart large product labels in such a way that phonograms, root words, affixes and other elements are separate. Put all these items into a box and have each child in turn draw out a stipulated number of them, in a random manner. Then ask him to put them together as words, or make up expressions that he can read because of his phonics abilities, even though some of them may be nonsense items, without real meaning.

Lift-Ups: Young children like hidden pictures. Adapt this appreciation to phonics by taking a piece of plain paper, folding it in half lengthwise, and then cutting from the edge straight toward the fold and perpendicular to it, making a series of three or four flaps that lift up, with the fold as the hinge. On the face of each flap write the phonic element being studied, and then ask each child to lift up the flaps on his paper and draw a picture underneath of something that contains the stimulus element. Use this same approach to making a house with windows and doors. Have each hinged place labeled with a different phonic element, and ask children to find pictures of things that may or may not qualify for each generalization. Let the children slip these pictures behind the openings, shifting them from place to place, to see if they can find where each one belongs.

Puppets: Make a series of simple puppets from discarded materials, and decorate each one according to his own character, complete with a name appropriate to a phonics generalization. At the beginning level, this might be "Short 'A' Sam" or "Digraph Ralph." Use these puppets to quiz the children, asking them for words or pictures that belong with each element being studied in class. Or, let the children "feed" these puppets appropriate pictures, letters, or words.

Sliders: Make a sliding card that can be placed over words on vocabulary cards and slid gradually from left to right in such a way that the word underneath is revealed only one letter at a time. Use this to give children practice in sounding shorter phonic elements that increase in length and complexity until the entire word is finally revealed. See how the pronunciation of the word changes as new letters are added. Another type of slider is made from two circles of cardboard, connected in the center with a brass fastener. Be sure they are the same diameter, and cut from the one on top a wedge-shaped piece, allowing part of the bottom circle to show through. On the bottom piece of cardboard write different word endings or any other phonic generalization. At the center of the top circle write one letter or combination of letters, permitting the individual child using this slider to slip the circle around, revealing different word endings underneath the opening.

Sorters: Young children like to sort things. Adapt this interest to phonics by arranging a series of containers, each coded with a different phonetic element. For example, make a collection of coffee cans, and place a letter stimulus on the lid of each one. Have the children find miniature toys, doll furniture, or pictures or words that can be sorted into the correct containers. Or have a large box or bag labeled with a phonic element and ask the children to bring things each day to fit that day's phonic generalization. To add interest to this type of sorting, have unusual containers for each day's collections: for example, have a jar for the "J" words, a basket for the "B" words, a purse for the "P" words, a shoe for the "Sh" words.

Trains: Make a three-car train for speech sounds to help the children identify the relative position of consonant sounds in words. Let the engine represent the initial consonant, the box car can be the medial one, and the caboose can serve as the final consonant sound. Use individual letters to put in or on each of these train cars and let the children manipulate them as they experiment with new words. Another adaptation of the train idea involves labeling each car of a long train with different letters or other phonics elements, and requires the children to find things to put into or onto the cars that qualify appropriately.

Wheels: A phonics wheel gives children practice in substituting various phonetic elements in different word settings. The simplest kind of a wheel is one that has two concentric circles cut from cardboard, with one circle somewhat smaller in diameter than the other. Fasten the two circles together in the center with a brass fastener so both circles move freely. On the inner circle have one type of phonic element, such as initial consonants, and on the other wheel have another kind. As the children become more skilled in their use of these wheels, increase the difficulty by having three concentric circles instead of only two. As variations of circles, make a phonics aid in which two circles serve as the wheels of a car or a locomotive, allowing the children to move them to make new words.

PHONICS GAMES Capitalize on children's game sense by adapting many commonplace fun activities to phonics learnings. Some of these might include:

Acting Game: Combine the children's listening skills with their phonics abilities in a game in which they are asked to listen to individual words and act according to a stimulus that has been pre-announced. For example, "If you hear a long vowel sound in this word, do whatever the word tells you, but if you do not hear a long vowel sound, stay where you are and do nothing. Here are some words: 'sit, ride, run, slide, fight, race.' " Another possibility for acting out might involve challenging the children to think of ways they could move appropriate to phonics generalizations. For example, ask the class to move to words that start with the letter "T." They might think of "tiptoe, tumble, or touch." Later on, add other words to the challenge, such as "Bounce backwards bashfully," or "Munch a marshmallow." Or, have the children working in pairs to form with their bodies the letters they hear in stimulus words.

Belonging Game: A variety of guessing activities can be used to check the children's phonic skills. One simple game is to pronounce several words and ask the child to identify the one that does not belong; or, pronounce a word and ask a child to cite another word that does belong. Too, place labels on actual objects in the classroom and give the children several minutes to notice phonic clues in the words. Then remove the labels, mix them up, and help the children to tell which ones belong with the appropriate objects in the array.

Feeding Game: Provide a series of shallow boxes, such as hosiery boxes, each of which is labeled with the name of an animal, and a picture to match. Cut a slit in each box top to represent the animal's mouth. Ask each child to feed the animals by inserting into the mouth picture cards or word cards naming things that start with the same letter the animal represents, or that have other similarities discussed before the game begins. Allow the children also to make replicas of their own faces and encourage them to feed each other's mouths. Label each child's face with his name or with some other phonic element that is contained in his name.

Silly Sentence Game: Make up silly sentences in which every word contains the same phonic element—for example, the same initial consonant. To illustrate the point, help the children to think of the name of a person whose name starts with "S" ("Sam"), then to suggest an activity that starts with the same sound ("Swims"), and finally for a time of the year ("Summer"). Later you might add adjectives ("Sweet"), and adverbs ("Slowly"), and eventually come up with a silly sentence such as "Sweet Sam swims slowly in the summer."

Traveling Game: One type of traveling game is "Suitcase," in which the child who is the leader has a suitcase that he is packing for a trip. He may say something like, "I'm going to Paris," whereupon the other children in the group suggest things he would need to take with him, such as "pajamas, paper, pencils, popcorn." To make a travel-type game more challenging, drop hints to the children concerning what they might want to take on a trip, but do not give away the clue unless it becomes too difficult for the children to guess it. For example, "I'm going on a trip. I plan to take boots, but not rubbers; food, but not lunch; roots, but not stems. I'll go to the pool, but not the beach, and watch the moon, but not the stars." The children will then have to deduce that you will take and do only those things that have a long double "o" sound in them.

SEQUENCE ACTIVITIES Develop a sense of the order of events that is important in stories and in daily routines by asking the children to draw a series of pictures of commonplace activities, such as eating breakfast, getting dressed for school, eating lunch, watching evening television, going to bed. Use a piece of paper that is folded into sections, and when the children are done with their drawing, cut the pictures apart and give each student practice in putting them back into sequence.

Involve the children in acting out things in order by asking one child to perform several simple tasks in the classroom, and then challenging other children to repeat in the same order these same actions. Or, let one child pack for a pretend trip, using a real suitcase and clothing from the play center; then see if any other child can duplicate the order in which the items were placed in the container.

Adapt familiar incremental songs, such as "Old MacDonald Had a Farm," to a series of words, activities, or picture, requiring the children in the group to recall the order in which the objects or actions were mentioned in the song.

Another activity is the use of a filmstrip of a story shown in class. After discussing the story and the strip, have the children cover their eyes, and move the filmstrip backwards or forwards. Ask the students to identify a certain frame in its proper sequence: "Did this picture come before or after the picture of Snow White eating the apple?"

SEQUENCE AIDS   Cut apart an old discarded reader. Take the story one paragraph at a time and glue each piece to a section of cardboard. Shuffle these cards and see if the children can read the paragraphs and put the story back into its correct order. Or, use the pictures in this discarded book, and have the pupils draw other pictures, or tell the happenings, that occurred just before and just after the events pictured on the page.

Sequence cards are available commercially from school supply houses. However, it is possible to make original sequence cards by taking a comic strip, pasting it to a piece of tagboard, and cutting it apart into several panels. Let the children see if they can put these panels back into their appropriate order. Or, have the children make their own pictures and simple narratives that retell a story they have read. Tell them to cut these apart and give them to another child who has read the same story for reassembling.

Give the class other experiences with putting things into sequence by cutting apart the lines of a familiar poem, or the words or a special song. Add picture clues with each line, where needed.

WORD STUDY ACTIVITIES   Help the children increase their vocabularies and improve their word attack skills with involvements such as these:

Antonyms: Give the children a series of simple sentences and see if they can change just one word in each one to change the meaning of the sentence. For example, use statements such as, "I saw a big fish. It was a cold day. We went in a dry boat." As they gain experience in this type of change, introduce sentences with several words that could be changed to make opposite meanings. See if the class members can change every single word in the statements offered. Also, ask the children to make "opposites" word cards, with one word on one side of the card, and an opposite word on the reverse side. Suggest that some words have more than one possible opposite meaning. Also propose that the children draw pictures on some of these cards to illustrate their antonyms.

Compound Words: Draw silly pictures interpreting the literal meanings of common compound words, particularly those that can be separated in such a way that the first part is a noun and the second part is a verb. Make a chart with expressions such as, "Did you ever see a house fly, a cat fish, a ski jump, a fish bowl?" As another idea, take some of the more usual compound words, print them on cards, and then cut the main elements apart. Then challenge the children to reassemble these elements into new and unusual combinations to invent words that are not in the dictionary. For example, some of the new combinations might include: "post-boy, wall-man, cow-paper"; suggest that the children make up original definitions for these inventions. A third activity is to make a flap card for compound words. Take a strip of cardboard or stiff paper, rectangular in shape, and fold the ends of the strip over to meet each other in the center of the strip. On these two flaps have the child write the two elements of a compound word, and underneath each flap, have him draw a picture appropriate to the portion of the compound word written on the covering flap.

Homonyms: Make a set of homonym cards, front and back, with meanings written at the bottom of each side of each card. Flash these cards and ask the children to define them, or to give the other word on the other side of the card. Another idea is to have the children make pictures of the homonyms to give visual reinforcement to their meanings. Where possible, include both words in the same expression and in the pictures: "a pair of pears, the sun on a son, some hair on a hare, a bored board, a hoarse horse."

Syllables: Show the children how to test for the number of syllables in each word by touching lightly the bottom of their chins as they are saying it. The chin will usually bob slightly for each syllable in the word. You might also make a little puppet, "Simon Syllable" who can demonstrate the point. Or, let the children clap their hands or bounce a playground ball to indicate the number of syllables.

Synonyms: Help the children with synonyms by taking objects found in the classroom and asking the children to think of other names for them. For instance, a scissors might be called a cutter, a paintbrush might be referred to as a spreader, a car is an auto, a penny is a cent, a pillow is a cushion, and a sack is a bag. Ask the children to suggest other examples.

part seven

SCIENCE:
Examining the Physical
World

Wondering About AIR And WATER

AERODYNAMICS   Make a simple toy parachute and let the children toss it up and watch it fall. Compare the speed of fall of a toy figure attached to the parachute and one that is not attached. Purchase a toy glider, or make a paper airplane and experiment with it. Ask a local light-plane pilot to come to class to explain how an airplane is able to stay up in the air. Illustrate airflow with a ping pong ball placed in a funnel. Hold the funnel upright and challenge the children to blow the ball out of it. The airflow should make it impossible. Juggle this same ping pong ball over a column of air from a vacuum cleaner with the air flow reversed. Or, suspend two ping pong balls on strings about an inch apart. Blow hard enough directly between them to blow them apart—however, they should draw closer together instead.

AIR ABSORPTION   Show that air is absorbed in all types of materials. Fill an aquarium with water and immerse items such as a brick, a sponge, volcanic rocks, styrofoam, loose soil, or bread. Check the air bubbles rising to the surface. Notice that water itself has air dissolved in it: fill a glass tumbler or jar with water and place it in strong sunlight. The air bubbles should begin to form on the sides of the container.

AIR EXPANSION   Show the expansion of air by placing a small balloon on the top of an empty Pyrex baby bottle. The balloon should not be inflated and should be placed tightly over the neck of the bottle. Place the bottle in a small pan of water and heat it. The balloon should gradually enlarge. Then remove the bottle carefully from the hot water and watch the balloon gradually deflate.

AIR PRESSURE Explain to the children that everywhere on earth there is air pressing against surfaces. Demonstrate this by placing your finger on the top of a soda straw which has been immersed in liquid. When the straw is removed from the container, and the finger remains tightly on top of the straw, the liquid does not come out because air pressure pushes it. Similarly, punch one small hole in a can of soda. Invert the can quickly; the liquid should not come out. Then punch a second hole in the opposite end; the liquid should come out readily. As the liquid is coming out, place a finger firmly over the second hole in the top, and the liquid should stop flowing again.

AIR SPACE Show that air occupies space by opening both double doors of a storage cabinet. Leave one door only slightly ajar, and open the second door wide. Quickly slam shut the second door; the first door should open, illustrating that even an empty cabinet has air in it. Similarly, an empty plastic sack is not really empty. Blow it up and tie it tightly at the top after the children have established there is nothing else inside it. When the sack is tied shut, let them feel the air pushing against their hands as they try to collapse it. Do the same thing with a balloon.

Use a balloon also to let the children see the bubbles of air escaping from it as it is released under water in an aquarium. Blow up another balloon and tie it shut. Let it hang a few days until it becomes wrinkled. Explain that the air has seeped out of the balloon. Another balloon activity is that of moving a book. Place a balloon underneath a book on a table. Blow into the balloon and the air pressure will visibly raise the book. Use a sturdy balloon that is inflated to support a child sitting on it.

Involve water in other experiments to show that air occupies space. One activity is that in which a paper napkin in a clear glass tumbler is inverted in a container of water. Be sure the napkin is crumpled so it stays in the bottom of the glass. Push the glass all the way to the bottom of the aquarium; the air in the inverted glass will keep the paper napkin dry. Another idea is to insert a funnel in a soda bottle, packing the outside of the funnel with plastic clay as it rests in the neck of the bottle. Take a glass of water and pour it quickly into the funnel. If the packing is tight and the pouring is quick, the water will stay in the funnel and will not run into the bottle because the air that occupies the bottle cannot get out and cannot be compressed.

AIR WEIGHT   Tell the children that on each square inch about 15 pounds of air are resting. Compare this area with that of a postage stamp. Get several heavy books and see if anyone can lift them with just two fingers. This should help the children appreciate the equalization of pressure inside and outside our bodies which keeps us from being crushed by air. Weigh a football that is deflated; then blow it up and weigh it again. Or, find two large balloons of the same size. Blow up both of them and balance them on a yardstick suspended as a balance beam. Then pop one of the balloons, releasing its air; that end of the balance beam should rise slightly.

ATOMIZERS   Illustrate the atomizer principle by blowing across the top of a soda straw that has been immersed almost completely in a bottle filled with water. Pinch the top of the straw together and blow carefully. A fine mist should appear. Find examples of other atomizers and fill them with water for the children to use.

BUOYANCY   Weigh an object out of water, using a spring scales, then weigh it again immersed in a container of water. Test different items on this scale and make a graph of the differences in the weights both in and out of the water. The children should begin to understand some relationship. Ask them to recall feelings when they go swimming, and to suggest why their bodies do not sink in the water. Set up an interest center in which the children experiment to see which objects naturally float and which ones sink. Give a child a lump of clay or a wad of crumpled aluminum foil and challenge him to make a shape that will float and a shape that will not float. Or, have a boat-making contest with sheets of aluminum foil to see which child can make a boat that will carry the most paper clips.

CLOUDS   Discuss the concept that clouds are really water vapor. Compare them with fog that does not rest on the ground. Observe different cloud formations. Make a chart of the basic types. Notice the speed of the clouds by watching cloud shadows race across the land. Ask the children to name the imaginary shapes they see in clouds. Notice the direction in which the clouds tend to move, and include this information as a part of a classroom weather observation program.

Show the relationship of clouds and the water cycle. Make a chart of a drop of water made from aluminum foil: show it falling from a cloud, then running on the ground, flowing into a lake, and finally evaporating back into a cloud. Make a miniature version of the water cycle by suspending in strong sunlight a plastic sack half full of water. The moisture should begin to condense on the upper side of the sack and run down. Notice this same effect in a terrarium.

CONDENSATION   Demonstrate water condensation by boiling a teakettle and holding a pan full of ice cubes over the steam rising from the spout. Water should begin to condense and drip from the bottom of the pan. Or, breathe on a window pane during cold weather to show condensation of water vapor that is produced by the body systems. Another illustration is a glass of iced drink sweating on a hot summer day.

DISSOLVED MINERALS   Show that water has dissolved mineral matter in it by boiling water in an open pan until there is a light-colored powdery residue. Explain the presence of these minerals by making a simple diagram of how rainfall seeps into the earth and follows underground rock strata, picking up minerals. Taste distilled water and then tap water, and compare the two.

EVAPORATION   Suggest the notion that evaporation is important in the water cycle and also helps people to be comfortable in hot weather. Let the children fold accordion-pleated fans and fan each other vigorously. Or, blow on a wet fingernail and dry one to feel the cooling effect. Recall that we are colder on windy days than still days. Another series of evaporation experiments involve the variables which influence the process. For example, use the same amount of water, but place it in different shapes of containers, such as saucers, bottles, or bowls. Or, with the same types of containers, test the effects when one of them is placed in a warm place and the other is placed in a refrigerator, or one container in a windy place and another in a still location. Still another possibility is to have one container covered, and the other uncovered, or place one in the shade and a comparable one in a sunny spot.

PRECIPITATION   In a large tin can collect snowfall in a sheltered location. Measure the depth of the snow, and then melt the snow to see how much water is produced. Or, during a snowfall, give each child a piece of black velvet and take the children outside to catch and examine individual snowflakes. Make a gauge for measuring rainfall from a plastic bleach bottle that is about 8 inches in diameter. Invert this bottle, with the bottom cut out of the bottle, into a funnel that drains into a glass jar, such as an olive jar, that is about 2½ inches in diameter. Five inches of water in the glass jar will represent about a ½ inch of actual rainfall.

SUCTION   Apply the children's understandings of air pressure to water activities. For example, make a simple siphon with a short length of plastic hose immersed completely in a filled aquarium. Be sure the entire hose is completely full of water. Pinch off both ends of the hose, leaving one end immersed and placing the other end into a container lower than the aquarium. Then release both ends of the hose and watch the water flow up and over the edge of the aquarium.

Another suction activity is sucking the air from a paper cup held against the mouth. It should stay in place a few seconds until the air pressure finally equalizes. Also, experiment with a rubber plumber's plunger: place it on a wet smooth surface, force it down, and see how long it takes for the air to seep back in. Ask the children to look for examples of suction devices from their personal toy collections.

SURFACE TENSION   Explore surface tension of water by filling a glass tumbler to the brim with water. Then carefully add paper clips until the surface of the water bulges upward and finally overflows. Another activity is to gently lay a piece of window screening or a small needle on the top surface of a container of water—or, can lids with tiny nail holes punched in them can also be used. Lay these items on the water with a fork. Also, place drops of water on a waxed paper or on a polished metal surface. Notice how the water beads. Find pictures of waterbugs that skate on the surface of a pond, using surface tension.

WATER PRESSURE   As a simple application of water pressure, bring some water pistols to class, or find plastic squeeze bottles for the same purpose. Show how water flowing creates power to move the vanes of a turbine: a model can be made from a bleach jug of plastic with vanes cut into the sides. Insert a broomstick or a dowel rod into the jug, nailing it at one end to keep the jug in place. Direct a stream of water against the vanes and watch the wheel turn.

WEATHER   Relate wind and water to a study of weather in a variety of activities. For one thing, maintain a regular weather watch as a part of the regular classroom routine. Ask one child daily to serve as a weather observer, making notations from simple weather instruments, or bring weather news from the daily newspaper. Display a large weather map in the room, and make simple notations on it concerning what is happening in the elements. Use simple symbols for high winds (a kite), rain (an umbrella), floods (a rowboat), snow (a snowman), unusual heat (a fan).

Record and graph the temperatures registered in your area. Compare them with temperatures from other areas of the state or the nation. Make large cardboard figures of children wearing clothing suitable for the weather each day. Make these items of clothing as you might for doll clothing. Assign one child the responsibility of dressing these figures each day. As a further guide for appropriate clothing and activities for different temperatures, make a large thermometer with a list of typical temperatures, each with a small figure of a child dressed appropriate to the temperature:

90	hot and sweaty	swimming
70	comfortable	take a walk, have a picnic
55	sweater	sit by a fire outdoors
40	coat	play in the leaves
32	water freezes	make a snowman
20	heavy coat, hat, gloves	go ice-skating
0	very cold	stay inside

WIND   Demonstrate the energy in moving air by flying a kite on a windy day. Let the children feel the pull of the kite on the string. Or, make pinwheels and let the wind turn them. On a gusty day have large sections of old sheets and let pairs of children hold the corners and let the wind push them along. Check wind direction with a cardboard weather vane, and measure windspeed with a set of paper cups stapled to a cardboard square nailed to the top of a dowel, for example.

What to Teach About ANIMALS

AGES   Use an encyclopedia or some other science reference book to find out how long different kinds of animals live. Make a simple bar graph of these findings and label each bar with a picture of that particular animal. Also include the life expectancy of the typical human being and note which animals live longer than people. Ask the children to contribute information about the ages of the pets they own and make appropriate predictions as to the probable life expectancies of these animals.

BABIES   Show the children that animal babies resemble their parents, although there are some differences between the adult and the infant animals. Make a game with pictures cut from magazines such as *National Wildlife, Audubon,* and *Field and Stream,* and ask the class to match the baby animal with the adult animal; adapt this to Lotto or to "Old Maid."

CATEGORIES   Help the children classify animal life by making a chart with compartments for each type of animal life. This chart can be in the form of a charming replica of Noah's Ark. Place over each compartment labels such as Insects, Birds, Fish, Reptiles, Mammals. Ask the children to find pictures of the members of each category. After the pictures are pasted onto cards and the chart is done, have the children have a game of sorting the cards into the correct compartments. As a part of this chart, have a simple legend at the bottom of each compartment that mentions briefly the characteristics of each type of animal life.

COMPANIONS   Discuss the role of animals as pets. Explore reasons why it is important to have friends from the animal life. List general suggestions for taking care of animals. Schedule an occasional visit from a pet that belongs to one of the children. Enumerate the special needs of that particular creature: food, environment, safety, handling. Find pictures in newspapers of unusual pets.

COMPASSION   Have the children make posters for a week of special emphasis such as ''Be Kind to Animals Week.'' Contact persons who represent local humane societies to talk about the need for compassion for pets: a regard for population control in order not to produce unwanted animals; the need not to abandon pets in the wild; adequate veterinary care; adequate space and appropriate diet; choosing pets that are easy to care for; and leaving wild animals in their native habitats.

DEFENSES   Study the ways in which animals protect themselves from their natural enemies. Make headings for lists of animals, include: Strong Odor, Running, Sharp Teeth, Speed, Pretending, Coloration. See if you can locate examples of animals that might fit under more than one category. Relate these kinds of defenses to human interactions, both physical and verbal.

DISEASES   Contact a local pet store or a science library for booklets that tell about diseases found among animals. Be particularly aware of those diseases that may occur in pets, especially rabbits, turtles, parrots and related birds. Emphasize with the children the need for them to wash their hands after handling any animal. Have a veterinarian discuss with the class some of the more commonplace health problems experienced by pets, and give suggestions for proper health care.

ENEMIES   Stress the fact that animals in the wild are wary of humans and generally should be avoided. Be sure the children understand, however, that most animals do not threaten people unless they feel that they are in danger, or if their babies are young, or if they are wounded or sick. Point out that each animal has its own natural enemies from which it must protect itself. However, make the children aware that these natural enemies keep each species under control, from a population standpoint. Find pictures of situations in which natural enemies were removed and the balance of nature was upset. (One such example is the rabbit population explosion in Australia.)

ENTERTAINERS Identify different kinds of animals that help make life more interesting, particularly those that can be trained to perform, such as circus animals. Collect pictures of such performers and post them in a "Circus Corner" in the classroom. Let the children dramatize animals they would be if they could be in a circus troupe. Let the children whose pets are trained to entertain demonstrate their tricks for the class. Ask a local kennel owner to give a simple explanation of how to train a dog.

ENVIRONMENTS Involve the class in a study of the various natural environments for animals. Enlist their aid in providing appropriate environments for the animals that are a part of the classroom collection. As another activity, have the class develop a cooperative mural which shows where common animals live. One committee, for example, might work on "Creatures of the Sky," another group might select, "Land Animals," while still a different group might choose "They Live in the Water." Suggest to these groups that they make holes in the mural and paste underneath these flap-covered holes cutout pictures of the animals that live there. For example, a hole in the trunk of a tree might hide a squirrel or an owl, a flap protecting a hole in the ground might shelter a turtle or a mole. Point out that some of the animals are at home in more than one environment.

FOOTPRINTS Compare the footprints of different small animals by recording them with a commercial stamp pad or with a folded paper towel serving as the inking device. Paint the animal's foot with a paintbrush, if necessary. Record these footprints on notebook paper and combine them into a loose leaf collection. See if some of the children can match the prints with pictures of the animals to which they belong.

As a related activity, after a fresh snowfall or a soaking rain, explore the soft earth in a garden or a woods for animal tracks. If the surface is suitable, pour some plaster of Paris into the depression caused by the animal's foot and see if the track can be preserved for further study. Or, make a plaster impressions box and take it along on a visit to a farm or a wildlife refuge.

HANDLING   In situations where there may be a possibility of a child being bitten by a nervous animal he is handling, provide a pair of leather gloves, explaining to the child that gloves make it easier for the animal to feel comfortable when being held. Also, ask the children who are handling animals to do so only when they are seated on the floor so they will not drop their young charges from any height, nor step on them when walking about. Designate only a special area in the classroom for handling animals, and stress the idea that such creatures need constant attention when they are out of their cages. When an animal escapes from its cage, show the children how to throw a soft cloth over the escapee to prevent injury. Or, place a cardboard box in a strategic corner, since many animals will naturally run to this type of shelter.

HISTORY   Develop an understanding of the animal ancestors that lived long before the recording of history. Establish the notion that fossil remains enable scientists to reconstruct the skeletons of dinosaurs. Compare pictures of these ancestors with their present-day counterparts. To suggest the tremendous size of many of these monsters, trace with chalk their general dimensions in a shape on the hard surface of a playground or parking lot or floor. Then outline the current dimensions of a blue whale, an elephant, or a horse. To make a modern-day display, use scale models of these animals, or have the children make some of their own from plastic modeling clay. Place these figures of dinosaurs into a classroom terrarium for a simulated jungle habitat.

MOVEMENT   Discover different ways in which animals move. Ask the children to name an animal that jumps, another that slides, another that gallops, and one that swings through the trees. Let each child choose one animal and imitate its movement; then have the other members of the class see if they can guess the name of the animal being imitated. As a movement experience, suggest that an animal might move in a variety of ways, depending on its feelings from time to time. Elicit a variety of interpretations.

OBSERVATIONS   Set aside a part of the room as an animal center. Label this center with a special name, such as "Whose Zoo?" or "Animal Farm." Find interesting pictures and cartoons of animals and post them prominently in the area. Also post a list of questions for children to answer based on the observations of the creatures. Encourage the children to maintain regular diaries of these observations, including the feeding habits, movements, weight, sleeping patterns, and physical changes from infancy to adulthood.

PRODUCTS Explore the ways in which animals contribute to the welfare of people. For example, help the children find pictures of foods that originate as parts of animals. Match each animal with the cut of meat. Check with a local grocery store for posters that present this information. Also ask the children to find pictures and samples of clothing fabrics that are used: fur, wool, leather, for example.

SIZES Use a standard reference work to discover the sizes of different animals. Make a simple bar graph indicating the heights of these creatures, and compare their sizes. Or, mark a place on a wall representing different creatures, and attach a picture of the animal at each spot. Compare their height or length with a human being. See if you can find examples of how the animal has learned to adapt to and use its size. A giraffe, for example, can feed from the treetops, while a hippopotamus uses water to support its bulk.

SOUNDS On a field trip to a farm, zoo, or a circus use a tape recorder to register the sounds of the animals visited. Involve the children in guessing the names of the animals as they listen to these sounds. Then challenge the children to imitate these sounds. Use the same tape recordings as background noises for dramatizations of stories.

SPEEDS Find information about the relative speeds of different creatures and combine the data into a graph. Place a picture of each animal on its respective bar on the graph. Compare the speed of these creatures with the speed of a man on foot, the speed of an automobile, or the speed of a light airplane. When the class is traveling as a group on a trip to the zoo, relate the speeds of the creatures they might be visiting by pointing out the speed of the vehicles in which they are traveling.

TRANSPORTATION Think of ways in which animals help people move from place to place. Try to locate pictures of unusual animal transportation: on water buffalo, reindeer, camels; in goat carts, dog sleds. Find other pictures indicating the historical applications of animal power in our own country: oxen, horses and buggies, and mules are good examples. Compare how long it might take to get to school on a horse with the time it takes on a bus or in a car.

VARIETIES   Demonstrate that each species has many different variations. Using a book about cats, for instance, show that there are many different breeds. Discuss the notion that animals seem to have their own unique personalities as well. In addition, some animals of a given breed are more intelligent than other members of the same breed; some dogs are friendlier than other dogs; some cats are more independent than other cats. Draw a parallel between animals and people in these areas of growth and development.

WORKERS   Use magazines such as *National Geographic* to find pictures of oxen pulling plows, donkeys drawing carts, horses carrying soldiers, as well as other animals that do work for people. Suggest ways in which these types of work are done in our own country, or find ways in which animals are still being used to do work. As another application of the idea of work, make a special study of insects such as bees and ants to appreciate the organization of their work habits.

PHYSICS:
Experiments with Forces

CONVECTION Explore the air currents caused by heated air rising. Burn incense in the classroom and watch the smoke rise. Post a thermometer at the ceiling of the room and another one at the floor level. Compare the two readings. Ask the children to take the temperatures of their attics and basements on a day when heating devices or cooling units are not in service. Hang a paper spiral cut from a circular piece of paper over the rising air coming from a heating unit in the cold weather. Also check convection in water by tinting a container of warm water. Then slowly pour this warm water into a container of cold water. See if the colored water tends to rise to the top of the second container.

ELECTRICAL CIRCUITS Ask an electrician to discuss in simple terms the operation of electrical circuits. Have him show the wires, tools, and switches he uses as he installs new wiring. Discuss the purpose of insulation on wires. Set up a simple battery-operated electrical circuit with a bell, buzzer, or light. Set up and tip over a circle of vertical dominoes to illustrate the sense of an electrical impulse traveling along a wire.

As a game application of this concept have the children stand in a circle and hold hands. The person who is the leader starts the impulse traveling about the circle by squeezing the hand of the person standing next to him. This child, in turn, squeezes the hand of his neighbor; in this manner the impulse goes all the way around the group. To add interest, ask one child to race the impulse around the circle, seeing which arrives at the starting place first.

ELECTRICAL SPEED Discuss the relative speeds of light and sound. Help the children to understand what happens during a thunderstorm: the light is seen almost instantaneously while the sound usually takes more time to reach the ears. Suggest that the light, which could travel around the earth seven and one-half times with every second on the clock, requires over eight minutes to arrive from the sun. Set a kitchen timer to illustrate this length of time. Show the children how to count seconds to estimate the distance of a lightning flash.

ELECTRICAL STORAGE Make a collection of different kinds of storage batteries. Cut open a dry cell with a hacksaw to see what is inside it. Find pictures of automobile batteries. Have an auto mechanic explain to the class how this battery works. Obtain a charger used to restore small batteries and explain its operation. Try to find pictures of solar batteries, such as have been used in conjunction with space exploration.

FREEZING Check the properties of water at cold temperatures by placing water in different sizes and shapes of containers. Find out which container of water freezes first in a freezer compartment. On a cold winter day place outdoors three equivalent cans filled with soil, water, and air. Using thermometers, see which one cools the fastest. Have the children make their own icicles in the spring by punching a small drip hole in a bucket of water placed on a window sill. Still another experiment involves covering different containers of water with foil, fiberglass, styrofoam, paper, or cloth and waiting to see which water freezes first and last.

FRICTION Demonstrate the need to lubricate moving parts to reduce friction. Bring a tricycle, wagon, bicycle, or other toy vehicle and ask the children to locate the moving parts. Lubricate these elements with light oil and see if they move more readily. Compare surfaces that are wet or dry, soapy, oily or rough. Point out that friction causes heat and heat causes wear. Demonstrate this heat by rubbing the hands together briskly, or by rubbing together two wooden blocks. Then try the same thing after having coated both surfaces with salad oil and rub them vigorously. Notice that heat does not build up.

GASES Watch gas forming by putting two or three seltzer tablets into a soda bottle filled with water. Cover the opening quickly with a small balloon. Note that the balloon begins to enlarge. Use carbon dioxide to shoot a cork. Find a cork that fits snugly into the neck of a pop bottle. Put a solution of half water and half vinegar into the bottle. Wrap some baking soda in tissue paper and place the soda in the bottle. Put the cork on tightly. The gas should expand and shoot the cork across the room.

GEARS Find examples of gears and demonstrate them for the class. A jeweler might be able to provide clock and watch gears, while a salvage dealer might be able to find automobile gears. Attach several wooden spools to the face of a plywood panel, using large nails as the axles on which the spools rotate. Connect the several spools with rubber bands and show how power is transmitted from one element of a machine to another one.

GRAVITY Compare the force of gravity with that of magnetism: both forces cannot be seen but both can be felt. Make a simple parallel with a magnet on a metal globe. (The magnet remains upright even when it is on the underneath part of the globe.) Similarly, a person stays on the earth because of the force of gravity pulling him down toward the center of the earth. To measure the strength of gravity use several different kinds of scales. Explain that a person's weight is a measure of this force. A very simple scale can be made with a long rubber band and a paper clip. Mark a scale on a cardboard strip to enable you to compare the weights of small objects.

INCLINED PLANE Fill a large box with books and let the children try to lift it up onto a low surface, such as another box or a step. Then, using a smooth board from the play center, see if these same children can slide the box up the inclined plane. Ask the children to find pictures of an inclined plane: ramps and conveyor belts are two examples.

INSULATION Examine the heating system to see where insulation is used to prevent heat loss. Sometimes insulation is wrapped around heating ducts, sometimes it is used in the attics. Get examples of some of these insulating materials from a building contractor. Have the children hold a container of warm water in their hands, and then surround the container with insulation and ask them to note the difference.

LEVERS   Ask the children if they can think of ways to lift someone as heavy as an adult. Provide a long board from the building block collection and experiment with one child and one adult, with a block as the fulcrum. Move the weight closer to and farther away from the fulcrum and see if the job becomes easier or harder. Make a chart of things that use leverage: crowbars, claw hammers, wrecking bars, a screwdriver prying open a paint can.

LIGHT ABSORPTION   Show that color depends on the degree of absorption of light. Arrange a series of colored pieces of construction paper and then darken the room. See if the colors are as bright as they were before. Explain that in complete darkness there is no color because there is no light to cause reflection.

LIGHT COMPOSITION   Explore color mixing by covering three flashlights with colored cellophane: yellow on one, blue on a second, and red on a third. Shine the three flashlights in a dark room onto the same spot on a white surface. Use any two flashlights at one time, and find out what happens when colors overlap. A similar effect is produced by mixing and matching color paddles made of cellophane and cardboard. Hold these paddles over different colors of construction paper and check the results.

MAGNETISM   Hide a large magnet inside a paper bag and perform "magic" by placing the sack into a small pile of paper clips. Some of the clips will adhere to the surface of the sack. Try the magnet in different media: immerse it in a tank of water, bury it in sand, cover it with cloth. Check to see if its pulling power is diminished. Experiment with the magnet to classify the types of things it will attract. Let the children sort objects into boxes in response to this experiment. Ask the children to find out if a magnet will attract another magnet: reverse the poles and check the results.

Place a compass near a magnet and see what happens. Discuss the fact that the magnetic poles of the earth are large gigantic magnets. Embed a bar magnet in plastic clay shaped like a globe to demonstrate this concept. Suspend a bar magnet from a string, twirl it gently, and see if it eventually points North as it comes to rest.

Wrap a large iron nail with bell wire and connect this wire to the terminals of a dry cell. See if the nail will pick up paper clips, and count the number. Increase the number of windings about the nail and see if the power of the magnet is increased.

MAGNIFICATION Examine different items with magnifying glasses: fingerprints, pores, coins, feathers, pollen, insects, sawdust, insect eggs, salt, mold, hair, leaves are a few examples. Change magnified images by placing two magnifying glasses one on top of the other, turning them at different angles for different effects. Examine an old pair of eye glass lenses to show how they magnify. Try a glass bead or a large marble as a magnifier. Or, locate a round glass bottle. Fill it with water and close the opening very tightly. Hold different objects up to the opposite side of the bottle and examine them.

PULLEYS Show how work is made easier by pulleys. Change the crossbar of a swing set into a simple pulley by throwing a rope over it. Have the children try to lift each other by pulling down on this rope. Demonstrate this same effect by making a wire frame for a wooden spool, running the wire through the spool hole and twisting the wire together again, allowing the spool to rotate freely. Experiment with raising small loads tied to string wound around the pulley.

REFLECTION Check the reflection of light with a mirror. Explore the symmetry of various letters and pictures. Place a mirror at the midpoint of each element to see how the appearance changes if the object is not symmetrical. Use a mirror in a beam of strong light and reflect light into corners of the classroom. Show how the angle of reflection changes the shape of the reflected light image. Look at multiple images formed by using several mirrors together. For example, place two mirrors at right angles to each other and examine the effects. Or, set up three mirrors in the arrangement of a looking glass in a clothing store. Too, use two mirrors facing each other to produce an image-within-an-image, disappearing forever in the distance.

As other applications of the reflection of light, invent a simple kaleidoscope by taping three pocket mirrors together, reflective surfaces toward the inside in a triangular arrangement. Cut small bits of colored paper on other geometric items and look at them through this device, turning it slowly in the hands as it is passed over the objects. A similar fun experience is to make a periscope from a quart milk carton and two small pocket mirrors taped inside the carton in proper position. Let the children use the periscope to see around corners.

REFRACTION Observe the apparent bending of light as you immerse a pencil in a glass of water or in an aquarium. With care, a pencil placed in the corner of a filled aquarium will become two different pencils. Fill a tall narrow olive jar with water and place your finger in it for another interesting effect.

SCREWS Locate commonplace examples of screws and compare them with an inclined plane. Think of jar lids, corkscrews, woodscrews, faucet handles, light bulb sockets. Show the relationship between a screw and an inclined plane by taking a triangular piece of paper and wrapping it around a pencil so the screw effect is shown. Get examples of tools that use the screw principle: automobile jacks, certain types of wrenches. Have a carpenter or a mechanic come to class to demonstrate these tools.

SHADOWS Show the children the relationship between a strong light source and a cast shadow. Have a game that involves the children in casting shadows of common objects onto a sheet hung up in the room. Use a filmstrip projector as the source of light. Let the children also use their hands to caricature animals and people. Outdoors have the children cast shadows of their bodies onto a large piece of paper. Outline these shapes and cut them out. Do this activity at different times of day and at different seasons to show that shadows vary with the declination of the sun.

SOUND AMPLIFICATION Show how sound can be controlled and magnified with a megaphone, cupped hands, or a rolled paper cone. Fashion another type of megaphone from a plastic bleach jug. Or, borrow a megaphone from a cheerleader and let the children experiment with it. Find a discarded loudspeaker, or borrow a battery-operated bullhorn, and show how the sound is amplified.

SOUND PRODUCTION Make a series of charts illustrating how sounds are made: by people, animals, machines, nature. Classify these sounds as those of the city, those from a farm, or sounds at school. In connection with a music class have older students in the school demonstrate different musical instruments and classify them according to the way their music is produced. Similarly, have the children feel their vocal cords when they speak or sing. Compare the lack of vibrations when they whisper. Find a picture or a model of the vocal mechanism and point out the parts of the speech apparatus that are involved in producing sounds.

SOUND RECEPTION Explore a model of the human ear. Point out the parts that vibrate and transmit sound impulses to the brain. Ask the children to put their fingers in their ears, or to place their hands over their ears and see how the quality of sound is affected. Compare the ear to a large seashell, an empty water glass, a funnel, or any other comparable device that gathers sound waves. See if any members of the class can suggest why elderly people sometimes cup their hands behind their ears. Find a picture of an old-fashioned ear trumpet. Ask a hearing specialist to demonstrate a hearing aid, particularly if there are hard-of-hearing children in your class. Construct a simple stethoscope using a funnel attached to a short piece of garden hose. Listen to a heartbeat, a pocket watch, or a whisper. Or, borrow a real stethoscope. Ask a doctor to visit the class to explain how he uses this instrument.

SOUND RECORDING Examine a record player and a record to see how sound is recorded. Place some old 78 rpm records on the turntable and see if the children can produce a sound using a small sewing needle inserted through the narrow end of a megaphone made from a cone of paper. Look at the grooves on the record with a magnifying glass. Use a tape recorder to register the voices of different children. See if others in the class can associate the correct voice and child. Compare the quality of the voice on the recording with the natural voice.

SOUND TRANSMISSION Explore some of the variables of sound transmission to see which media are best suited. For one experiment, turn on a small transistor radio and place it inside different kinds of containers: a large jar with the lid screwed on tightly, a shoebox wrapped in quilting, or a styrofoam picnic chest. Or, place the radio inside a watertight jar and submerge the jar in a filled aquarium and see if there is a noticeable reduction in sound. Try the same experiment with two large rocks, clapping them together under water.

Explore the transmission of sound over distances by setting up a simple telephone with tin cans or paper cups and a wire or stout string. Remind the children to hold the string taut if the sound is to be transmitted. Another interesting activity is to suspend a stainless steel knife, fork, and spoon on ordinary string. Hold the ends of two strings in such a manner that they are plugged in to their ears. While the strings are being held this way, let the implements clang together. The strings will transmit the sound and magnify it, so they will sound very much like church chimes. See if wood will transmit sound over a distance by putting a pocket watch or a kitchen timer on a wooden table. Ask the children to place their ears to the surface of the table and listen for the ticking.

SPECTRUM   Cast a rainbow on the ceiling of your classroom by immersing a mirror part-way in a pan of water, with the mirror at about a 30 degree angle. Be sure the mirror is in direct sunlight. Or, break a beam of light into its component parts by placing a clear glass of water on a window sill in direct sunlight. Put the glass slightly over the edge of the sill. Position a large piece of white paper on the floor and ask the children to name the colors they see cast upon it. Try the same thing with a prism. Match the colors with crayons.

VIBRATIONS   Help explain the production of sound with demonstrations concerning vibrations. For example, strike a tuning fork against a hard surface, then immerse the fork quickly into a container of water and notice the water droplets fly, even though the vibrations themselves cannot be seen. Another activity is to cover a margarine tub with plastic wrap securely and tightly fastened with a rubber band. Place grains of salt, sugar, sand, or tiny seeds on the taut plastic surface and talk against it with an improvised megaphone, trying to make the tiny particles dance. Or, place fine sand on a flat metal cookie sheet. Draw across the sheet with a violin bow. If the vibrations are right, the sand will arrange itself into patterns.

WHEELS   Demonstrate the value of wheels in making work easier by placing a handful of marbles on the top of a large unopened can. Place a second can on the top of the marbles and rotate it carefully. Note the ease with which the top can moves. Or, use roller skates, a board, and a box of books. A coaster wagon is another possibility to demonstrate wheels' value.

Investigating PLANTS

AGES See if any of the children know how to tell the age of a tree. To illustrate the process of counting the rings of a tree, ask a member of a local forestry department or conservation agency to cut a tree "round" for the class when they are removing trees. Let this tree round dry thoroughly, then sand and shellac it. Count the rings and see how old the tree was. See if all the rings are the same size. Indicate on the tree round the date when your children in the classroom were born. Depending on the age of the tree, also indicate on it other important historical dates of recent history.

ARBOR DAY Plan a special observance in the spring with poems, songs, and stories about plant life, particularly trees. Plant a tree or a shrub as a part of this simple ceremony. Suggest that the children make individual contributions to a fund for purchasing a tree or shrub. Make a small permanent label or plaque indicating the name of the tree, the group responsible for its purchase and planting, and the date. Encourage the children to adopt this tree, recording observations about its leafing and flowering, and the bird and insect visitors.

CAPILLARITY Use lamp wicks, paper toweling, or sugar cubes to suggest how liquids rise in the stalks of plants. Add food coloring to the water to make the result more visible. Use this same approach with the split stem of a piece of celery, putting a part of the stem in blue-tinted water, and the other section into red-tinted water. Examine the leaves at the top of the stalk to see if they have changed color. Then cut the stalk crosswise to see if the tints have appeared there also.

CROPS   Discuss the variety of plants that are raised for human consumption. Visit the same farm two or three times during different seasons to see the changes in these plants. Compare the appearance of each crop at the different times of year. Collect examples of seeds, stalks, and harvested product for a classroom display. Ask a food processer or distributor or merchandiser to explain to the class how these crops find their way to the store and to the home.

DECORATIONS   Bring fall weeds indoors for inside greenery: yarrow, dandelions, daisies, mullein, or mint can be planted in pots in the room. Press other flowers for a room collection: daisies, azaleas, begonias, buttercups, pansies, clover, ivy, and verbena can be used for this purpose. Another idea is to use fresh-picked daisies, zinnias, mums, marigolds, and other hardy flowers. Stand them in water for several hours, then remove the heads and thread them onto a wire for a homemade wreath that will last for several days. Still another possibility is drying flowers by hanging them head-down in a box and covering them gently with a mixture of cornmeal and borax.

DIRECTIONAL GROWTH   Explore the influence of gravity on plant growth. Plant seeds upside down and see if they grow upward. Or, take a potted plant, turn it on its side, and see how long it takes for the plant stalk to attain vertical growth again. Another activity is to find out what happens when a plant is deprived of light. Using two comparable plants, place one in the sunlight and the other under a lightproof covering that has a small hole in it. Check the plants after a week or two to see if one plant looks as healthy as the other, and if the covered plant has grown toward the light hole.

DISTRIBUTION   Demonstrate different ways in which seeds travel: in the water, in the wind, or by animals or humans. Dandelions, milkweed pods, and maple seeds demonstrate wind-borne seeds, while burrs and stickers are carried by animals and humans. Other seeds are deposited by birds after eating. Some bird nests can be planted in sterilized soil and the small seeds that are in the nesting materials will grow.

DYES Show how plants used to be utilized for coloring garments as you obtain pieces of muslin or other light fabrics and dye them with plant parts in boiling water. Some of these plants produce these colors:

goldenrod	yellow
dandelion taproot	magenta
dahlia blossoms	orange-yellow
lily-of-the-valley leaves	green-yellow
sumac berries	purple
sunflower seeds	blue
pear leaves	dull yellow

EDIBLE PARTS Make a chart or a table display illustrating the notion that different parts of plants are edible. Ask for examples of roots (potatoes, yams), stems (celery), seeds (nuts), flowers (cauliflower), or leaves (spinach). Caution the children against eating parts of plants of which they are not sure, particularly in cases where one part of a plant is all right to eat, and another part of that same plant is poisonous: potato eyes and rhubarb leaves are two cases that illustrate this problem.

ENEMIES Present the notion that plants have enemies that tend to destroy them—these could include insect pests or plant diseases. Find examples of galls or other insect damage on nature walks, or ask a nurseryman or conservation agent to describe and illustrate these plant enemies. Also suggest that some plants are enemies of man, particularly those that infest crops and crowd out the good plants. Other plants are enemies because they are poisonous to touch. Make a display of these latter plant enemies just before vacation times when the children might be outdoors in the woods.

ENVIRONMENTS Develop a mural or an exhibit that points out the different places in which plants are found. Headings might include Water, Land, or Air, or might relate to climate with a title like Desert, Cold, or Jungle. Also have an experience in examining the immediate environment of plants where you live. Mark off a small section of ground near the school, and count all the different kinds of plants you can find growing there. Describe the soil, moisture, and amount of sunlight available, also. Dig down a few inches to see the depth of the topsoil.

EXPANSION   Show that seeds and plants expand. Fill a small glass jar with bean seeds and then add water to the very brim. Screw the lid on very tight. Place the jar in a cardboard box. Within a short while the seeds will absorb the water and will swell with enough force to shatter the glass. Relate this to the expansion of seeds planted in moist soil: the plant must expand in order to grow. Also bring to the children's attention that plants expand in cracks of rocks and sidewalks with enough force to raise and break these solid objects.

FOSSILS   Compare present-day plants with prehistoric plants by showing pictures in reference works that demonstrate fossils. Discuss coal as a fuel and its origin as plant material. Make your own fossils by imprinting ferns and leaves in a box of plaster of Paris mixture. Coat the leaves or ferns with petroleum jelly first to permit easy removal from the hardened plaster. Place the object in the bottom of a shallow box lid and pour the plaster mix carefully on top of it. Or, use a clay mold on which you print the leaf or fern or twig. See if you can find examples of real plant fossils to show the children.

GARDENING   Allow space for each child in a garden in the corner of the school yard or in a neighbor's yard. Show the class that gardening is a year-round activity: preparing the soil, planting, weeding, watering, picking the vegetables or flowers, spraying for insects or diseases, turning the soil in the fall and adding compost. To add interest to this gardening, let the children use their own personal implements: shovels, rakes, and hoes. Set up a routine for watering and providing other care that must regularly be provided.

GERMINATION   Check the germination time of seeds you buy for the children to plant. Young children find it difficult to wait for plants to grow. Also check the percentage of germination; look at the seed packet for this information. In the event that some seeds may not germinate, give each child more than one seed. Larger seeds may germinate better if they are soaked in water before planting. If more than one plant grows in the individual container, the extra ones can be thinned out. As a controlled experiment, plant a wide variety of seeds and make a daily notation of which ones have sprouted. Make a chart or graph of the results.

IDENTIFICATION   Plan a tour of the school grounds, a neighborhood park, a backyard garden, or a forest preserve. Study plant and leaf shapes before the trip and then see how many the children can identify on the walk. Give the children cut-out shapes that match those taken from standard reference books to aid in this identification. Encourage the children to collect samples of each type of plant or leaf: use adhesive cellophane for small seeds, plastic clear bags for larger specimens. After the walk make a chart on which the specimens are displayed and labeled.

LANDSCAPING   Find a small plot of earth that is in need of improvement. Contact a professional nursery worker for advice. Examine the soil for insects. Bring in better soil if it is needed. Purchase inexpensive plants that require very little care. Take a field trip to a nursery to select the plantings, or visit a landscaping site to watch a landscaper at work.

LEAF ACTIVITIES   Fall leaves present a wide variety of interesting activities, many of them involving art media. Here are some useful suggestions:

Patterns: Randomly cover a piece of white paper with red, orange, and yellow crayoning. Then cover this entire area with heavy black crayoning or black tempera paint. Next, outline a leaf pattern using something sharp, such as the point of a pair of scissors. Finally, scratch away the entire area inside the leaf pattern and see a lovely multicolored leaf emerge.

Pressings: Collect large leaves and press them using a warm iron on a pad of paper toweling. Enclose these leaves between two sheets of waxed paper or plastic wrap. Before pressing, add bits of grass, flower petals, or crayon shavings for extra effect. Place these pressings in a light source.

Printings: Using diluted poster paint mixed with liquid starch, paint the veined side of a leaf with a paintbrush. Set out pieces of absorbent paper, such as newsprint or paper toweling. Print the leaf, veined side down, by pressing it onto the paper. Another kind of print is made by spattering the leaf with a toothbrush dipped into tempera paint and rubbed over window screening. Or, press the leaves, veined sides down, into Play dough or clay.

Rubbings: Place leaves on top of several paper towels, veined sides up. Using onion skin paper or tracing paper, rub over the leaves lightly with crayon, chalk, or charcoal, holding the coloring implement in a flat position. Another approach is to rub over leaves that are underneath aluminum foil, veined side up.

Skeletons: Dry large leaves thoroughly, having pressed them carefully. When they are dry to the point of crispness, take a wire brush and strike the tines of the brush against the dried leaf material between the veins. These leaf skeletons may be used for leaf rubbings, or spray paint them for room decorations.

Stencils: Rub over the edges of leaves with colored chalk, charcoal or crayons, moving the instrument from the center of the leaf outward onto the paper. Or, outline the leaf on paper, cut out the shape, and use that shape as the stencil. To add further interest, let the children overlap these stencil figures in a variety of ways and use different colors to make the shape on the paper.

MOISTURE   Cover a plant with a clear plastic covering and see if moisture forms on the inside surface of the covering. Using a terrarium, demonstrate that a plant environment can become almost self-supporting as the moisture from the plants is condensed and falls back into the soil. Demonstrate the importance of moisture to plant growth by using matched sets of plants: let one plant get too dry, let one have correct water, and overwater the third plant. Compare their appearance and growth after several weeks of this treatment.

OVERCROWDING   Demonstrate the effects of crowding on plants. Place one or two seeds in one container, and place a handful of seeds in a comparable container. After several weeks of growth with similar care, see which plants are more fully formed. Plant some vegetable in a garden and show the children how to thin the rows.

PARTS   Make a chart that compares the parts of the typical plant to a factory. Indicate that each part has a special job to do: lifting water from the soil, producing food for the plant to use. Look carefully at each part of a plant using a magnifier or a microscope. Dig up a large plant growing in moist soil. Carefully wash off the roots and examine the root hairs. Compare the length of the taproot with the height of the plant. Bring to class a variety of seeds and compare them. Find pictures of the adult plants and tape the seeds to these pictures.

PRESERVATION   There are a variety of ways of saving leaves, flowers, and weeds for display or for teaching. For example, leaves may be dipped into paraffin melted on a double boiler.

Dandelion puffs may be sprayed with hairspray or spray shellac. Or, soak leaves in a solution of one part laundry bleach to 12 parts of water for two days. Rinse the leaves thoroughly in water. Then soak them in a solution of two tablespoons of glycerine to two quarts of water. Pat them dry without rinsing. Magnolia, laurel, holly, ash, and rhododendron leaves can be preserved by standing branches of foliage for two weeks in a mixture of one part of glycerine to two parts of water.

Dry flowers by preparing a mixture of two-thirds borax to one-third of dry, clean, sifted sand, or silica gel acquired from a florist. Cut the flowers and insert florist's wire into the stems for support. Gently sift the mixture about the flowers which are suspended head-down in a box. After two or three weeks of drying, remove the flowers carefully and brush them off with a soft brush. Try cornmeal and sand as an alternate medium. When the flowers are dried and cleaned, spray them with shellac for further preservation.

ROLES Discuss the importance of plants to the survival of mankind. Help them to enumerate and discuss some of the uses of plants:

> They hold water on the soil, preventing erosion.
>
> They enrich the soil with their leaves.
>
> They produce fruit, flowers and other items to use.
>
> They make water and oxygen.
>
> They provide shade.

As an elaboration of products, find pictures and realia that illustrate food, clothing, and shelter that can be traced to plant life.

SEASONS Make a mural with four panels showing the changes that occur as a fruit tree experiences the changing seasons. Discuss what is happening at each stage of development. Explain the need for a cycle of activity and rest among both plants and humans. Relate the special seasons to certain types of plant life: pumpkins, mistletoe, evergreens, holly, poinsettias, clover, and lilies are some examples. Use the seasonal weeds, nuts, and grasses in a variety of holiday decorations and craft items.

SOIL Have a local geologist or soil conservation agent bring to class samples of different types of soil in your area and explain which are best for growing plants. Ask him also to tell what measures are used to prevent soil erosion. Find a source of potting soil that can be used for classroom projects. One possibility is field soil that is sterilized by heating it in an oven for a half hour at about 400 degrees.

TREES Keep a diary of a tree, making observations on the date when it begins to bud, when the leaves emerge, when the blossoms open, when the seeds fall, when leaves change colors, and when the leaves begin to fall. Another activity is to check the grain of wood in furniture, a baseball bat, or lumber. Contact a cabinetmaker for samples of different kinds of wood. Obtain a variety of low-grade lumber from a lumberyard, especially that which has loose knots. Cut this lumber into short sections, sand it carefully, and let the youngest students use the knots and knotholes as matching experiences.

WATERING Make a sprinkling bottle by punching several holes into the metal cap of a plastic bleach bottle. Use a small bottle for ease of handling. A bottle with a handle on it makes it simple for even the youngest child to do the watering. Other sprayers can be made from plastic squeeze bottle, oil cans, or even water pistols. Instruct the children in proper watering techniques for indoor plants: keep the dust off the leaves, remove small insects, and provide moisture, but do not overwater the plants.

WINDOW BOXES Set up a plant center on the window sill facing a strong light source and cleverly name each plant. When all the plants are in place, drape a large plastic sheet over the window sill, and tape this drape in position to produce a type of a hothouse for the plants. Post a series of questions on cards around the area to help children to think about how plants grow. As a decorative touch, make window boxes and attach them to the outside of the building. Keep them filled with seasonal potted plants. The window box will keep them elevated for everyone to enjoy, and will discourage dogs and other animals from destroying the garden in miniature.

part eight

SOCIAL STUDIES:
Encouraging Awareness of Others

COMMUNITIES
and the World of Work

ADVERTISEMENTS As an occupational involvement, let each child choose a special product to advertise—this can be either a real product or an imaginary one. Let each person plan a simple campaign to sell his item: make up a slogan, a television or radio commercial, a trademark, a poster, and a designed container. Set up a storefront display for each of these items, and let the class indicate which products they might like to purchase.

BANKING Set up a play bank in the classroom and allow each child to make deposits and withdrawals, using small coins brought from home, or with tokens issued in the classroom in recognition of tasks accomplished. Keep records of each transaction and offer interest earned at the end of each week, utilizing small pieces of candy or pennies as evidence of the interest. Let the children spend their real money for objects donated by parents or for objects purchased for this purpose; let the children spend their tokens for privileges in the classroom.

As another banking activity, visit a bank to negotiate a small loan to purchase supplies to make something for sale, such as a large batch of holiday cookies. Then sell the products that are made, involving the children in planning the expenditures and the profit. Repay the loan and keep the promissory note as a reminder of the experience. Let the children help decide how to spend the profits of the sale.

BUDGETING   Give the children some appreciation of the different decisions wage earners must make regarding the distribution of their funds. Make a large chart with different headings, each one illustrated with an appropriate picture. Divide the chart into columns for expenditures such as: housing, food, clothing, travel, fun, charity. Under each column place replicas of pennies that suggest the proportion of the typical salary that is spent on each of the categories; use an encyclopedia or other standard reference work to find this information. Or, as another variation of this same chart, let the children suggest items to include under each heading, and write words in where they belong, or paste or draw pictures under the appropriate categories. Let children suggest, from their own families' experience, general variations in expenses that might occur due to different sizes of families, or ages of the children, for example.

CIRCUS   Circus-related occupations are always popular with young children. Develop this theme with music and artwork. Encourage the children to bring to class their own stuffed animals for a menagerie made of cardboard boxes decorated as cages. Or, construct your own large animals from cardboard boxes stapled together and painted appropriately. Use dress-up materials and salvaged costumes for the different performers and circus workers. Identify the variety of circus people and discuss each new responsibility: performers, laborers, ringmaster, animal trainers, concessionaires, cooks, and ticket takers are just a few possibilities. Convert the center area of the classroom, especially if it has a rug, into a performance arena. Use the under-table areas as cages for the animals. Decorate the room with pennants, flags, and crepe paper streamers.

CLOTHING MANUFACTURE   Discover where different clothing fabrics originate. Get samples of cloth and match them with a set of pictures of their sources: leather, silk, rubber, cotton, wool, nylon, and linen all have interesting stories connected with their development. Make a picture chart of machines that help care for clothing: sewing machine, iron, dryer, and washing machine are obvious selections. Have a seamstress or a tailor show the children how to make simple garments for themselves or for doll play. Locate samples of materials for the children to use in their own sewing activities. Make simple shapes for them to outline, cut out, and sew together to dress a simple cardboard doll with a head cut from a mail order catalog page.

COMMUNITY CHANGES   Discuss the notion that towns are always changing. To substantiate this idea, contact a long-time resident of your area and ask him or her to tell the children about some of the changes. Think in terms of buildings that have been erected or torn down or remodeled; identify families that have moved in or out; ask the children for examples of adults who have changed their jobs. Ask parents who have newly moved to the community or to the area tell the class why they have changed places. Ask them also to discuss with the children why they prefer a rural area, small town, or city.

DIVISION OF LABOR   Explain in simple terms the division of labor and the specialization that characterize many occupations. Set up a small assembly line in the classroom in which two groups of children cut out and assemble jointed cardboard puppets. Run off a ditto master with all the parts to be used. With one group give each child a pair of scissors, brass fasteners, paper punches, and sets of the papers with the outlined parts. Ask each child in this group to do all of the manufacturing processes, with each child putting together his own puppet. With the other group, however, ask several children to cut apart the pieces of the puppets, another child or two to punch all the holes, and several other students to assemble the objects. See which group can put together the most puppets in the same period of time. Adapt this same approach to other projects, such as making no-bake cookies.

ECONOMIC NEEDS   Elicit discussions of economic needs by cutting out a series of pictures and pasting them onto small cards. Have a variety of items included: foods, hardware, toys, television sets, record players. Use a mail order catalog as a source of some of these pictures. Give each child a small amount of play money. Make up different situations and see if the children can tell the difference between what they might want to buy and what they might need to buy. Propose a series of hypothetical situations such as these:

> You are very sick with a serious disease. Would you buy medicine or a toy to play with?
>
> You need to build a doghouse. Which would be more important to you, a hammer, or a yo-yo?
>
> Your fire at camp has gone out. Would it be best to buy matches or marshmallows first?

ELECTIONS   Be aware of the different elections that occur in most areas in the spring and in the fall. Arrange to have the mayor or other municipal employees come to your classroom to tell the children in simple terms what issues are involved in the elections, and what each municipal or other civic job entails. Visit the offices of these workers, and make a display of news pictures devoted to the election.

Apply the democratic process in your own classroom by having your own elections. This could be something as simple as a campaign by two children for the position of room captain. Give each child a symbol as an identification badge, and let the children in the class vote for the candidate of choice by marking a simple ballot with "Yes" or "No," or by using a smiling face or a frowning face. Also involve the children in other decision-making in the classroom, as, for example, in letting them decide procedural matters, such as planning games, parties, projects, or other special events.

FARMS   Study the variety of farms represented in your local area and let the children identify the different items these farms produce. Help the class to see the importance of each type of crop in the total food supply or commercial industries. Contact a farm implement dealer for a catalog and pictures of different kinds of machinery used in farming operations. Discuss some of the natural hazards to which crops are subject: drought, flood, disease, hail, frost, pests. Ask farm workers to come to the room as resource persons and describe the skills and information they must command in order to be successful at their jobs. Take the class on a visit to a farm at different seasons of the year to see the various activities and stages of crop development.

FOOD PROCESSING   Make a chart or diagram of where different foods come from. Trace a certain food from its source through the different stages of the milling, processing, packaging, and merchandising, and transportation. Contact some of the major food producers for flow charts and pictures of the food products in different stages of preparation.

INTERDEPENDENCE   Show that all workers need each other, and that producers are also ultimately consumers. Label each child with a badge or a headband to identify a different occupation. Place all the children in a circle formation and give one child some play money. Ask him to turn to the child next to him and purchase by name either some goods or services, exchanging some of the money for the purchase. In turn, the second worker turns to the third child in the circle and continues the process. In this way some money goes all the way around the ring, returning to its starting point. To make the demonstration even more graphic, try the same procedure, only this time interrupt the money flow to show that without money the purchasing cannot continue.

JOB CHANGE   Bring to the children's attention the fact that adults often change their jobs. Have the students help make a survey of the different kinds of work their parents have performed over the course of the years. Ask them also to indicate the reasons for some of the major changes that have occurred, and suggest that they specify which changes necessitated moving home locations.

JOB DIGNITY   Develop the notion that all work has its own dignity and there is no occupation that should be demeaned. Let the children suggest what would happen if there were no garbage collectors, no doctors, no teachers, no laborers, no farmers. Consider these occupations one by one. Show the children that work is dignified if the person involved enjoys himself and does the best he can at it.

JOB DIRECTORY   Make a classified directory of the jobs held by the parents of the children in your class. Use yellow tablet paper and reserve one page for each parent. Arrange these pages alphabetically. On each page list the name of the adult, the name of the job, the place where the work is done, the special skills that are needed, the hours and days of work, the things that the adult enjoys about the job, and the ways in which the job helps other people. Also add pictures of the work place, the products made, and ask each child to draw an original illustration of his parent at work.

JOB HANDS   Make an interesting display by asking each child to have his parents trace around their hands and reply to the heading, "What My Hands Do." Have each parent write a brief statement on this tracing telling the nature of his or her job. Combine these tracings into a simple booklet about work. Then have the children in the class trace their own hands, and make some statements about their own responsibilities in the school or at home; this should help them to understand that they have a job to do, just as their parents have their own jobs to do.

LOCAL INDUSTRY   Make a collection of all the items that are commercially grown or manufactured in your area. Think in terms of crops from farmland and goods made in shops and plants. Where these products are too cumbersome to bring to class, contact the local producers and ask them to supply literature, descriptions, and pictures about each item. See if any of the children's parents help to make these goods. If so, make a display in which the picture of the parent is connected to the picture of the product with a piece of colorful yarn.

PURCHASING   Encourage the children to evaluate the things they buy, and thereby develop more discretion in their purchasing. Suggest that they inspect the qualities of the toys they buy; consider the price, durability, safety, simplicity of operation, and variety of uses. Examine the quality of the inexpensive toys offered in cereal boxes, as well as those advertised in special offers on these same containers.

As another activity, have the children cut out food prices and food advertisements and compare the different items offered. As you compare the advertisements, discuss the variations in prices for the same goods. Point out that price alone is not a reliable indicator, as the purchaser must also consider the quality of the item, the selection of merchandise, the personal services offered, the convenience, cleanliness, and friendliness of the store.

ROLE PLAY   Set up a series of play centers geared to the children's parents' occupational specialties. Let each child act the role of his own parent at work. Decorate each work center appropriately to the job being portrayed. Include pieces of uniforms, and add actual objects produced by the parents. Let the child indicate the type of work he might choose to make other play centers appropriate to these personal selections as well.

In conjunction with this role play, discuss with the children the fact that roles in work are increasingly not associated with either boys or girls exclusively. Show pictures and news articles about men becoming chefs, designers, nurses, telephone operators, and kindergarten teachers. Demonstrate also that girls are now choosing to be pilots, jockeys, telephone repair persons, and truck drivers. Stress the fact that jobs should demand only competency rather than a person of a given sex.

SALES   Make a collection of different sale flyers, advertisements, and posters from local stores and use them in the store play in the classroom. Or, schedule a "white elephant" sale in the classroom. Issue the children play money or scrip accumulated for specific achievements in the class; or let the children invest their own money in purchasing inexpensive items, with the understanding that all profits from the venture will go toward some predetermined project. Encourage the children to make good decisions concerning the expenditure of their money.

STORE PLAY   Make a large department store replica by stapling together a series of shoeboxes or other standard-size cartons into a vertical arrangement of open-faced compartments, each one representing a different story of a building. In each room place doll furniture or other miniatures to suggest a store area. Display small picture cards of the goods sold there. Make a directory of the store, listing the different floors and departments.

As another type of store play, take some sections of large packing cartons and accordion-fold them, with each section decorated and labeled appropriate to the various occupational interests. Cut out a window in each section, and place a child proprietor behind each one. Give each child pictures or replicas of products to sell. Give the children play money or money adapted from the coupons and premiums that come with bulk mailings as part of advertising campaigns.

TOOLS   Ask different workers to come to the class and bring their tools of their trade along with them to demonstrate. Relate each tool to the children's knowledge of simple machines. Cut out other pictures of other tools and assemble them in a notebook. Or cut out tools and cut out pictures of uniformed occupations; ask the children to match correctly each tool with the worker who uses it. Make a collection of discarded tools to use in role play, and make another collection of miniatures of tools.

TRAFFIC PLAY   Make a series of streets and alleys in the classroom or on the playground by using wide rolls of paper and laying them flat on the play surface, or paint or tape permanent traffic lanes and pedestrian crosswalks. Involve the children with bicycles, tricycles, wagons, and other large toys, instructing them in observing the proper rules of the road. Try to arrange these roadways in replicas of the principal thoroughfares around the school. Label each roadway. Use them to show the safest routes to school and the best way to cross a street. Designate some of the children to serve as safety officers to watch for poor driving habits or improper pedestrian practices. Set up a juvenile court to deal with offenders.

TRAFFIC SURVEY   Set up two or three groups, each with adult supervision, at each of the corners near the school. Ask the children to record the number and kinds of vehicles passing each point. Where feasible, put up a larger poster labeled "Traffic Survey" at a nearby stop sign or stoplight; ask drivers their destinations. Ask some of the children to record and graph the colors of the cars, or to count and graph the number of passengers each vehicle is carrying.

TRANSPORTATION PLAY   Set up play areas for imaginative vehicular play involving boxes, chairs, and other simple equipment. To make a bus or a train, for example, find a carton in which a refrigerator has been shipped and cut a doorway and windows in it. Place chairs inside the box, and label the outside of the box with names and numbers to simulate a vehicle. Establish a station with wrapped packages to deliver, and tickets for the passengers. Make tags to attach to the packages indicating final destinations. Find a discarded military hat to use for the conductor or the engineer or truck driver. Using large sections of discarded cardboard, cut out large stand-up replicas of people and other vehicles, to further populate the transportation center.

TRANSPORTATION TOYS   Designate a day when the children are to bring their transportation toys to school. Instruct them to label each item with tape to indicate its ownership. Then assemble and classify the toys according to their use: buses, airplanes, trains, cars, boats, and trucks are good examples. Within each of these categories point out the wide variety of vehicles: boats, for instance, might be represented by a ferry, a tug, a liner, a freighter, a submarine, or a sailboat. Encourage the children to discuss each type of vehicle according to how it travels and how it works. Let the children play with these vehicles, and suggest that they be shared with all students, in the event that some children do not have these kinds of toys.

As a related activity, take a tape recorder on a trip to the business section of your town and record the different sounds for the children to identify and use in their imaginative play. Look for sounds produced by the vehicles themselves, as well as those made by safety signals, such as railroad bells, an ambulance siren, or a police whistle.

UNIFORMS   Draw a series of community helpers by tracing around children's bodies on large paper or cardboard. Have the children decorate each cutout figure appropriate to a different occupation. Point out that sometimes a uniform suggests a specific job, but sometimes it is impossible to tell. After these cardboard figures are completed, cut holes into their faces, and hand holes for the children to hold, and have the pupils use these figures for dramatic play relating to the world of work.

WORK CONDITIONS   Identify some of the conditions under which work occurs. Make a series of charts on jobs that must be done during the daylight and those that must be done at night. Ask the children to identify the times of day their own parents work. Make another series of charts concerning jobs that are done in the home, such as appliance repair, telephone installers, cleaning, and carpenters working on remodeling of houses. Still another approach to this concept is to identify persons who work for others, as different from those who are self-employed. Or, suggest that some work seasonally, while others are employed the entire year around.

WORKER DISPLAYS   Make a "Worker of the Week" display in which a child can be honored for a special job he has performed in the classroom. Or, adapt this same idea to honor an individual child's parents. Check the newspapers for special news about parents who are involved in community affairs, and keep on the lookout for news of promotions. Use photographs of the parents being honored in the display.

WORK HATS   To enhance role play in occupations make a series of hats for the children to wear. For example, from a white paper sack, cut out one side completely and roll up the others for a nurse's cap. Use a large oval of red construction paper with an inner oval cut away and folded up in front for the fireman's hat. Adapt a discarded plastic bleach jug for a spaceman's helmet.

ENVIRONMENTS
and Ecological Responsibility

BEAUTIFICATION Ask the children to join in a competition to find in the natural environment the ugliest thing they can locate. Require that each child tell why he thinks his find is the least beautiful object found, and have the other children agree or disagree with his opinion. Discuss what mankind has done to scar and disarrange the beauty of the outdoors. Involve the children in a major campaign to beautify the classroom or the school grounds or the neighborhood. This might be something as simple as a clean-up effort, or it might involve earning money for shrubbery, a tree, or flowers. Still another project might be to find an eroded area and plant grass or make a small dam to interrupt the free flow of water. Organizing a short-term effort at recycling paper, glass, or metal is another possibility.

COMPOST Make a compost heap for a class garden project by placing leaves, grass clippings, water, soil, and fertilizer underneath a plastic cover in the fall. Add clean garbage such as apple cores and vegetable scraps. Contain the material in the pile by putting it inside a wooden baffle, or use a discarded sandbox. Add this compost to the soil in the spring.

CONSERVATION Help the children identify ways of saving resources in the environment. Let them make a list of ways showing how to conserve clothing, for example, by keeping it clean, wearing it correctly, keeping it repaired, marking it for identification of ownership. Suggest ways of conserving food, such as taking only as much as can be eaten, using leftover items, avoiding convenience foods, if there is time to prepare them otherwise. Challenge the children to think of ways to conserve resources, homes, machinery.

DUST POLLUTION In a darkened room use a strong projector beam to show the tiny specks of dust that float in the air. Ask the children to suggest where the dust might come from. Pick up a rug and shake it gently. Or, clap two erasers together, and then look at the beam of light again. Examine the dust bag from a vacuum cleaner. Let objects stand on a dark surface for several days, then lift them off and see the patterns in the dust.

To check outdoor dust pollution, on a dry, windy day hang up a soaked sheet in such a way that it will catch dust particles falling from above. Be sure it is thoroughly wet so the dust particles and soot particles adhere to the surface. Collect another type of dust by placing a wet paper towel over the exhaust pipe of a running car. Check it after a brief period to see if carbon has collected on the surface of the towel. Or, examine a rusted-out muffler from a junkyard or service station to see the soot particles inside it. Still another possibility is to carefully blacken a piece of paper with a lighted candle.Explain that the carbon residue from fires floats through the air and some of it settles in the lungs.

ENDANGERED SPECIES Get pictures and other information on endangered species and discuss with the children why each type of creature is on the verge of extinction. Find pictures of other animals that no longer exist, such as the passenger pigeon or the dodo bird. Help the children to think of human beings as still another endangered species and make suggestions for our own survival.

GARBAGE Demonstrate the impact of different kinds of garbage on the environment by burying in marked spots in a handy garden plot different kinds of refuse: bones, orange peels, leafy vegetables, paper, tin, glass, aluminum, plastic, for example. After the passage of several months, dig up each spot and observe the degree of deterioration of each type of material. Consider the percolating of water through these discards. Suggest alternate ways of disposing of garbage: dumping at sea, landfilling, burning, and recycling. Identify problems involved in each of these possibilities.

INTERDEPENDENCE Compare the different elements of nature with the different aspects of a community where everyone has his own job to perform. Show that plants, animals, air, water, and sunlight all have a particular job to do. Point out that the community of nature cannot properly function without one of the elements. Ask the children questions such as, "What would happen if there were no air?", "Could the world get along without trees?" or "How would life be changed if all the world's water disappeared?"

LITTER Stimulate the children's interest in trash by making a container from a cardboard box or a fiber drum decorated as a "Trash Troll," "Litter Eater," or "Mess Monster." Have a poster contest to advertise the importance of a clean environment. As a variation of a poster contest instruct the children to make their posters using only discarded trash items as their design items. Relate this contest to the children's immediate environment by asking them to use only the discards they have collected during a clean-up campaign in or around the school building. Still another approach to the litter problem is to have the children assume roles of various pieces of trash and ask each one to tell his own or her own sad story of polluting the environment. Or, have the children use discards as puppets to tell this same ecological tale.

Another activity is to point out the differences between natural litter and man-made litter. Make posters on which each type is displayed. Find examples of ways in which natural litter conserves the environment even when discarded: old logs serve as homes for insects, dead leaves turn to soil. As an extension of this activity, make a class collection labeled "Scrap Book" and ask the children to see which person or which group can assemble in a specified period of time the widest collection of man-made debris or litter.

NATURAL ELEMENTS Make a bulletin board labeled "Hurt or Help?" and ask the children to find examples in picture form of ways in which fire, wind, water, and earth are helpful, and ways in which they are sometimes harmful. They may find pictures of floods, blizzards, earthquakes, forest fires, or hurricanes. Or, they may come up with pictures of crops growing, boats sailing on lakes, windmills, fireplaces, or spring showers. Point out that man-made elements are also helpful at times, and at other times they can be harmful.

Another activity related to natural resources is to make a chart showing the origins of many of our commonplace inventions and foods. Show that metals come from the earth in the form of ores; that paper and lumber originate as trees; that plastics can be traced to petroleum and other chemicals. Help the children to realize that these materials are limited in their supply and they must be used wisely.

NOISE POLLUTION   To explore the effects of noise, assign the children some intellectual task that ordinarily requires careful attention: a timed test in mathematics might be a good example. While the class members are working at this job, deliberately play a loud distracting record to see if it impedes their speed and accuracy. Another activity is to use a tape recorder at a busy corner to capture the noises from traffic or trains, or tape record the noise in a crowded cafeteria. Ask the children to suggest other noises that are bothersome at times. See if they can think of reasons to explain why hospitals are marked with ''Quiet Zone'' traffic signs.

OPEN SPACE   Point out that people as well as other creatures need enough space. Place one child in a designated part of the classroom, and ask that child to move about freely, or to play a game, such as jumping rope. Then gradually add other members of the class in the same floor space and note the changes in mobility and safety as the area becomes more crowded. Encourage discussion from pupils who find it necessary to share rooms with siblings; have them suggest some of the problems that occur in crowded quarters. See if the children can think of reasons to have parks and open land in and around cities.

PAPER CONSERVATION   Help the children to be especially aware of the proper use of paper in the classroom. For practice activities and just for fun experiences, let them utilize the backs of used pieces of paper obtained from the school office, or accumulated in the classroom. Let children practice difficult cutting or other art experiences on inexpensive and discarded paper before attempting them on the more expensive types. Encourage the children also to use paper scraps for mosaics, collages, and simple pasting and sculpturing activities. Keep these paper scraps in a special drawer and allow the children free access to these remnants. Encourage the children to save papers at home for recycling. Show the class items in the classroom that have been made from or that have been printed on recycled paper.

RECYCLING   Help the children to think in terms of recycling commonplace materials as a part of their responsibility to the environment. For example, show them how they might make do without certain items. A paper sack might be used more than once to contain a lunch, as one possibility. Toys, hats, and costumes for play and for Halloween can be made from discarded materials rather than bought in the store. Still another idea is to encourage the children to bring to school their outgrown or discarded clothings, books, and toys for a classroom exchange, thereby multiplying the use of these items. Or, have the children purchase these items from their own funds to give them added mileage, or donate them to children who are not able to buy their own clothing and playthings. Use any moneys realized from sales of such items in some designated beautification project selected by the members of the class.

SOIL EXPERIMENTS   Prepare several simple experiments to show the nature and the purpose of soil. Dig down through the topsoil until you reach subsoil, and compare the color and texture of the different types of earth. See if there are stones, clay, or sand underneath the topsoil. If so, plant some plants in this inferior earth and compare their growth with that of plants in potting soil.

Another activity is to take some loose soil and put it into a jar, then fill the jar with water. Shake the jar vigorously and let the contents settle. Check to see which size of particles settle to the bottom first, and which ones remain in suspension longer. Come back to the jar the next day and inspect the clarity of the water.

At another time, dig up sod and compare the root structure present with the lack of root structures where soil has been badly eroded. Show how roots can hold back water runoff. Prove that there is water dissolved in soil by filling a jar full of freshly dug dirt. Then tightly cap the jar and place it in direct sunlight. The water should condense on the inside of the jar.

TECHNOLOGY   Help the children list the major inventions, such as the labor-saving devices found in the typical home. Help them to suggest alternate ways of doing work that would not require the same consumption of commercial energy nor the consumption of raw materials in producing the implement. Ask a person who is experienced in antiques to bring to class some examples of predecessors of modern-day inventions, or pictures of them, and explain or demonstrate their functions. Let the class make as gift items decorated reminder cards for the purpose of conserving energy and materials in their homes.

TRANSPORTATION   Have the children bring to class examples of different ways of traveling, using either pictures cut from magazines or models and toys from their personal collections. Talk about each method in terms of types of energy required, speed of travel, kinds of pollution, and general impact on a person's health.

TREES   Find out from a science book or a science teacher how many pounds of air an average person breathes every day. Then find out how many pounds of oxygen are produced by a typical shade tree in your area. Make this interdependence apparent to children by identifying a tree or a group of trees that produce the designated amount of air. Suggest that each child adopt a tree and help to take care of it in appreciation for this life-giving service. Also consider the value of trees in terms of their service to animal life, to water conservation, and the shade they provide to people. Also consider their products, including those that can be replaced, such as fruits and nuts, as well as those that cannot be replaced unless a similar tree is planted in the place of every tree that is consumed. Encourage the school to purchase a balled and bagged evergreen tree for the winter holiday displays, and then plant this living tree, instead of cutting down another one, as a mark of respect for the natural environment.

WATER EROSION   Set up a drip pail so it drips on a piece of soft rock, gypsum, sand, or clay to check the effects of dripping water. Also, look for examples of water damage and aging in weathered bricks and cracks in the sidewalk. Take a field excursion to an eroded field and find water-washed gullies. Ask a soil conservation agent to explain to the children how such erosion might have been prevented and how it might be controlled.

Another activity is to make a simple splash board on a dusty board held at different angles to the drip of an outside faucet or a sprinkling can. Compare the effects to see which angle produces the most erosion of the dust. Show the children commercial splashboards made from stone or concrete that are used to prevent erosion underneath downspouts and drains.

Help the more ambitious students to make a simple erosion box from a wooden plant box. Fill it with different kinds of soil, such as loam, sand, or clay. See which soil absorbs the water best, and which permits the greatest runoff. Use a watering can to control the amount of water and the rate of flow. Cut a piece of sod to fit exactly into the box and pour the same amount of water again. See if the sod holds the water best of all.

As still another water erosion activity, take the children on an "erosion walk" just after a heavy downpour. Instruct the class to look for signs of erosion on the playground and elsewhere in the neighborhood. Check for signs of heavy runoff, as suggested by large puddles and by swirls of sand and silt. Compare the amount of water that runs off paved areas with that which runs off grassy areas.

WATER POLLUTION   Set up two bowls of water and add a variety of trash items to one of the bowls, especially those that discolor the water. Ask the children if they would like to drink the dirty water. Put some fish in the two bowls and see which ones live more normally in terms of the number of times they might surface to breathe air directly. Later, filter the dirty water through a coffee filter and see if the apparent quality of the water improves.

Another experiment with water involves adding phosphates to one of two comparable bowls. Place both these bowls in direct sunlight and compare the growth of algae in them. Discuss how algae tends to contaminate the water and suffocate the fish.

A final experiment is one in which the effects of polluted water on plant life is explored. Place some waste matter into one container of water and keep a second container pure. Obtain from a florist or nurseryman two inexpensive plants of comparable size, and water them the same amount each day. Examine their rates of growth, with all other variables being held equal. Be sure the chemicals used in the contaminated water are not those that would enrich the soil. Also, be sure the children understand the parallel you draw between this type of pollution and industrial wastes that similarly pollute water that is sometimes used by plant life, both natural vegetation as well as crops under cultivation.

WATER WASTE   Find a leaking faucet and place a container under it to see how much water is wasted every day. On the basis of a year, compute for the children how much water would be wasted if the faucet is not repaired. Then find a way to make a graphic representation of this amount of water. Take the children to a water treatment plant to help them visualize the source of the community water supply; or draw a cross-section of a well. Make a diagram of the water cycle to show the children the ultimate source of all water in the world.

NATIONS: Understanding Maps and People

AERIAL MAPS Contact community officials for a copy of an aerial map of the region in which the school is located. Look for landmarks that are familiar to the children to see what these points look like from above. Convert this map into a pin map with each pin bearing a label appropriate to the main points of interest, with special attention given to the individual children's homes.

CLIMATE MAP Make a simple climate map of the world. Cut out pictures of the sun, jungle vegetation, Eskimos, desert animals, and other symbols of varying climates and paste them onto the map in appropriate locations. In the instance of the United States climate map, attach pictures of crops and outdoor activities associated with each area, such as citrus fruits and water sports for Florida and California, skiing and apples for Maine and Washington. As another variation of this type of map, find a puzzle map of the United States and cover each puzzle piece with a cutout picture. Challenge the children to reconstruct the map in terms of climate-related ideas instead of the names of states. Also, contact a local television station or a university department for a copy of a weather map and discuss its use in predicting changes in the weather.

COMMUNITY MAP Find or make a map of the local community, including the entire school attendance area. Locate addresses for all children and have each student place a miniature of his home on the map in its proper place. Using a string thumbtacked to a small wood block representing the school, see which child lives farthest away. Attach to the map small pictures cut from magazines to represent the major stores and industries in the community, and any other important natural or man-made features.

DIRECTIONAL ORIENTATION   Develop an orientation to maps by always placing the map on the floor flat, properly related to the directions the map represents. Never discuss the directions on a map while it is hanging up vertically. It is confusing for the young child to hear that the top of a map stands for north, and as he looks at a map hanging on the wall, the top of it is pointing up to the sky. As another simple aid to orient the children to the cardinal directions, place labels and symbols on the four walls of the classroom: "East" might be represented by a rooster crowing to the world; "North" might be suggested by a polar bear; "South" might be indicated by something tropical; and "West" might be pictured by a child going to bed after sundown.

DIRECTIONS   Help the children learn the main directions by asking one person to pose as a sergeant, adapting military commands such as, "South face! West face! North face! East face!" Another idea is to print directions for the children to read and follow, such as, "Run west to the big tree, then walk south to the school." Or, adapt oral commands to the use of miniature vehicles along a road map, as if the child were taking a trip, turning east or west, for example, at major intersections.

Still another idea is to play the game "Weather Vane" in which the children pretend to be a wind indicator at the top of a building. The leader of the game calls out different directions and the players must point that way with one hand, while holding the other hand upright behind their heads like the feathers on the cock. Encourage the leader to try to fool the players, and challenge the children not to be fooled. Combine this directional game with a physical activity in which the children must respond motorically to commands such as, "The duck flies south," "The sun rises in the east," or "The wagons rolled west." At each command the players must turn the correct direction and perform the simple action suggested by the leader.

ETHNIC TRADITIONS   Locate sources of information, especially at holiday seasons, that show how people in other lands celebrate

Christmas or Easter, for example. Survey the families represented in your classroom to discover traditions observed in eating, housing, or mode of dress in their own national origins or ancestors in this country. Find pictures of typical families in other countries and make a display. Search for pictures in copies of travel magazines, as one possible source.

EXCHANGES   Help the children become more aware of foreign countries and customs by having them exchange information through an "Adopt-a-Ship" or an "Adopt-a-Child" program advertised in professional teachers' magazines. Or, suggest that they exchange letters with international pen pals, or participate in an art exchange. Or, when your children move away from your school to attend in distant communities, make arrangements with the receiving teacher to exchange letters, information, and regional products.

FAMILY ORIGINS MAP   Ask your children to find out where they were born, where their parents were born, and where their grandparents were born. Cut out small paper-doll figures for each person in the family. Using a world map or a national map, stretch yarn or cord from the point of family origin to the present community. Count the different countries or states represented by the families of your children. Use a similar map to see where grandparents are presently living.

FLOOR MAP   Obtain or make a large map of the United States or of the world. Draw wide roadways and waterways with a felt-tip pen. Find miniature blocks or boxes to represent principal cities. Have the children use tiny toys, such as cars, trucks, boats, and airplanes, in their map play. Label the principal cities and pose questions such as, "Is it possible to travel from Chicago to New York by boat?" or, "Can you go from Miami to London by car?" Let the child who is answering the question act it out, using the toy miniatures to check the accuracy of his reply.

FLOOR PLAN   Check in the school office for a copy of the floor plan of the building, or obtain a blueprint which provides the same information. Place small stand-up cutout figures of each school helper in the appropriate location on the map of the school. Discuss each person's job when his figure is put in place on the map. As another activity, staple together a series of shoeboxes or other cartons to represent the rooms in the school. Label each room in the assemblage and furnish each area appropriate to its function using cutout pictures and furniture cut from small boxes. Encourage the children to use this replica in their role play.

FOREIGN FLAGS   Find pictures of the flags of other countries, and encourage the children to make flags from construction paper. Compare the symbols and colors in the various pennants to find similarities. See if you can discover the meanings of the symbols used in the flags as you check the encyclopedia. When all the flags are assembled, have a parade around the room, playing a variety of national music. Correlate this activity with a study of the United Nations in October.

FOREIGN FOODS   Make a collection or a listing of foods that have been adopted by our country from foreign origins. Some will be obvious, such as tacos, sauerkraut, and weiners, while others will be less obvious, such as noodles, corn, doughnuts, and potatoes. Invite resource persons to the class to prepare national or ethnic dishes for the children to sample. Be sure the children understand the idea that each ethnic group develops its own unique food items.

FOREIGN HOUSING   Find pictures of homes in foreign countries or in different parts of this country and make a chart identifying the area in which each type of housing is used. Develop with the children the idea that the availability of materials and the climate, as well as custom, help the people in each area to decide what type of housing to build. Let the more able children make miniature houses from pieces of cardboard.

FOREIGN LANGUAGE   Have someone from a foreign culture talk with the children in his native tongue. Help the class to see how important it is for people to have a common way of communicating with each other. Contact an amateur radio operator to tape record a foreign-language broadcast and play it in the class. Or, obtain from a language teacher commercial records of different languages. Teach the children simple words and phrases in a language that is appropriate to their social studies. Remind the children that our language sounds just as unusual to other people as their speech seems to us.

FOREIGN PRODUCTS   Collect a variety of imported products and discover where each one comes from. Make a list of these foreign countries, and find them on a map. Attach a string to each country as it is located, and tie the string to a pin on the map and the other end of the string to a product that has been placed on a display table. Also ask the children to look for foreign stamps on letters, or to collect examples of currency and coins. Contact parents for dolls, handcrafts, travel posters, and stickers. Make still another display with pictures and real examples of foods, animals, natural resources, or any other aspect of human interdependence.

FOREIGN SONGS   Locate examples of songs from other countries, or ask a music teacher to help the children learn some. Try to sing some of these songs in the original language. Ask resource persons to demonstrate foreign folk dances, and national or ethnic dress appropriate to these countries. If your school is located in a metropolitan area, you may be able to find representatives of different cultures to perform this service for you.

MAP GAME   Make a simple map game by using any large map and then drawing a series of straight lines connecting the cities located prominently around the map. Then, by tossing dice or spinning a spinner, let the children have a "race" around the nation or the world to see which player can get "home" first. Have a variety of routes for the individual players to follow and vary the procedure by having bonus cards or penalty cards for them to follow, such as, "You drove too fast. Go to jail for one turn," or, "The road was downhill. Take another turn."

MAP PUZZLES   There are many inexpensive commercial map puzzles. It is also easy to make a puzzle by gluing a map to a large piece of posterboard and then cutting out the pieces with heavy-duty shears. A more sturdy map puzzle can be made by salvaging a large wall map from a social studies department and gluing it to a thin sheet of hardboard or plywood. Shellac the surface after the glue is dry and cut out the pieces with a jigsaw or saber saw.

MAP SOURCES   Free maps are usually available from major oil companies, from state departments of tourism, from foreign embassies, from major transportation organizations, and from travel agents. Maps are also included as occasional inserts in *National Geographic* magazine.

MAP SYMBOLS   Teach the use of map symbols by making them into a card game. To illustrate: cut out a picture of mountains and paste it onto a card. Cut out a symbol for mountains and paste it onto a similar card. The object of the game is to match symbols with the appropriate pictures to win the game.

MODELS Help the children to understand that maps, globes, and other models are merely representations of large areas and large objects. Show them photographs of people and establish that a picture is a small representation of the larger item. Or, use a miniature toy and demonstrate that it is also a small replica of the actual object. Suggest that since it is impossible for people to see all the earth at one time, a globe is used to represent it; similarly, maps are used to suggest the main areas on the earth.

OCCUPATIONAL MAPS Make an occupational map of the community or of the main business district, or of the area immediately surrounding the school. In each appropriate block on the map draw or paste a picture of the businesses. Ask the children to report their own parents' involvements in the community's business life, and identify these relationships by placing photographs of the parents at the appropriate places where they work or shop. Or conduct a survey of shopping habits and draw lines with yarn from pictures of the children's homes to the shops and other community facilities most frequently used.

PLAYGROUND MAPS Using chalk and a grid arrangement for enlarging pictures, outline on the hard surface of the playground a large map. Make it permanent, where permissible, with paint. Label each important feature on the map, and suggest play activities appropriate to it, such as, "Show me how to swim down the Mississippi River," or, "Fly from New York to Los Angeles." A similar activity is to make a compass rosette on the playground surface and instruct the children to jump from one direction to another, skipping occasional markings of the rosette as they respond to you.

PLOT MAPS Have the children examine their family's property and draw a simple map of it. Or, encourage some of the parents to bring to school surveys of their plots. Ask each child to include on his drawing all the major buildings, the large trees, pathways, and other natural or man-made features on the property. Convert some of these maps into games by connecting the main elements with lines for moving markers in response to the numbers obtained from a spinner or the tossing of dice.

POST CARDS   Make a collection of post cards from distant states or from foreign lands. Locate each place on a map. Post some of the cards on the appropriate spots on a map. Classify the post cards by state or by country or by type of feature pictured. Cut apart some of the duplicate cards to make miniature puzzles; keep the pieces of these puzzles in small envelopes to prevent their loss.

RESOURCE PEOPLE   Check in your community for persons who may be able to bring both information and products from other areas or from different cultures. Inquire through local churches for missionaries, watch the local newspapers for notes about returning military personnel, contact airline employees, poll the parents of your children, ask other teachers for leads to volunteer agency workers, or contact the foreign language departments of local high schools and colleges for international exchange students or teachers with international experience.

SAND TABLE MAPS   Involve the children in simple mapping by using a sand table filled with moist sand. Help the class to identify and build various local physical features, such as roads, hills, rivers, and lakes. Discuss simple drainage patterns. Use miniatures from play sets to represent houses, vehicles, trees, and structures. When the discussion is done, place a large piece of paper over the sand table and help the children draw a simple map of the area.

SCALE DRAWINGS   Introduce map skills by making a scale drawing of the classroom. Spread a large sheet of paper on the floor in the middle of the room. Use large building blocks to represent the major items in the room and label each object. Then, draw a line around each object with a felt-tip pen and label each drawing, after the blocks have been removed. After discussing the drawing, make a much smaller scale drawing of the classroom. Suggest that the children make a simple scale drawing of one of the rooms in their own homes.

SPACE MAPS   Obtain copies of a moon map from a space agency. Or, make diagrams of constellations or charts of the solar system. Discuss the need for maps in space travel (for example, in the landings on the moon). Find a picture of the earth that was taken by a satellite, and compare it with a map of the same surface.

TOURIST MAP Contact the tourist department of your state and ask for information concerning the main travel attractions in each area, especially those located close to your own community. Make a large outline map of your state by projecting a commercial highway map onto a large piece of paper using an opaque projector. Ask the children to draw an outline of the different tourist features. Fill in the details on the map and attach pictures cut from tourist folders.

TRAFFIC CHANNELS Encourage the children to think of all the ways traffic moves in different channels. Help them to think of highways as channels, along with rivers and canals. Also suggest railroads, airline routes, sidewalks, stairs, bridle paths, and bike paths. Point out to children that the main thoroughfares in your local area were probably at one time the easiest pathway from one place to another. Some of these might date from earlier eras of history. Check your local history to see if there are any unusual facts connected with traffic channels in your area. Note that pathways are always being formed; inspect the grass outdoors near the school doors and see if pedestrian traffic has created new channels for foot traffic.

TRAVEL ROUTES Let each child who plans to take an extensive trip bring to class maps on which, with adult help, he can trace the general route taken. Ask the child to report something special about each principal stop along the way. Suggest that his parents help him to look for inexpensive educational souvenirs to share with the class when he returns.

TREASURE HUNT Adapt the children's map skills to a treasure hunt. Hide a series of small candies or other treats at different spots in the classroom or on the playground. Give each of several groups a map of where they are hidden and see if they can find the hidden items. One particularly appropriate treasure is foil-wrapped candy that resembles coins. Another variation of this game for older primary children is to write directions on a piece of paper, and require the group to read the instructions as they move about the area looking for clues.